# MILLER'S
## *Pine & Country Furniture*
## BUYER'S GUIDE

MILLER'S PINE & COUNTRY FURNITURE BUYER'S GUIDE

Created and designed by
Miller's
The Cellars, High Street,
Tenterden, Kent, TN30 6BN
Tel: 01580 766411

Consultants: Judith & Martin Miller

Project Editors: Lynn Bonnett, Jo Wood
Editorial Assistants: Wendy Adlam, Marion Rickman
Production Assistants: Gillian Charles, Karen Taylor
Advertising Executive: Elizabeth Smith
Advertising Assistants: Melinda Williams, Joanne Daniels
Index compiled by: DD Editorial Services, Beccles
Design: Jody Taylor, Matthew Leppard, Darren Manser, Kari Reeves
Additional photography: Ian Booth, David Copsey, Roddy Paine, Robin Saker

First published in Great Britain in 1995
by Miller's, an imprint of
Reed Books Limited,
Michelin House, 81 Fulham Road,
London SW3 6RB
and Auckland, Melbourne, Singapore and Toronto

© 1995 Reed International Books Limited

A CIP catalogue record for this book is
available from the British Library

ISBN 1-85732-684-9

Bromide output by Perfect Image, Hurst Green, E. Sussex
Illustrations by G.H. Graphics, St. Leonard's-on-Sea
Colour origination by Scantrans, Singapore
Printed and bound in England by Bath Press, Avon

Miller's is a registered trademark of
Reed International Books Ltd

# MILLER'S
## *Pine & Country Furniture*
# BUYER'S GUIDE

Consultants

## Judith and Martin Miller

Project Editors

### Jo Wood

### Lynn Bonnett

# ACKNOWLEDGEMENTS

*Miller's publications would like to acknowledge the great assistance given by our consultants:*

### COUNTRY FURNITURE
**Derek Green** of Cedar Antiques has been trading in Hartley Wintney for almost 30 years, specialising in Country Furniture and associated items. His wife Sally joined the company some 12 years ago adding a new design and furniture finding service.
**Cedar Antiques Ltd, High Street, Hartley Wintney, Hants RG27 8NY**

### EARLY PAINTED PINE & FRENCH PROVINCIAL FURNITURE
**Robert Young** left Sotheby's in 1975 to start his own business. In 1978 he opened a shop in Battersea specialising in Country Furniture and Folk Art. The following year he met his wife, Josyane, and business partner. Robert has written many articles for the *Antique Collector* and the *Antique Collectors' Club* magazine as well as lecturing at Sotheby's and the Women's Institute.
**Robert Young Antiques, 68 Battersea Bridge Road, London SW11 3AG**

### KITCHENWARE
**Christina Bishop** has been one of London's top kitchenware dealers for over 20 years. She can be found every Saturday at her stall in the popular Portobello Road Antiques Market, where she attracts customers from as far afield as Japan, Australia and America. Christina was born and brought up in Lancashire and her enthusiasm for kitchenware stems from an interest in social and domestic history, as well as a passion for baking. In 1994, Christina acted as a consultant to Phillips for their auction of Elizabeth David's Kitchenware. She is the author of *Miller's Collecting Kitchenware*.
**Christina Bishop Kitchenware, Westway, Portobello Road Market, London W11**

### OAK & COUNTRY FURNITURE
**Patrick Robbins,** from his busy shop in Tenterden, began dealing in antiques in the late 1960s. His interest in Oak and Country furniture has grown over the past 15 years. He also specialises in 18th and 19thC furniture and works of art. Patrick has contributed many articles to antiques publications.
**Sparks Antiques, 4 Manor Row, Tenterden, Kent TN30 6HP**

### PINE FURNITURE
**Ann Lingard** began collecting needlework tools and samplers 25 years ago. She then moved on to Pine and Country furniture and has run her shop in Rye for the past 20 years. She sells to top dealers all-over the world but in particular to the US and Japan. She writes for the *Antiques Bulletin* and other antiques publications.
**Rope Walk Antiques, Rope Walk, Rye, Sussex, TN31 7NA**

### WELSH FURNITURE
**Richard Bebb** has been dealing in Welsh furniture and Folk Art for the last 25 years, and is the author of *Welsh Country Furniture*. He also contributes regularly to many antiques magazines.
**Country Antiques, Castle Mill, Kidwelly, Dyfed, Wales SA17 4UU**

# CONTENTS

MILLER'S

# KEY TO ILLUSTRATIONS

*Each illustration and descriptive caption is accompanied by a letter code. (Auctioneers \* and Dealers •). In no way does this constitute or imply a contract or binding offer on the part of any of our contributors to supply or sell the goods illustrated, or similar articles, at the prices stated. Advertisers are denoted by †.*

| | | |
|---|---|---|
| A | * | Aldridges of Bath Ltd. The Auction Galleries, Bath BAI 5BG. Tel: 01225 462830 |
| AD | | Alan Douglas. PC |
| Ad | | Adams Furniture Centre, The Old Post Office, Huntingdon PE18 6AW. Tel: 01480 435100 |
| AF | †• | Albert Forsythe, Mill House, Saintfield, N. Ireland BT24 7EX. Tel: 01 238 510398 |
| AG | * | Anderson & Garland, Marlborough Cres., Newcastle-upon-Tyne, NE1 4EE. Tel: 0191 232 6278 |
| AGr | * | Andrew Grant. PC |
| AH | * | Andrew Hartley Victoria Salerooms, Little Lane, Ilkey W.Yorkshire LS29 8EA. Tel: 01943 816363 |
| AH | • | Abbotts Antiques & Country Pine, 109 Kirkdale, London SE26 Tel: 0181 699 1363 |
| AHA | • | Ashleigh House Antiques 5 Westbourne Road, Birmingham. Tel: 0121 454 6283 |
| AHL | • | Adrian Hornsey Three Bridge Mill, Twyford, Bucks. Tel: 01296 738373 |
| AI | • | Antiques & Interiors Romney Bay House, Coast Rd, New Romney, Kent TN28 8QY. Tel: 01797 364747 |
| AL | †• | Ann Lingard Ropewalk Antiques, Ropewalk, Rye, Sussex. Tel: 01797 223486 |
| AnD | †• | Antique & Design, The Old Oast, Hollow Lane, Canterbury, Kent CT1 3TG. Tel: 01227 762871 |
| AP | * | Andrew Pickford The Hertford Salerooms, 42 St Andrew St, Hertford, SG14 1JA. Tel: 01992 583508 |
| AP | • | Angela Page, 15 Cumberland Walk, Tunbridge Wells, TN1 1VJ. Tel: 01892 522217 |
| ARK | • | The Ark Antiques. PC |
| AS | • | Arthur Seager Antiques, 50 Sheep Street, Stow on the Wold, Glos. Tel: 01451 831605 |
| B | * | Boardmans, Station Road Corner, Haverhill, Suffolk. Tel: 01440 730414 |
| BA | • | Bratton Antiques. PC |
| BA | • | Barlow Antiques. PC |
| BB | • | Bernice Barker. PC |
| Bea | * | Bearnes, Rainbow, Avenue Road, Torquay, Devon. Tel: 01803 296277 |
| BEL | †• | Bell Antiques, 68A Harold Street, Grimsby, Humberside, DN35 OHH. Tel: 01472 695110 |
| Ber | • | Berry Antiques, The Old Butcher's Shop, Goudhurst, Kent TN1 1AE. Tel: 01580 212115 |
| BH | †• | Bob Hoare Pine Antiques. |
| HOA | • | Phoenix Place, North Street, Lewes, |
| BOA | * | Sussex, BN7 2DQ. Tel: 01273 480557 |
| BHW | * | Butler & Hatch Waterman now Lambert & Foster, 102 High St, Tenterden, Kent. Tel: 01892 832325 |
| BMM | * | Button, Menhenitt & Mutton Ltd. PC |
| Bon | * | Bonhams, Montpelier Galleries, London, SW7 1HH. Tel: 0171 584 9161 |
| BR | • | Bed of Roses, 12 Prestbury Road, Cheltenham, Glos. Tel: 01242 231918 |
| Bro | * | Brocklehursts. PC |
| Byl | †• | Bygones of Ireland, Westport Antiques Centre, Westport, County Mayo, Eire Tel: 00 35398 26132. |
| C | * | Christie, Manson & Wood Ltd, 8 King St, St James's, London SW1Y 6QT. Tel: 0171 839 9060 |
| CAL | †• | Cedar Antiques, High St, Hartley Wintney, Hants, RG27 8NY. Tel: 01252 843252 |
| CC | • | Chalon UK Ltd., Old Hambridge Mill, Hambridge, Somerset. Tel: 01278 788590/788605 |
| CCA | • | Combe Cottage Antiques, Castle Combe, Wilts. Tel: 01249 782250 |
| CCP | †• | Campden Country Pine Antiques, Chipping Campden, Glos GL55 6HN. Tel: 01386 840315 |
| CDC | * | Capes Dunn & Co, The Auction Galleries, Charles St, Grtr Manchester, M1 7DB. Tel: 0161 273 1911 |
| CDE | • | Colin Dyte Export Ltd, Huntspill Road, Highbridge, Somerset. Tel: 01278 788590/788603 |
| Ced/CAL | †• | Cedar Antiques, High Street, Hartley Wintney, Hants. Tel: 01252 843252 |
| CEMB | • | Christina Bishop's Kitchenware, Westway, Portobello Rd Market, London, W11. Tel: 0171 221 4688. |
| CGC | * | Cheffins Grain & Comins, The Cambridge Salerooms, Cambridge CB1 4BW. Tel: 01223 213343 |
| CHA | • | Chapel House Antiques. PC |
| CI | • | Country Interiors, 10 Great Western Antiques Centre, Bath, Avon, BA1 2QZ. Tel: 01225 310388/421505 |
| CNY | * | Christie Manson & Wood Int Inc., 502 Park Ave, New York, NY 10022, USA. Tel: 001 212 546 1000 |
| CoA | †• | Country Antiques (Wales), 31 Bridge St & Castle Mill, Kidwelly, Dyfed, SA17 4UU. Tel: 01554 890534 |
| COP | • | The Antiques Centre, Stephen Copsey, George St, Huntingdon, Cambs. Tel: 01480 435100 |
| COT | †• | Cottage Pine Antiques, 19 Broad Street, Brinklow, Warwicks CV23 0LS. Tel: 01788 832673 |
| Cou | †• | Country Homes, 61 Long Street, Tetbury, Glos, GL8 8AA. Tel: 01666 502342 |
| CPA | • | Country Pine Antiques, The Barn, Upper Bush Farm, Upper Bush, Kent. Tel: 01634 717982 |
| CSK | * | Christie's South Kensington Ltd, 85 Old Brompton Rd, |

| | | |
|---|---|---|
| | | London, SW7 3LD. Tel: 0171 581 7611 |
| CUL | †• | Cullompton Old Tannery Antiques, Exeter Rd, Cullompton, Devon, EX15 1DT. Tel: 01884 38476 |
| CW | * | Cubbitt & West. PC |
| DA | * | Dee Atkinson & Harrison, The Exchange Saleroom, Driffield, Yorkshire, YO25 7LJ. Tel: 01377 253151 |
| DDM | * | Dickinson Davy & Markham, Wrawby St, Brigg, S Humberside. Tel: 01652 653666 |
| DDS | • | Dorking Desk Shop, 41 West Street, Dorking, Surrey. Tel: 01306 883327 |
| DEB | • | David E Burrows, Manor House Farm, Osgathorpe, Nr Loughborough, Leics. Tel: 01530 222218 |
| DEL | • | Anne Delores, Bartlett Street, Antiques Centre, Bath, Avon. Tel: 01225 310457 |
| DFA | †• | Delvin Farm Antiques, Gormonston, Co Meath, Eire. Tel: 00 353 184 12285 |
| DM | * | Diamond Mills & Co, 117 Hamilton Road, Felixstowe IP11 7BL. Tel: 01394 282281 |
| DMA | * | David Masters Antiques, Elm Tree Farm, High Halden, Kent, TN26 3BP. Tel: 01233 850551 |
| DMe | †• | Daniel Meaney, Alpine House, Carlow Road, Abbeyleix, Co Laois, Eire. Tel: 00 353 502 31348 |
| DN | * | Dreweatt & Neate/Dreweatts Watson & Barton, |
| DWB | | Donnington Priory, Donnington, Newbury, Berks. Tel: 01635 31234 |
| EEW | * | Eldon E. Worrall, Worralls, 15 Seel Street, Liverpool, L1 4AU. Tel: 051 709 2950 |
| EL | * | Eldred's, Robert C Eldred Co Inc, 1475 Route 6A, East Dennis, Massachusetts 0796, USA, 02641. Tel: 001 508 385 3116 |
| EM | • | Eythorne Manor, Hollingbourne, Maidstone, Kent. |
| ERA | †• | English Rose Antiques, 7 Church Street, Coggeshall, Essex, CO6 ITU. Tel: 01376 562683 |
| FA | • | Frank Andrews, 10 Vincent Road, London, N22. Tel: 0181 881 0658 |
| FAG | †• | Fagins Antiques, The Old Whiteways Cider Factory, Hele, Exeter, Devon EX5 4PW. Tel: 01392 882062 |
| Far | • | The Farmhouse. PC |
| FF | • | Fritz Fryer, 12 Brookend Street, Ross on Wye, Hereford & Worcs. Tel: 01989 567416 |
| FHA | • | Flower House Antiques, 90 High Street, Tenterden, Kent, TN30 6JB. Tel: 01580 763764 |
| FOX | • | Foxhole Antiques, High Street, Goudhurst, Kent TN30 6JB. Tel: 01580 212025 |
| FP | • | For Pine, 340 Berkhampstead Road, Chesham, Bucks, HP5 3HF. Tel: 01494 776119 |
| FRM | * | Frank R Marshall & Co, Marshall House, Knutsford WA16 6DH. Tel: 01565 653284 |
| GA | • | Greenmill Antiques. PC |
| GA(W) | * | GA Property Services, Phillips, The Red House, Hyde Street, Winchester, Hants SO23 7DX Tel: 01962 862515 Fax. 865166 |
| GC | | PC |
| GD | * | Garth Denham, Horsham Auction Galleries, also Warnham, Horsham, Sussex RH12 3RZ. Tel: 01403 55699/53837 |
| GD | †• | Gilbert & Dale Antiques, The Old Chapel, Ilchester, Yeovil, Somerset, BA22 8LA. Tel: 01935 840444 |
| GPA | †• | Graham Price Antiques, Unit 4, Chaucer Trading Est, Polegate, Sussex BN26 6JD. Tel: 01323 487167 |
| GRF | | Grange Farm Ltd. PC |
| GT | • | Garrod Turner. PC |
| GWe | • | Gerald Weir, 7-11 Vermont Rd, Ipswich, Suffolk. Tel: 01473 255572 (Trade Only) |
| H | • | Huntington Antiques, The Old Forge, Church St, Stow on the Wold Glos. Tel: 01451 830842 |
| HeR | †• | Heritage Restorations, Maes Y Glydfa, Llanfair, Caerinion, Welshpool, Powys, SY21 0HD. Tel: 01938 810384 |
| HG | • | The Hay Galleries. PC |
| HGN | †• | Hungerford Pine Company, 14/15 Charnham St, Hungerford, Berkshire. Tel: 01488 686935 |
| HOA | †• | Bob Hoare Pine Antiques. BH and BOA |
| HON | †• | Honans Antiques, Gort, Co Galway, Eire. Tel: 00 353 091 31407 |
| HSS | * | Phillips Incorporating Henry Spencer & Sons, 20 The Square, Retford, Notts, DN22 6XE. Tel: 01777 708633 |
| HWO | * | Hall, Wateridge & Owen, Welsh Bridge Salerooms, Shrewbury Salop. SY3 8LA. Tel: 01734 231212 |
| IW | • | Islwyn Watkins, 1 High Street, 39 High St, Knighton, Powys, LD7 1AT. Tel: 01547 520145 |
| JAC | • | John & Anne Clegg, 12 Old Street, Ludlow, Salop. Tel: 01584 873176 |
| JBL | • | Judi Bland, Durham House Antiques Centre, Stow on the Wold, Glos. Tel: 01451 870404 |
| JD | • | Julian Dawson, Lewes Auction Rooms, Garden St, Lewes, East Sussex. Tel: 01273 478221 |
| JeB | • | Jean Brown. PC |
| JH | * | Jacobs & Hunt, Lavant Street, Petersfield, Hants. GU32 3EF. Tel: 01730 62744/5 |

JHW • John Howkins, 1 Dereham Road, Norwich, Norfolk. Tel: 01603 627832

JMW * J M Welch & Sons, now Hamptons Fine Art, Gt Dunmow, Essex, CM61AU. Tel: 01371 873014

KEY * Key Antiques, 11 Horse Fair, Chipping Norton, Oxon. OX7 5AL. Tel: 01608 643777

L * Lawrences of Crewkerne, Fine Art Auctioneers, South St, Crewkerne, Somerset, TA18 8AB. Tel: 01460 73041

LA • Leominster Antiques. PC

LAC • Leicester Antiques Centre. PC

LAM • Penny Lampard, High St, Headcorn, Kent. Tel: 01622 890682

LAM • Lambrays, R J Hamm, Polmoria Walk, Wadebridge, Cornwall, PL27 7AE. Tel: 0120 881 3593

LAY • David Lay ASVA, Auction House, Penzance, Cornwall. Tel: 01736 61414

LC • Luckypenny Antiques, PC

LHA • Lesley Hindman Auctioneers, 215 West Ohio St, Chicago, Illinois, USA IL60610 Tel: 001 312 670 0010

LIB †• Libra Antiques, 81 London Road, Hurst Green, Sussex, TN19 7PN. Tel: 01580 860569

LL • Lowe of Loughborough, 37–40 Church Gate, Loughborough, Leics. Tel: 01509 212554

LRG • Lots Road Galleries, 71 Lots Road, Worlds End, London SW10 0RN. Tel: 0171 351 7771

M * Morphetts of Harrogate, 4-6 Alberts Street, Harrogate, N. Yorks. Tel: 01423 502282

MA • Manor Antiques. PC

MA • Mercury Antiques, 1 Ladbroke Rd, London, W11. Tel: 0171 727 5106

MA • Morgan Antiques. PC

MAT • Christopher Matthews, 23 Mount St, Harrogate, Yorkshire, HG2 8DQ

Max • Maxey & Sons. PC

MCA * Mervyn Carey, Twsyden Cottage, Benenden, Kent. Tel: 01580 240283

MCA • Miller's of Chelsea, Netherbrook House, also

MofC • 86 Christchurch Rd, Ringwood, Hants BH24 1DR. Tel: 01425 472062

MGM * Michael G Matthews,/Bonhams West Country, Dowell St, Honiton EX14 8LX. TEL: 01404 41872

MIL †• Milverton Antiques, Fore St, Milverton, Taunton, TA4 1JU. Tel: 01823 400592

MM • Mark Maynard, 651 Fulham Rd, London, SW6. Tel: 0171 731 3533

MMB • Messenger's, 27 Sheep Street, Bicester, Oxon. OX6 7JF. Tel: 01869 252901

MMG • Morton M Goldberg, 547 Baronne St, New Orleans, USA, LA70113. Tel: 001 504 592 2300

MofC • Miller's of Chelsea see **MCA**

MPA • Market Place Antiques. PC

MS • Mary Sautter, 6 Station Street, Lewes, Sussex. Tel: 01273 474842

N * Neales, 192-194 Mansfield Road, Nottingham, HP7 OAH. Tel: 0115 962 4141

NCr • Nigel Cracknell Antiques Ltd. PC

NSF * Neal Sons & Fletcher

NWE †• North Wilts Exporters, Farmhill Hse, Brinkworth, Wilts SN15 5AJ. Tel: 01666 8241335/510876

OA • Odiham Antiques. PC

OB • Oola Boola Antiques

OB • The Old Bakery, St. David's Bridge, Cranbrook, Kent. Tel: 01580 713103

OC • Olwen Carthew PC

OCP †• Old Court Pine, Alain & Alicia Chawner, Collon, Co Louth, Eire. Tel: 0141 26270

OL • Outhwaite & Litherland, Kingsway Galleries, Liverpool L3 2BE. Tel: 0151 236 6561

OMH • Old Mint House, High St, Pevensey, Eastbourne BN24 5LF. Tel: 01323 762337

OPH †• The Old Pine Hse, 16 Warwick St, Leamington Spa, Warwicks CV32 5LL. Tel: 01926 470477

OSc • Simon & Penny Rumble, Old School, Chittering, Cambridge CB5 9PW. Tel: 01223 861831

P • Phillips, Blenstock House, 7 Blenheim St, London W1Y 0AS. Tel: 0171 629 6602

P(L) * Phillips Leeds

P(M) * Phillips Manchester

P(S) * Phillips Sevenoaks

PA * Pamela Aitchison. PC

PAC • Polegate Antiques Centre. PC

PC • Private Collection

PC • Peter Cheney

PC †• Pine Cellars

PCA * Paul Cater Antiques. PC

PCh * Peter Cheney, Western Road Auction Rooms, Littlehampton, BN17 5NP. Tel: 01903 722264

PCL • Peter Collins, 92 Waterford Rd, London SW6. Tel: 0171 736 4149

PD • Pine and Design. PC

PEN †• Pennard House Antiques, 3/4 Piccadilly, Bath BA1 6PL. Tel: 01225 313791/01749 860260

PF • Paul Fewings Ltd. PC

PH †• Pennard house Antiques, Temple Bank, Milnthorpe, Cumbria. Tel: 015395 62352

Ph • Phelps Ltd., 133 St. Margaret's Rd, Twickenham TW1 1RG. Tel: 0181 892 1778

PHA • Paul Hopwell Antiques, 30 High St, West Haddon,

Northants NN6 7AP. Tel: 01788 510636

PIN • Pine Finds. PC

PM • The Pine Merchants. PC

PM • Peter McAskie. PC

POT †• The Pot Board

PS * Phillips Cheshire

PWC * Parsons, Welch & Cowell, Now Phillips Sevenoaks

R * Rendells, Stone Park, Ashburton TQ13 7RH. Tel: 01364 653017

RA • Roberts Antiques, Lancs. Tel: 01253 827794

RBB * Russell Baldwin & Bright, Ryelands Rd, Leominster, Hereford & Worcs. HR6 8NZ. Tel: 01568 611166

RdeR * Rogers de Rin, 76 Royal Hospital Rd, London SW3 4HN. Tel: 0171 352 9007

RIT * D & J Ritchie Inc (Canada), 288 King St East, Toronto, Canada M5A 1K4. Tel: (416) 364 1864

RK • Richard Kimbell, Riverside, Market Harborough, Leics. Tel: 01858 433444

RP • Robert Pugh, Avon. Tel: 01225 314713

RYA †• Robert Young Antiques, 68 Battersea Bridge Rd, London SW11. Tel: 0171 228 7847. Fax 585 0489

S * Sotheby's, 34–35 New Bond Street, London W1A 2AA. Tel: 0171 493 8080

S(NY)* Sotheby's, 1334 York Ave., New York, NY 10021, USA. Tel: 212 606 7000

S(S) * Sotheby's Sussex, Summers Place, Billingshurst RH14 9AD. Tel: 01403 783933

SA †• Somerville Antiques & Country Furniture Ltd.,

SAn †• Moysdale, Ballina, Co Mayo, Eire. Tel: 010 353 96 36275

SBA • South Bar Antiques. PC

SC • Simon Castle Decorative Antiques. PC

Sca • Scallywag, now Pine Country, 22 High St, Beckenham BR3 1AY. Tel: 0181 658 6633

SHA • Shambles, 22 North St, Ashburton, Devon. Tel: 01364 653848

SK(B)* Skinners Inc., 357 Main Street, Bolton, USA, MA 01740. Tel: 0101 508 779 6241

SKC * Sotheby's King & Chasemore, Sussex

SPA • Station Pine Antiques, PO Box 177, South PDO Nottingham NG2 3BB.

SPa †• Sparks Antiques, 4 Manor Row, Tenterden, Kent TN30 6HP. Tel: 01580 766696

SS • Shirley Smith Antiques. PC

SSD • Smith & Smith Designs, 58A Middle St North, Driffield, Yorks.. Tel: 01377 256321

SSP • Stanley Stripped Pine. PC

SV • Sutton Valence Antiques, Sutton Valence, Maidstone, Kent. Tel: 01622 843333

SWN • Swan Antiques, Kent. Tel: 01580 291864

TaB • The Tartan Bow, 3a Castle St, Eye, Suffolk. Tel: 01379 870369

TEN * Tennant's, The Auction Centre, Leyburn, Yorks. DL8 5SG. Tel: 01969 623780

TJ • Tobias Jellinek, 29 Broadway Ave, St. Margaret's, Twickenham. Tel: 0181 892 6892

TM * Thos, Mawer & Sons, The Lincoln Saleroom, Lincoln. Tel: 01522 524984

TPC †• The Pine Cellars, 39 Jewry Street, Winchester, Hants SO23 8RY. Tel: 01962 777546

TPF • Traditional Pine Furniture, 248 Seabrook Rd, Hythe. Tel: 01303 239931

TRU • The Trumpet, West End, Minchinhampton, Glos. Tel: 01453 883027

UC †• Up Country, The Old Corn Stores, 68 St. John's Rd., Tunbridge Wells, Kent TN4 9PE. Tel: 01892 523341

UP • Utopia Pine & Country Furniture, Lake Rd, Bowness, Cumbria. Tel: 015394 88464

VV • V & V Chattek Auctioneers. PC

W * Walter's, No 1 Mint Lane, Lincoln LN1 1UD. Tel: 01522 525454

W • Woodstock. PC

WAC • Worcester Antiques Centre, Worcester WR1 4DF. Tel: 01905 610680

WaH †• The Warehouse, 29/30 Queens Gdns, Dover, Kent CT17 9AH. Tel: 01304 242006

WAT †• Crudwell Furniture Strippers, Oddpenny Farm, Crudwell, Wilts SN16 9SJ. Tel: 01285 770970

WEL • Wells Reclamation Co., The Old Cider Farm, Coxley, Nr. Wells, Somerset BA5 1RQ. Tel: 01749 677087/677484

WHA • Wych House Antiques, Wych Hill, Woking, Surrey. Tel: 014862 64636

WHL * W H Lane & Sons, 65 Morrab Rd, Penzance, Cornwall TR18 2QT. Tel: 01736 61447

WIL * Peter Wilson, Victoria Gallery, Nantwich, Cheshire. Tel: 01270 623878

WL * Wintertons Ltd., Lichfield Auction Centre, Wood End Lane, Fradley, Lichfield, Staffs WS13 8NF. Tel: 01543 263256

Wor * GA Property Services (Worsfield) - see

DA & GA (Worsfolds) ALSO **CAG**

WRe • Walcot Reclamations, 108 Walcot Street, Bath, Avon BA1 5BG. Tel: 01225 444404

WV †• Westville House Antiques, Littleton, Somerton, Somerset TA11 6NP. Tel: 01458 273376

WW * Woolley & Wallis, Salisbury Salerooms, 51/61 Castle Street, Salisbury, Wilts SP1 3SU. Tel: 01722 411422

# INTRODUCTION

In recent years there has been a distinct move away from the emphasis on luxury and extravagance which dominated the 1980s. The growth in popularity of pine and country furniture is an indication of our changing tastes, which have become increasingly focused on simplicity, versatility and practicality.

Country furniture was designed to be plain, solid and functional, and was made for use in ordinary houses and cottages rather than stately homes, mansions or palaces. The oldest pieces that are available to buy today date from the early 17th century. The fact that furniture in this style continued to be made and used in the 18th and 19th centuries, principally in rural areas, has led to the somewhat misleading term 'country furniture'. The most commonly-used wood was oak, but pieces were also made in chestnut, beech, walnut, elm, ash, yew and the fruitwoods. Craftsmen used designs which reflected the natural properties of the materials available, such as the suppleness of beech, and the wonderful rich colours of the fruitwoods.

There is a wide variety of styles and forms that exist in British country furniture – Welsh-made pieces are particularly characteristic, and even have their own names. Country furniture was also produced in the United States and in the rest of Europe, and French Provincial Furniture in particular has lately become more readily available.

Although sometimes not as old as some oak and country furniture, pine has also become more popular. Solid wood has a universal appeal, and the warm, golden colour of pine is easy to work with when decorating a room, a flat or a whole house. The functional nature of the designs means that pieces will not go out of fashion, and also gives them a great deal of versatility – a pine side table will look equally good in a living room, bedroom or bathroom.

Pine furniture exists in many different types: antique, old Continental, 'antique' and reproduction, and may be painted or unpainted. Depending on your tastes or your budget, these can be mixed and matched: the timelessness of pine furniture means that an antique table can sit quite comfortably with a set of 20th century pine chairs.

When buying country furniture, bear in mind that for 17th and 18th century pieces, the colour and patina (the glow the wood develops over the years from an accumulation of wax, polish and dirt) account for around fifty per cent of the value. This is particularly true of oak which will not withstand cleaning and French polishing like mahogany. Other important factors include the condition, the quality of the carving or decoration, and the existence of carved dates and inscriptions.

Pine is likely to be found in almost any condition, and the original quality may also be variable: some pieces were skilfully-made, while others were hastily nailed together.

If a piece of pine furniture has not already been stripped down to the natural wood, then it may be covered with paint, or black or brown varnish – to find out what the bottom layer is, remove part of the paint or varnish in a concealed place with the edge of a coin, for example, taking care not to damage the wood itself. If you want to buy a piece you can strip down, look for plain wood, and avoid pine which has a red stain – this will have been caused by the pigment of an old paint or brown stain. However, if you are after a piece which you can repaint then this will not matter, and you may be able to buy the piece for a lower price.

If you are buying stripped pine, check that the arms and legs are secure as the chemical process of stripping the wood can loosen joints. The softness of pine also means that on older pieces, parts such as feet and cornices may have been replaced. Check that the workmanship is good, and the colours match.

There is a wide variety of items available in both pine and country furniture suitable to furnish any room. For kitchens there are tables, chairs, dressers, serving tables, benches, and settles (wooden settees with high backs). Originally designed to divide the cooking area from the dining space, dressers are an attractive addition to any kitchen, and allow you display crockery and other items. Depending on their age, country chairs, especially matching sets, can become expensive. It is possible, however, to buy single, non-matching chairs for relatively modest amounts, particularly those from the 19th century, and these can look very effective. Even in a small kitchen, shelves or wall cabinets provide space for storage or display without making the room feel cluttered.

If you decide to give your living room a country theme, side tables, bureaux, Windsor and other armchairs, stools and small tables can all help to the effect. Again, if you have a limited budget, you could concentrate on small and non-matching pieces, and build up the look slowly. Chests are always good value and can serve as low tables.

Small pieces of pine or country furniture can also transform the feel of a bedroom: a box can sit at the foot of a bed (and provide useful storage for bedding), and old shelves and chests of drawers are also an attractive addition. Other accessories can help to build up the look, such as folk-style decorations, old prints, baskets, candlesticks and country fabrics (particularly patchwork).

Whether you are buying from an auction, dealer, second-hand shop or a warehouse, always buy the best that you can afford, and take comfort in the knowledge that your fruitwood stool from c1800, you three-legged elm cricket table, or your pine pot cupboard from c1870, are likely to maintain, if not increase, their value in the present market.

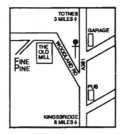
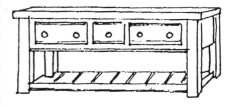

# PINE FURNITURE

Over the past 10 years or so, the pine trade has become established in its own right with pine furniture a popular choice for houses both old and modern. Pine itself falls into several categories: antique, old, Continental, 'antique' and reproduction. A variety of size, design and finish ensures that there is something for everyone within this thriving market.

It is helpful to bear a few pointers in mind when buying a piece of pine furniture, as style, availability, condition and age all have a bearing on the price and value of a piece. In addition, the modern-day requirements of individuals, interior designers and fashion trends, tend to dictate and have an effect on price and availability of styles.

An example of the above is seen in the present-day demand for turned leg pine dining tables, measuring between 72–96in (182.5–243.5cm) long and 36in (91.5cm) wide. Such pieces are greatly sought after as most tables of these dimensions were made in mahogany. On the other hand, the honest straight leg pine kitchen table is readily available – a factor reflected in its lower price. Sometimes the straight legs are removed on such tables and replaced with turned legs partly to be fashionable, and partly to add height under the apron of the table.

The proportion and condition of a piece are important to its value and price. For example, a wardrobe that is not deep enough to take a coat hanger, or a table of the right height with insufficient leg-room, or one that is not tall enough, is not a practical piece of furniture. Some people like pine to look pristine and in mint condition, others prefer the worn and slightly battered look – whatever your preference, do ensure that the piece is in a sufficiently good condition to stand up to its proper use. If in doubt, ask the dealer or auction house for guidance, they should be happy to advise you.

Much old pine has been painted, and a great deal comes to the trade with as many as twelve coats of paint (on top of the original), which should be removed. There are two basic ways of doing this. It can be done painstakingly by hand with a sharp knife or razor blade, in order to retain as much of the original paint as possible, or, it must be dipped and washed off well. However, it is usually these coats of paint which have, over the years, protected the soft wood underneath. When the paint has all gone, one hopes that the beautiful original wood will be revealed; on the other hand, you may find that the piece has been made up from different, mismatching pine or, worse, not from pine at all!

Once the wood is quite dry, it can be gently sanded and finished with a wax polish. It will soon mellow to its own unique colour and, if kept polished, will take on a glowing appearance. Be wary of any pine that needs repairing: it is difficult to match woods for invisible restoration, particularly as it may have mellowed with the passing years. Pieces which have been used in a workshop and have oily patches are also problematic areas – oil is very difficult to remove, and produces a sticky finish when waxed.

The price of antique pine has continued to increase in value in line with, and sometimes ahead of other woods. Many pieces which were widely available ten years ago are now relatively difficult to find: linen presses, good dressers, press tables, pot cupboards and chairs are prime examples. Although this may be a relatively expensive collecting area, there is nearly always something interesting, unusual and useful to be found. More everyday furniture, such as tables, chests of drawers and boxes, are still in plentiful supply.

The diverse origins of pine furniture, and numerous types of pine trees, all contribute to its varied repertoire. Pine, or deal as it was known in early times, was partly home-grown, with some imported from Scandinavia and North America. This accounts for its wide variety of colour and grain. Pitch pine, another variety, is a dark, grainy wood and, although very hard, is not as popular since its unique colour does not mix well with other woods.

Apart from Maples, Heal's, Shoolbreds of London and Gillows of Lancaster, there are few well-known makers of pine furniture in Britain. Some furniture was made in country workshops, giving us engaging primitive pieces; some was made for 'the big house' by estate carpenters and joiners, who produced free-standing furniture, one-off pieces, and built-in panelling and shutters. Fine cabinet makers also used pine as a carcass for exotic and expensive woods.

British pine furniture can largely be divided into regional types, for example, in the south of England one can find conventional chests of drawers, tall closed and open dressers, and pot board bases; Wales has superb conventional dressers, and many unusual chests of drawers; Scotland boasts a great deal of quality pine, including huge chests of drawers with twisted panels and various drawer arrangements, wall racks and wall shelves, and low Scottish dressers. Irish pine has its own primitive charm, with one-piece dressers, primitive chairs and substantial food cupboards.

With such a diverse and versatile wood as pine, there will be something to appeal to everyone. The wide range available means the piece that you choose, as well as being pleasing to the eye, should serve a long and useful life.

Ann Lingard

A pine Winchester haberdashery chest, with glazed sliding doors above 12 graduated drawers, on bun feet, c1860, 72in (182.5cm) wide.
**£1,200–1,500**   *TPC*

An Irish pine dresser, with glazed doors to top, 2 drawers and cupboards to base, 19thC, 54in (137cm) wide.
**£700–900**   *TPC*

A Continental pine dresser, with glazed doors to top, on turned supports, over carved, piano fronted two-drawer, two-door base, 19thC, 50in (127cm) wide.
**£700–900**   *TPC*

A pine dresser, with pierced and fretted frieze above an open delft plate rack and 4 spice drawers, on a base with a central cupboard flanked by 3 drawers each side, on bun feet, 19thC, 52in (132cm) wide.
**£900–1,200**   *TPC*

A pine dresser, with open delft plate rack and spice drawers, on base with 2 drawers above a pair of double panelled doors, 19thC, 52in (132cm) wide.
**£700–900**   *TPC*

*r.* A pine open potboard dresser, with 2 drawers, on square legs, 19thC, 48in (122cm) wide.
**£500–700**   *TPC*

*r.* A pine farmhouse dresser, with stepped delft plate rack above a three-drawer, three-door base, 19thC, 78in (198cm) high.
**£1,400–1,800**   *TPC*

*l.* A country pine dresser, with open delft plate rack, on unusual base with centre cupboard flanked by stepped and graduated drawers, early 19thC, 90in (228.5cm) wide.
**£1,400–1,800**   *TPC*

An Irish pine dresser, c1840, 55in (139.5cm) wide.
**£1,100–1,300** *UP*

A West Country cottage glazed pine dresser, with cupboards below and applied split mouldings, 19thC, 48in (122cm) wide.
**£2,000–3,000** *CC*

A pine free-standing base, c1860, 46in (116.5cm) wide.
**£450–550** *AL*

An Irish pine dresser, c1840, 68in (172.5cm) wide.
**£1,100–1,300** *UP*

A German pine breakfront dresser, 19thC, 59in (149.5cm) wide.
**£1,000–1,500** *PC*

An Irish one-piece pine dresser, with a plate rack, c1860, 54in (135cm) wide.
**£900–1,000** *PIN*

A Cornish pine dresser, 18thC, 58in (147cm) wide.
**£1,800–2,500** *PH*

A North Wales pine dresser base, with a thick sycamore top, 90in (228.5cm) wide.
**£1,500–2,000** *PH*

A miniature pine dresser base, c1840, 25in (63.5cm) wide.
**£350–450** *AS*

A long pot board dresser base, c1830, 134in (340cm) wide.
**£2,000–3,000** *PH*

A North Country enclosed dresser, 19thC.
**£1,200–1,500** *JMW*

A pine base unit, c1870, 60in (152cm) wide.
**£500–650** *SSD*

A pine dresser, 48in (122cm) wide.
**£1,100–1,300** *LAM*

A Welsh pine half glazed dresser, early 19thC, 72in (182.5cm) wide.
**£1,200–1,400** *TPC*

An early Victorian Irish pine dresser, 54½in (138cm) wide.
**£900–1,100** *WAT*

A Victorian Welsh pine dresser, with 3 drawers, c1860, 48in (122cm) wide.
**£600–700** *CUL*

An Irish pine dresser, with fretted top and fiddle front, c1860, 58in (147cm) wide.
**£800–1,250** *HON*

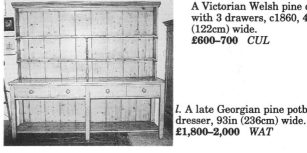

*l.* A late Georgian pine potboard dresser, 93in (236cm) wide.
**£1,800–2,000** *WAT*

*l.* A pine dresser, with 3 central drawers flanked by 2 cupboards to base, late 19thC, 43in (109cm) wide.
**£600–700** *CUL*

A pine dresser, c1850, 88in (223.5cm) wide.
**£2,500–4,000** *Sca*

An Irish pine dresser, c1880, 63in (160cm) wide.
**£1,000–1,300** *UP*

An Irish pine dresser, c1860, 52in (132cm) wide.
**£1,000–1,300** *UP*

A pine dresser, 19thC, 60in (152cm) wide.
**£1,000–1,200** *PH*

A George III pine dresser, with moulded cornice above a plate rack, the lower section with 3 frieze drawers above a pair of fielded arched panelled cupboard doors, on square section feet, 54in (137cm) wide.
**£2,500–3,500** *Bon*

A Yorkshire serpentine front pine dresser, 54in (137cm) wide.
**£2,000–2,500** *SSD*

A Dutch pine dresser, with green textured glass doors, 19thC, 41in (104cm) wide.
**£500–700** *CI*

An Irish pine dresser, c1880, 62in (157cm) wide.
**£1,500–2,000** *CPA*

A pine display dresser, c1880, 76in (193cm) wide.
**£1,200–1,500** *SPA*

A pine dresser base, c1830, 60in (152cm) wide.
**£400–600** *SPA*

A pine dresser base, c1875, 60in (152cm) wide.
**£800–1,000** *SPA*

A Flemish pine dresser base, c1890, 34in (86cm) wide.
**£300–350** *AnD*

A pine dresser, with glazed doors, 3 drawers and cupboards to base, late 19thC, 66in (167.5cm) wide.
**£600–700** *CUL*

A Cornish glazed dresser, 19thC, 48in (122cm) wide.
**£850–1,100** *WV*

A pine dresser, with 3 frieze drawers and 3 cupboards, 19thC, 60in (152cm) wide.
**£1,250–1,350** *WV*

*l.* A pine dresser, early 19thC, 72in (182.5cm) wide.
**£1,250–1,450** *WV*

A Georgian pine dresser base, 72in (182.5cm) wide.
**£1,300–1,650** *PEN*

A pine dresser, 19thC, 120in (304.5cm) wide.
**£2,000–3,000** *WV*

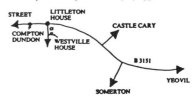

A Devonshire pine dresser, with glazed top, 51in (129.5cm) wide.
**£1,500–2,000** *PH*

A pine dresser, c1890.
**£1,000–1,500** *CPA*

An Irish pine dresser, c1880, 37in (94cm) wide.
**£1,000–1,200** *UP*

A pine dresser, c1870.
**£1,100–1,500** *CPA*

A pine dresser, 18thC, 58in (147cm) wide.
**£2,000–3,000** *VV*

A glazed two-piece pine dresser, c1850.
**£900–1,100** *CPA*

A pine dresser, c1880.
**£900–1,100** *CPA*

A glazed two-piece pine dresser, unrestored, c1860.
**£800–1,000** *CPA*

A pine dresser, c1840, 42in (106.5cm) wide.
**£950–1,150** *AL*

*r.* An Irish pine one-piece dresser, with original feet and cornice, c1840.
**£1,000–1,300** *GPA*

*l.* A Victorian Irish pine dresser, 49in (124.5cm) wide.
**£1,500–2,500** *Ad*

An Irish pine dresser, c1860, 52in (132cm) wide.
**£1,000–1,300** *LC*

A pine dresser base, with 7 drawers and central cupboard, c1860, 71in (180cm) wide.
**£550–650** *ASP*

An Irish pine dresser, c1870, 47in (119cm) wide.
**£650–750** *ASP*

A pine dresser base, c1880, 85in (216cm) wide.
**£500–700** *OCP*

*r.* A Victorian dresser base, with 9 drawers and 1 door, c1870, 85in (216cm) wide.
**£650–750** *ASP*

An Irish pine dresser, with rope-twist shelves, c1840, 66in (167.5cm) wide.
**£1,100–1,500** *LC*

A pine dresser base, c1840, 39in (99cm) wide.
**£600–700** *SSD*

A North Wales pine dresser, with a potboard, c1780, 78in (198cm) wide.
**£2,500–3,500** *HG*

A French pine dresser, c1900, 74in (188cm) wide.
**£800–1,000** *AD*

A Lincolnshire pine chiffonier, with a carved back board, 60in (152cm) wide.
**£1,200–2,000** *PC*

A pine dresser, with a shaped top, c1800.
**£1,200–1,500** *AL*

An early pine base, 52½in (131cm) wide.
**£500–700** *AL*

*r.* An Austrian dresser, 40in (101.5cm) wide.
**£900–1,000** *RK*

An Irish country pine dresser, 54in (137cm) wide.
**£675–750** *RK*

A Victorian pine buffet, on 5 legs, fitted with 7 drawers, 71in (180cm) wide.
**£500–600** *AL*

A Welsh breakfront pine dresser, Anglesey, c1830, 80in (203cm) wide.
**£3,000–4,000** *HG*

A Scottish dresser, 51in (129.5cm) wide.
**£750–1,000** *RK*

A French dresser, c1860.
**£600–700** *TPF*

A Shetland Islands dresser, with iron handles, c1880, 51in (130cm) wide.
**£750–1,000** *AL*

A Bavarian pine kitchen dresser, handles replaced, 49in (124.5cm) wide.
**£700–800** *CHA*

A Scottish pine dresser base, with inlay to drawers, c1860, 43in (109cm) wide.
£400–500 *HOA*

A Victorian pine dresser, with 4 small, 4 large drawers and a central cupboard, c1860, 60in (152cm) wide.
£700–750 *COT*

A Polish pine kitchen dresser, with drawers and glazed doors, c1830, 39½in (100cm) wide.
£525–625 *POT*

A mid-Victorian pine potboard dresser, c1870, 60in (152cm) wide.
£2,500–2,750 *POT*

*l.* An early Victorian pine single drawer dog kennel dresser, with wide boarded rack, c1850, 56in (142cm).
£1,000–1,225 *POT*

A pine dresser base, c1850, 42in (106.5cm) wide.
£440–500 *GD*

A Polish pine country dresser base, with one drawer and 2 panelled doors, c1870, 51in (129.5cm) wide.
£325–375 *ASP*

A fiddle front dresser, c1780, 54in (135cm) wide. **£900–1,200** *UP*

A two-piece pine dresser, c1780, 90in (229cm). **£2,000–3,500** *UP*

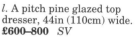

A George III pine dresser, the later raised open shelved back with a moulded cornice, c1790, 66in (168cm) wide. **£3,000–4,000** *SS*

*l*. A pitch pine glazed top dresser, 44in (110cm) wide. **£600–800** *SV*

A scratch carved pine dresser, c1780. **£900–1,200** *UP*

*l*. An Irish pine dresser, 18thC, 54in (135cm) wide. **£900–1,100** *PCL*

A pine pot board dresser, with a new base, 83½in (212cm) wide. **£1,200–1,500** *AL*

A pine dresser, with new drawers and back boarding, 19thC, 84½in (216cm) wide. **£1,500–2,000** *AL*

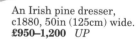

An Irish pine dresser, c1880, 50in (125cm) wide. **£950–1,200** *UP*

An Irish pine dresser, with new handles, c1840, 48in (122cm) wide. **£1,500–2,000** *AL*

A Lancashire pine dresser, with 3 bowfront drawers, c1860, 59in (147.5cm) wide. **£1,000–1,200** *Sca*

A Yorkshire serpentine front dresser, c1850, 54in (135cm) wide. **£1,200–1,500** *SSD*

## Continental Pine

Mainly from Eastern Europe, much of which is relatively recent, the styles and construction of Continental pine are very suitable for today's smaller houses, such as knock-down wardrobes, and smaller glazed kitchen dressers.

*r.* A pine dresser, with boarded back, 19thC, 60in (152cm) wide.
**£1,250–1,350** *WV*

A pine dresser, with original decorative frieze, wide back boards, c1840, 61in (155cm) wide.
**£750–950** *OCP*

A pine dresser, with plate rack, c1890, 57in (144.5cm) wide.
**£700–900** *OCP*

A pine dresser, the open base with stretchers, early 19thC, 78in (198cm) wide.
**£1,350–1,550** *WV*

A pine chicken coup dresser, c1860, 59in (149.5cm) wide.
**£600–900** *OCP*

A pine dresser, with plate rack and 4 spice drawers, c1870, 58in (147cm) wide.
**£450–550** *OCP*

An Irish pine dresser, with fretwork top, 2 drawers and 2 panelled doors to base, c1880, 48in (122cm) wide.
**£450–485** *SA*

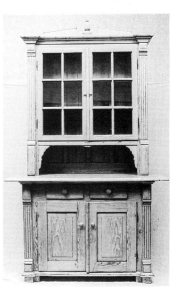

A Continental pine kitchen dresser, with glazed doors to top and 2 panelled doors to base, c1870, 92in (233.5cm) high.
**£750–850** *ASP*

An Irish pine cottage dresser, Co. Galway, c1840.
**£1,100–1,500** *HON*

A Scottish pitch pine dresser base, with 7 drawers and shaped back, c1870, 80in (203cm) wide.
**£1,150–1,350** *LRG*

A late Victorian pine dresser, 53in (134.5cm) wide.
**£2,000–3,000** *W*

A West Country pine dresser, c1790, 88½in (225cm) wide.
**£1,800–2,000** *BH*

A Lincolnshire pine low dresser base, c1870, 52in (132cm) wide.
**£900–1,000** *UC*

A Cornish pine dresser, late 19thC, 53in (134.5cm) wide.
**£1,500–2,000** *Ad*

A Scottish pine dresser, with spice drawers, c1850, 70in (177.5cm) high.
**£700–900** *BH*

A Victorian pine china cabinet, with unusual relief on cornice, 46in (116.5cm) wide.
**£1,500–2,000** *OA*

A pine dresser base, c1840, 44in (111.5cm) wide.
**£400–500** *AL*

An Edwardian breakfront pine Welsh dresser, with stained glass cupboard doors above, 59in (149.5cm) wide.
**£2,000–3,000** *OA*

A Victorian pine breakfront dresser.
**£3,000–4,000** *WEL*

A pine glazed two-piece dresser, c1840.
**£1,000–1,500** *CPA*

A pine dresser, Co. Longford, c1850, 47in (119cm) wide.
**£600–800**   *DMe*

An Irish pine dresser, single drawer, c1855, 37in (94cm) wide.
**£500–580**   *DMe*

A goose dresser, with 2 drawers and open base, County Laois, c1780, 60in (152cm) wide.
**£2,000–2,500**   *DMe*

*r.* A pine dresser, with six spice drawers, c1840, 83in (210.5cm) wide.
**£1,800–2,000**   *DMe*

*l.* A pine dresser, Co. Kildrare, c1845, 45in (114cm) wide.
**£600–650**   *DMe*

*l.* A pine dresser, with herringbone panels, Co. Tipperary, c1850, 40in (101.5cm) wide.
**£580–600**   *DMe*

A pine glazed dresser, c1860, 52in (132cm) wide.
**£2,000–3,000** *Far*

An Irish cottage dresser, c1850, 48in (122cm) wide.
**£3,500–4,500** *BR*

An Irish dresser, 18thC, 54in (137cm) wide.
**£2,500–3,500** *Ad*

A Victorian pine dresser, c1870s, 75in (190.5cm) wide.
**£2,500–3,500** *OA*

A mid-Victorian dresser, 76in (193cm) wide.
**£2,500–3,000** *Ad*

A Lincolnshire pine dresser, c1880, 60in (152cm) wide.
**£2,000–3,000** *W*

*l.* A Georgian astragal glazed pine dresser, 58in (147cm) wide.
**£3,500–4,000** *Ad*

An Irish pine dresser, 53in (137cm) wide.
**£2,000–3,000** *Ad*

A pine breakfront dresser, 56in (142cm) wide.
**£3,500–4,000** *Far*

An Irish dresser, 18thC, 56in (142cm) wide.
**£2,500–3,500** *Ad*

An early Victorian pine dresser, with ornate fretwork, Co. Laois, c1840, 63in (160cm) wide. **£1,400–2,000**  *DMe*

A pine dresser, c1860, 56in (142cm) wide. **£500–600**  *DFA*

A pine dresser, restored, c1890, 50in (127cm) wide. **£350–450**  *DFA*

An Irish pine open rack dresser, with reeded sides and top, the base with 2 drawers and 2 cupboard doors, c1850, 59in (149.5cm) wide. **£800–1,000**  *HON*

An Irish pine fiddle front dresser, with fretwork top and 2 drawers, c1840, 58in (147cm) wide. **£800–1,000**  *HON*

A pine dresser, with 2 glazed doors to top, 2 drawers and 2 cupboard doors to base, c1880, 41in (104cm) wide. **£350–450**  *Byl*

An Irish pine dresser, c1880, 52in (132cm) wide. **£400–600**  *Byl*

A pine dresser, with 2 panelled doors, c1865, 48in (122cm) wide. **£500–700**  *Byl*

An Irish pine dresser, with 3 shelves, 2 drawers and 2 panelled cupboard doors, c1860, 53in (134.5cm) wide. **£600–800**  *Byl*

An Irish pine dresser in 2 sections, c1840, 48in (122cm) wide.
**£1,500–2,500** *AL*

An Irish pine fiddle front dresser, c1840, 57in (145cm) wide.
**£1,100–1,500** *UP*

A pine dresser, the doors with leaded glass, c1890, 68in (172.5cm) wide.
**£1,500–2,500** *W*

A Scottish dresser, c1880, 49in (125cm) wide.
**£750–850** *RK*

An early Victorian pine dresser base, with original handles, c1840, 58in (147cm) wide.
**£950–1,200** *Sca*

A dresser base, c1840, 73in (185cm) wide.
**£800–1,100** *AL*

A Welsh pine dresser, with 2 glazed cupboards, original handles and hooks, c1790, 62in (157cm) high.
**£2,000–3,000** *Sca*

*r.* A mixed wood Irish dresser, c1800, 52in (133cm) high.
**£1,100–1,500** *UP*

A Welsh glazed dresser, c1880, 39in (99cm) wide.
**£800–1,000** *RK*

A late Victorian Cornish dresser, c1870, 78in (198cm) high.
**£1,500–2,500** *Ad*

A narrow cottage spice dresser, c1860, 34in (85cm) wide.
**£350–400** *PIN*

An Irish pine fiddle front dresser with 3 drawers, c1840, 78in (198cm) high.
**£1,200–1,400** *LC*

An Irish pine dresser, with
3 shelves and 2 cupboard doors,
c1880, 48in (122cm) wide.
**£400–600** *Byl*

An Irish pine dresser, with
2 drawers and 2 cupboard doors
to base, c1880, 43in (109cm) wide.
**£350–500** *Byl*

An Irish pine dresser, with
3 drawers and 2 cupboard
doors to base, c1860, 50in
(127cm) wide.
**£500–750** *Byl*

A pine dresser, the top with
glazed doors, the base with
2 drawers and 2 cupboard doors,
c1870, 50in (127cm) wide.
**£400–500** *Byl*

*r.* An Irish original
chicken coup dresser,
48in (122cm) wide.
**£950–1,200** *AF*

*l.* An Irish fiddle
front pine dresser,
with fretwork top
and 3 drawers to
base, c1800, 60in
(152cm) wide.
**£2,000–2,200** *SA*

An Irish pine dresser, with
fretwork top, 2 drawers and
2 doors with moulded panels to
base, c1870, 52in (132cm) wide.
**£480–550** *SA*

An Irish pine dresser, with
fretwork top, 2 drawers and
2 decorated doors to base,
c1870, 43in (109cm) wide.
**£380–420** *SA*

An Irish pine dresser, with
2 drawers, and 2 panelled
doors to base, feet replaced,
c1850, 56in (142cm) wide.
**£480–550** *SA*

A pine two-piece dresser,
with 18thC top, 57in
(144.5cm) wide.
**£400–600** *OCP*

An Irish pine fiddle front
dresser, with 2 drawers,
c1865, 55in (139.5cm) wide.
**£500–600** *Byl*

A pine cottage dresser, with
carving on cornice, 2 drawers
and 2 decorated doors, c1870,
42in (106.5cm) wide.
**£420–480** *SA*

A pine dresser, with 2 glazed
doors to top, 2 drawers and
2 panelled doors to base,
c1880, 48in (122cm) wide.
**£400–600** *Byl*

An Irish pine dresser,
with 2 cupboard doors
and shoe feet, c1860,
50in (127cm) wide.
**£500–600** *Byl*

## Make the most of Miller's

*In* **Miller's Pine &
Country Buyer's Guide**
*we do NOT just reprint
saleroom estimates.
Our consultants work
from realised prices
and then calculate a
price range for similar
items, avoiding
uncharacteristic 'one
off high or low results.*

A pine refectory table, with twin-plank top, plain moulded friezes and square chamfered legs, joined by flattened stretchers, 19thC, 160in (406cm) long.
**£1,400–1,800**  *C*

A pine drop-leaf table, c1880, 34in (86cm) long.
**£140–180**  *AL*

A pine side table, c1880, 36in (91.5cm) wide.
**£75–100**  *AnD*

A Victorian pine table with 4 frieze drawers, c1860, 63in (160cm) wide.
**£500–600**  *COT*

A Victorian pine side table, with 2 drawers, bamboo style legs, some repairs, 35in (89cm) wide.
**£200–350**  *HNG*

A pine side table, with single plank top, single drawer and porcelain handles, turned legs, late 19thC, 22in (56cm) wide.
**£150–300**  *HNG*

*r.* A German pine breakfast table, with twin pedalstals and heavily carved feet, c1850, 39in (99cm) wide.
**£400–600**  *HNG*

A Regency pine tilt-top table, on central reeded base, with 3 legs and original wood casters, 19thC, 46in (116.5cm) diam.
**£500–600** *CI*

A pine serving table, c1830, 96in (243.5cm) long.
**£500–600** *SPA*

A pine kitchen table, cut down for use as a coffee table, c1880, 39in (99cm) wide.
**£200–250** *SPA*

A pine serving table, c1900, 36in (92cm) high.
**£200–250** *MofC*

A pine kitchen table, c1875, 72in (182.5cm) long.
**£400–550** *SPA*

A Victorian pine side table, with 2 drawers, 46½in (118.5cm) wide.
**£350–500** *AL*

*l.* A farmhouse table, c1870, 66in (167.5cm) wide. **£700–800** *SSD*

A pine and elm tilt-top pedestal table c1840, 36in (91cm) wide.
**£500–700** *SSD*

A lift-top table, c1840, 34in (86cm) wide. **£350–400** *AL*

A drop-leaf table, with drawer under, c1840, 60in (152cm) wide.
**£300–350** *AL*

A pitch pine desk, with side flap and two porcelain inkwells, 19thC, 36in (91.5cm) wide.
**£300–400** *AL*

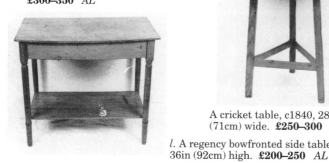

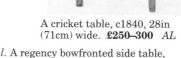

A cricket table, c1840, 28in (71cm) wide. **£250–300** *AL*

*l.* A regency bowfronted side table, 36in (92cm) high. **£200–250** *AL*

A country pine side table, stretchers restored, c1750, 30in (76cm) wide.
**£350–400** *PEN*

A pine cricket table, 24in (61cm) diam.
**£220–250** *GD*

A farmhouse table with elm single plank top, with 2 drawers and original brass handles, square tapered feet, 72in (182.5cm) long.
**£650–800** *HGN*

A Georgian pine kitchen table, with original brass bale handles, on square tapered legs, 28in (71cm) wide.
**£225–275** *ERA*

A Continental pine candle stand c1870, 13in (33cm) diam.
**£125–145** *PEN*

*r.* A Continental table, with cupboard below, c1820, 37½in (95cm) wide.
**£360–400** *GD*

A pine trestle refectory table, 1830s, 109in (276.5cm) long.
**£580–650** *GD*

An early Victorian pine flap-over tea table, with gateleg, hardwood legs, c1850, 36in (91.5cm) wide.
**£175–200** *POT*

A Victorian pine kitchen table, with drawer, c1860, 60in (152cm) wide.
**£340–400** *GD*

A Victorian pine occasional table, on turned fruitwood base, top damaged, 30in (76cm) wide.
**£150–175** *POT*

A pine cider table, with cross frame, c1910, 25in (64cm) wide.
**£125–140** *ASP*

A Victorian pine stretchered table, with 2 drawers, c1850, 48in (122cm) long.
**£350–390** *GD*

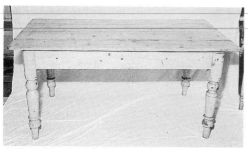

A Victorian pine kitchen table, on turned legs, c1880, 68in (172.5cm) long.
**£175–230** *POT*

An early Victorian pine side table, with simulated bamboo legs, c1840, 34in (86cm) wide.
**£75–120** *POT*

A cricket table, mid-19thC, 32½in (81cm) diam.
**£300–385** *POT*

A pine table, with beech legs, on original casters, c1905, 38in (96.5cm) wide.
**£200–300** *POT*

An early Victorian pine side table, on tapered square legs, c1850, 34in (86cm) wide.
**£100–150** *POT*

A pine table, with one drop-leaf and 2 drawers, c1890, 36in (91.5cm) wide.
**£200–250** *AL*

A pine cupboard, with one long drawer above a cupboard with pigeonholes, c1870, 38in (96.5cm) wide.
**£500–570** *AL*

A pine cupboard, with 2 panelled doors, c1870, 57in (144.5cm) wide.
**£200–220** *AL*

A pine table, with turned legs, cut down, c1890, 39in (99cm) wide.
**£100–150** *FAG*

A pine combination chest of drawers with a cupboard at the top, c1860, 42in (106.5cm) wide.
**£850–900** *AL*

A pine table, with one drawer, the legs cut down, c1890, 35in (89cm) wide.
**£125–175** *AL*

A pine washstand, with a marble top, a drawer, and a shelf beneath, c1880, 30in (76.5cm) wide.
**£250–300** *AL*

A side table, with one small drawer, c1880, 38in (96.5cm) wide.
**£200–260** *AL*

A pine side table, with 2 drawers and a drop-leaf, c1870, 42in (106.5cm) wide.
**£300–335** *AL*

A pine table, cut down, c1870, 46in (116.5cm) wide.
**£100–150** *AL*

A pine box, with 2 drawers, the interior with a candle box, the inside of the lid panelled, c1880, 42in (106.5cm) wide.
**£250–300** *AL*

A pine box, the interior fitted with a tray, c1860, 37in (94cm) wide.
**£180–220** *AL*

A set of pine shelves, c1890,
30in (76cm) wide.
**£100–125** *AL*

A pine cricket table, with 3 legs
and a shelf beneath, c1860, 28½in
(72.5cm) wide.
**£450–480** *AL*

A pine chest of drawers, with
2 drawers above a deep bottom
drawer, c1870, 26in (66cm) wide.
**£280–300** *AL*

A Continental pine pot cupboard,
c1910, 17in (43cm) wide.
**£90–110** *FAG*

A pine hanging cupboard, c1880,
16in (40.5cm) wide.
**£100–125** *COP*

A pine pot cupboard,
with a wooden knob,
15in (38cm) wide.
**£200–240** *AL*

A pine chest of 6 small drawers,
c1860, 23½in (60cm) wide.
**£200–300** *FAG*

A pine pot cupboard, with
brass handle, c1890, 14½in
(35.5cm) wide.
**£125–175** *AL*

A pine plate rack, c1880, 16in
(41cm) wide.
**£90–120** *FAG*

A pine chiffonier, with 3 drawers and one cupboard, and a shaped back, c1865, 42½in (108cm) wide.
**£350–380** *DMA*

A Dutch pine dresser base, c1840, 46in (116.5cm) wide.
**£250–300** *DMA*

A Louis Philippe style pine sideboard, of European origin, c1890, 42in (106.5cm) wide.
**£325–375** *AnD*

A pine side table, with 3 drawers, c1860, 45in (114cm) long.
**£180–300** *DMA*

A pine D-end breakfront sideboard, 19thC, 62in (157cm) wide.
**£700–900** *TPC*

A set of pine wall shelves, c1890, 18½in (47cm) wide.
**£60–70** *AL*

A pine swing mirror, c1880, 27in (58.5cm) wide.
**£200–235** *AL*

A pine stool, c1890, 12in (30.5cm) wide.
**£30–35** *AL*

A set of pine wall shelves, c1880, 36in (91.5cm) wide.
**£75–85** *AL*

A Continental pine plant stand, c1920, 45in (114cm) wide.
**£80–100** *FAG*

A set of pine steps, c1890, 17½in (44.5cm) wide.
**£30–35** *AL*

A pine cricket table, with a shelf, c1860, 25in (63.5cm) wide.
**£350–370** *AL*

A pine table, with straight legs, and one drawer, c1890, 36in (91.5cm) wide.
**£125–145** *AL*

A set of pine steps, c1890, 16in (40.5cm) wide.
**£30–35** *AL*

A set of pine shelves, by Liberty & Co., c1890, 20½in (52cm) wide.
**£100–115** *AL*

A pine stool, c1890, 17in (43cm) wide.
**£30–35** *AL*

An early Victorian pine cupboard, with 2 glazed doors, above a base with 2 long drawers and 2 cupboards, c1850, 48in (122cm) wide.
**£200–250** *DMA*

A Bavarian pine bread cupboard, once with wire panels to the front, 70in (177.5cm) high.
**£250–350** *AnD*

A pine panelled cupboard, with 2 doors, wooden knobs, 19thC, 72in (182.5cm) wide.
**£500–600** *TPC*

A Cornish pitch pine display cupboard on chest, the top with 2 astragal glazed Gothic style doors, 48in (122cm) wide.
**£800–1,200** *TPC*

A Continental pine vitrine, c1880, with a later top, 42in (106.5cm) wide.
**£450–600** *AnD*

A Dutch pine cupboard, with internal shelves and drawers, c1840, 48in (122cm) wide.
**£450–550** *AnD*

A Bavarian pine cupboard, with one panelled door, c1880, 36in (91.5cm) wide.
**£400–500** *AnD*

An early Victorian cupboard, with 2 doors above 2 different sized drawers, c1850, 48in (122cm) wide.
**£200–250** *DMA*

A Continental pine cupboard, with 2 doors glazed at the top, c1865, 48in (122cm) wide.
**£400–500** *AnD*

A pine side table, with 2 drawers, on turned legs, 19thC, 36in (91.5cm) wide.
**£150–200**  *TPC*

A pine table, with up-stand back, the drawer with pottery knobs, on turned legs, c1880, 37in (94cm) wide.
**£250–300**  *AL*

A pine table, with turned legs, c1880, 47in (119cm) wide.
**£300–325**  *AL*

A pine table, with one end drawer, on turned legs, c1890, 42½in (108cm) wide.
**£350–400**  *AL*

A pine cricket table, c1850, 24in (61cm) wide.
**£340–370**  *AL*

A pine table, with turned legs, c1880, 40½in (102cm) wide.
**£100–140**  *AL*

A pine table, with straight legs, c1890, 36in (91.5cm) wide.
**£100–125**  *AL*

A pine table, with one end drawer, on straight legs, c1890, 42in (106.5cm) wide.
**£280–320**  *AL*

A pine table, with a centre drawer, on tapering legs with stretchers, 18thC, 42in (106.5cm) wide.
**£200–250**  *TPC*

A pine glazed bookcase, c1840, 43in (109cm) wide.
**£550–650** *DMA*

A mid-European pine bookcase, with 2 glazed doors, and a drawer under, 1890, 36in (91.5cm) wide.
**£425–475** *AnD*

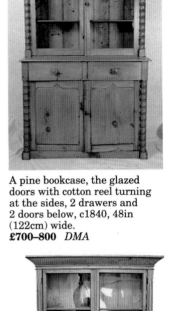

A pine bookcase, the glazed doors with cotton reel turning at the sides, 2 drawers and 2 doors below, c1840, 48in (122cm) wide.
**£700–800** *DMA*

A Czechoslovakian pine bureau/bookcase, with an inlaid walnut interior, c1875, 48in (122cm) wide.
**£1,000–1,250** *AnD*

A pine glazed bookcase, with reeded column supports, and one long drawer, c1870, 40in (101.5cm) wide.
**£300–350** *COP*

A pine glazed bookcase, with 2 short and 2 long drawers to base, with applied moulding, c1860, 48in (122cm) wide.
**£850–900** *MIL*

A Victorian Irish pine dresser, with glazed top, turned columns, 2 drawers and 2 doors, the panels carved, handles replaced, c1880, 49in (124.5cm) wide.
**£850–950** *OPH*

A Victorian pine glazed bookcase, c1860, 36in (91.5cm) wide.
**£200–300** *AnD*

An eastern European pine kitchen cabinet, with glass upper doors, 2 drawers and 2 cupboard doors, c1870, 39in (99cm) wide.
**£300–350** *NEW*

A pine armoire, with 2 doors, c1850.
**£500–550** *COP*

A pine dresser base, with one long drawer above 2 cupboard doors, c1870, 42in (106.5cm) wide.
**£225–275** *COP*

A pine corner cupboard, 19thC, 38in (96.5cm) wide.
**£450–550** *FOX*

A pine cupboard, with 4 doors, c1850.
**£700–750** *COP*

A pine dressing table, c1880, 54in (137cm) wide.
**£400–450** *COP*

A pine dresser, with 2 glazed cupboard doors above, turned columns, 2 drawers and 2 cupboards beneath, c1880, 45in (114cm) wide.
**£375–425** *COP*

A pine armoire, with 2 doors, c1880, 48in (122cm) wide.
**£350–400** *COP*

A Czechoslovakian food cupboard, c1860, 40in (101.5cm) wide.
**£450–500** *COP*

A pine sideboard, with a shelf between 2 cupboards, c1880, 54in (137cm) wide.
**£550–600** *AL*

A pine corner cupboard, with 4 doors and one drawer, c1865.
**£775–850** *COP*

A pine chest of drawers, with
2 short and 3 long drawers,
on bracket feet, c1820, 21in
(53cm) wide.
**£300–350** *DMA*

A pine chest of drawers, with 2 short
and 3 long drawers, on bracket feet,
c1880, 20in (50.5cm) wide.
**£500–600** *AL*

A pine chest with lift-up lid,
on a drawer base, the front
moulded, c1870, 38in
(96.5cm) wide.
**£300–320** *MIL*

A Dutch chest of 3 long drawers,
c1880, 40in (101.5cm) wide.
**£275–375** *AnD*

A Continental chest of
drawers, with 4 long drawers,
40in (101.5cm) wide.
**£275–375** *AnD*

A pine chest of drawers, with 2 short
and 2 long drawers, pottery knobs,
19thC, 34in (86cm) wide.
**£250–300** *LIB*

A pine chest, with 2 moulded long drawers,
on bracket feet, 19thC, 42in (106.5cm) wide.
**£300–350** *TPC*

A pine chest of drawers, with moulded drawer
fronts, 37in (94cm) wide.
**£280–300** *MIL*

A Georgian chest of drawers, with 2 short and
3 long drawers, 40in (101.5cm) wide.
**£350–450** *AnD*

A pine mule chest, with 2 drawers, the front
panelled, c1780, 45in (114cm) wide.
**£440–480** *MIL*

A pine corner cupboard, with a glazed door and brass knob, c1900, 13in (33cm) wide.
**£40–60** *FOX*

A miniature pine chest of drawers, with large wooden knobs, c1870, 13in (33cm) wide.
**£180–200** *MIL*

A pine hanging cupboard, c1850, 25in (63.5cm) wide.
**£120–150** *DMA*

A pair of pine hanging cabinets, with glazed doors, c1875, 14in (35.5cm) wide.
**£145–175** *AnD*

A Dutch pine cabinet, with locking door, originally used as the base for a safe, c1890, 27in (68.5cm) high.
**£235–265** *AnD*

A Victorian pine pot cupboard, c1840, 16in (40.5cm) wide.
**£100–130** *DMA*

A pine pot cupboard, with brass knob, c1880, 15in (38cm) wide.
**£150–185** *AL*

A pine pot cupboard, with scroll decoration, on turned feet, 15in (38cm) wide.
**£150–200** *AnD*

A pair of Continental pine bedside pot cupboards, c1890, 15in (38cm) wide.
**£200–250** *AnD*

A pine box, 19thC, 30in (76cm) long.
**£50–55** *LIB*

A pine mule chest, with brass handles,
early 19thC, 36in (91.5cm) wide.
**£250–350** *TPC*

A pine box, late 19thC, 16in (40.5cm) wide.
**£30–45** *FOX*

A pine wall hanging cupboard, with an interior
drawer, 19thC, 20in (50.5cm) wide.
**£70–100** *FOX*

A pine chest of drawers, with a bonnet drawer at the bottom, c1860, 36in (91.5cm) wide.
**£400–470** *AL*

A pine two-door cupboard, c1870, 42in (106.5cm) wide.
**£300–380** *AL*

A pine chest of drawers, with 2 long drawers, one short drawer, and a pot shelf, c1880, 33in (83.5cm) wide.
**£400–450** *AL*

A pine chest of drawers, with 2 short and 2 long drawers, c1880, 36in (91.5cm) wide.
**£350–400** *AL*

A pine chest of drawers, with 3 long drawers, c1850, 37½in (95cm) wide.
**£475–535** *AL*

A pine chest of drawers, with 2 short and 3 long drawers, c1830, 44½in (113cm) wide.
**£580–660** *AL*

A pine chest of drawers, with 4 long drawers and central handles, c1870, 49in (124.5cm) wide.
**£250–325** *COP*

A pitch pine desk, with 3 drawers either side and bookshelves in the kneehole, on casters, c1890, 49½in (126cm) wide.
**£680–730** *AL*

A pine chest of drawers, with 2 short and 2 long drawers, 39in (99cm) wide.
**£400–470** *AL*

A Victorian pine chest of drawers, with 2 short and 2 long drawers, 33in (83.5cm) wide.
**£230–260** *FOX*

A pine chest of drawers, with a marble top, tiled splashback, and 3 long drawers, c1890, 43in (109cm) wide.
**£400–460** *AL*

A pine armoire, with 3 mirrored doors, and 2 long drawers beneath, c1880, 63in (160cm) wide.
**£375–450** *COP*

A pine dresser, with 2 glazed doors above, 2 drawers and cupboard doors beneath, c1880, 50in (127cm) wide.
**£375–450** *COP*

A pine breakfront bookcase, with astragal glazed doors above, one long and 2 short drawers above 3 cupboards, c1870, 72in (182.5cm) wide.
**£800–1,100** *COP*

A pine armoire, with 2 doors, on bun feet, c1870, 46in (116.5cm) wide.
**£300–350** *COP*

A Lincolnshire pine chiffonier, c1860, 72in (182.5cm) wide.
**£700–750** *COP*

A pine dresser, with reeded and turned supports, 2 glazed doors above, 2 short drawers and 2 cupboard doors below, c1875, 52in (132cm) wide.
**£375–425** *COP*

A pine dressing table, with central mirror between 2 mirrored cupboards, 2 small drawers, and 2 cupboards below, c1870, 56in (142cm) wide.
**£400–450** *COP*

A pine linen press, c1865, 46in (122cm) wide.
**£475–575** *COP*

A pine armoire, with 2 doors, c1870, 46in (116.5cm) wide.
**£375–450** *COP*

A pine secrétaire, c1860,
42in (106.5cm) wide.
**£1,500–2,000** *UP*

A pine pedestal pub table,
c1880, 30in (76cm) high.
**£100–150** *AHL*

A pine dressing chest, the top with a
mirror on turned supports over a
drawer, a cupboard and 3 drawers to
a shaped plinth base, 19thC, 34in
(86cm) wide. **£300–400** *TPC*

A pine gallery back washstand,
with a shelf and drawer under,
on turned legs, 19thC, 24in
(61cm) wide.
**£200–300** *TPC*

A Welsh high backed
turned spindle
armchair, early 19thC.
**£200–300** *TPC*

A pine picture frame, c1870, 35in
(89cm) high. **£120–170** *AHL*

A Scandinavian pine dressing
chest, c1900.
**£250–275** *BEL*

A dairy table,
c1850, 28in
(71cm) wide.
**£100–120** *SA*

A pine mule chest, with 2 drawers,
early 19thC, 32in (81cm) wide.
**£250–350** *TPC*

A pine armoire, with 2 doors,
c1880, 55in (139.5cm) wide.
**£375–450** *COP*

A pine chiffonier, c1865,
44in (111.5cm) wide.
**£350–450** *COP*

A pine spice dresser, with
2 glazed doors, 6 small drawers,
above 2 short drawers and
2 cupboard doors, c1875, 58in
(147cm) wide.
**£625–675** *COP*

A pine bookcase, with 2 glazed
doors, c1880, 37in (94cm) wide.
**£300–375** *COP*

An eastern European pine dresser
base, c1850, 48in (122cm) wide.
**£375–450** *COP*

A pine dresser, with
2 glazed doors, 2 short
drawers, and 2 cupboard
doors beneath, c1880,
42in (106.5cm) wide.
**£350–425** *COP*

An Irish pine pantry cupboard,
c1870, 54in (137cm) wide.
**£375–450** *COP*

A pine armoire, with 2 doors, and
2 turned columns with urn finials,
c1870, 47in (119cm) wide.
**£400–450** *COP*

A pine food cupboard,
with 4 doors, c1870,
49in (124.5cm) wide.
**£1,000–1,125** *AL*

A pine chest of drawers, with 2 short and 2 long drawers, c1900, 34in (86cm) wide.
**£250–300** *Ber*

A pine sideboard, with 2 drawers above 2 cupboard doors, c1870, 41in (104cm) wide.
**£550–600** *AL*

A pine chest of drawers, with 2 short and 3 long drawers, and white pottery knobs, c1870, 40in (101.5cm) wide.
**£475–535** *AL*

A Scottish pine chest of drawers, with 2 jewellery drawers and a concealed drawer, c1870, 52in (132cm) wide.
**£850–900** *AL*

A pine chest of drawers, with 2 short and 3 long drawers, c1840, 43in (109cm) wide.
**£550–600** *AL*

A pine cupboard, with panelled doors, one with a brass knob, c1870, 49½in (125cm) wide.
**£400–435** *AL*

A pine chest of drawers, with 2 short and 2 long drawers, c1800, 31½in (80cm) wide.
**£550–600** *AL*

A pine chest of drawers, with 2 short and 2 long drawers, c1880, 36in (91.5cm) wide.
**£400–435** *AL*

A pine dresser base, with one long drawer above 2 cupboard doors, c1875, 40in (101.5cm) wide.
**£225–275** *COP*

A pine chest of drawers, with 2 short and 2 long drawers, c1870, 40in (101.5cm) wide.
**£200–225** *COP*

A pine sideboard, with one long drawer above 2 cupboard doors, with pine knobs, c1890, 39in (99cm) wide.
**£300–350** *FAG*

A mid-Victorian pine kitchen side table, with 2 drawers and turned legs, c1870, 34in (86cm) wide.
**£150–185** *POT*

A late Victorian table, on turned legs, 48in (122cm) wide.
**£200–275** *POT*

A Victorian Irish pitch pine farmhouse table, with turned legs, 96in (243.5cm) long.
**£680–850** *AF*

An early Victorian pine cricket table, c1840, 33in (84cm) diam.
**£150–185** *POT*

A pine oval drop-leaf supper table, c1900, 45in (114cm) long.
**£185–225** *OCP*

A pine coffee table, cut down to size, with single end drawer, on turned legs, c1870, 66in (167.5cm) wide.
**£110–135** *SA*

A pine drop-leaf table, c1860, 48in (122cm) long.
**£185–220** *OCP*

A pine tripod wine table, c1880, 27in (69cm) high.
**£130–150** *OCP*

*r*. A pine side table, with gallery back and single drawer, c1850, 24in (61cm) wide.
**£120–150** *DMe*

A pine side table, 33in
(84cm) wide.
**£130–180** *AL*

A pine cricket table,
c1850, 30in (75cm) high.
**£400–500** *PIN*

An Irish pine double stretcher table,
c1850, 84in (215cm) wide.
**£1,000–1,200** *PIN*

A pine and elm tilt-top,
pedestal table, c1860, 46in
(116.5cm) diam.
**£550–700** *SSD*

A pine writing table, with a
hinged drop leaf, c1820, 36in
(92cm) wide.
**£250–300** *AL*

A pine cricket table, c1850, 27in
(67.5cm) high.
**£350–500** *AL*

*l.* A pine table with bamboo
style legs, 21½in (54cm) diam.
**£200–300** *LAM*

A pine cricket table, c1850,
29in (73cm) diam.
**£400–500** *AL*

A pine lamp table, 22½in
(57cm) high.
**£100–120** *AL*

A bedside adjustable table,
c1850, 32in (81cm) high.
**£150–200** *AL*

A small pine base, c1880,
24in (61cm) wide.
**£150–200** *AL*

A pine dining table with one
drawer, c1840, 34in (86.5cm) wide.
**£350–400** *AL*

A pine table with slatted shelf, c1850,
59in (149.5cm).
**£300–350** *AL*

*l.* A two drawer work table, c1850, 72in (183cm) wide. **£600–700** *AL*

A shaped pine side table, c1870, 51in (130cm) long. **£250–350** *AL*

A Devonshire pine table, with shaped top rail and tapered legs, 108in (274cm) long. **£250–300** *PF*

A pine table, with concealed drawer at one end, late 19thC, 38in (96.5cm) wide. **£300–450** *AL*

A Georgian pine side table, on tapering legs, 23in (58.5cm) wide. **£400–550** *OA*

A German shoemaker's pine bench, 47in (119cm) long. **£100–150** *CHA*

A Welsh pine drop-leaf table, with one drawer and ogee scrolls each end, 30in (76cm) wide. **£250–300** *PF*

*r.* A pine dairy table, handles replaced, 19thC, 22in (55.5cm) wide. **£250–300** *AL*

A pine extending table, on dual scroll carved supports joined by lion's mask stretchers and iron cross struts, possibly Spanish, 122½in (310cm) wide extended. **£2,700–3,000** *CSK*

A Victorian pine tripod table, 33in (84cm) diam. **£500–700** *OA*

A pine side table, with one drawer and porcelain knobs, 36in (91.5cm) wide. **£250–400** *AL*

A Spanish pine table, with shaped side rails and one drawer, 24in (61cm) wide. **£150–250** *SM*

An Irish pine table, c1860, 31in (79cm) wide.
**£250–300**  *UP*

A pine side table, 33in (82.5cm) wide.
**£140–200**  *AL*

A pine and elm cricket table, c1840, 26in (66cm) high.
**£150–250**  *SSD*

A pine cricket table, 28in (71cm) diam.
**£350–500**  *PH*

A Georgian pine carving table, with 2 drawers and 6 legs, c1810.
**£700–800**  *PIN*

A Georgian pine cricket table, c1820, 29in (72.5cm) diam.
**£500–550**  *PIN*

A Victorian pine serving table, c1880, 40in (102cm) wide.
**£300–400**  *PIN*

A pine gateleg table, c1850, 34in (86cm) wide extended.
**£400–500**  *AL*

A pine gateleg table, with a drawer, c1850, 59in (150cm) wide extended.
**£450–550**  *AL*

A pine side table, with turned legs and double stretchers, 65in (165cm) wide.
**£500–700**  *PH*

A pine serving table, c1840, 63in (160cm) wide.
**£500–700**  *SSD*

A Victorian pine side table, c1880, 36in (92cm) wide.
**£300–350**  *PIN*

A pine farmhouse table, with stretcher,
66in (167.5cm) wide.
**£240–300** *OCP*

A pine side table, with single
drawer and turned legs, c1850,
31in (79cm) wide.
**£130–150** *DMe*

A pine cricket table, c1880,
27in (69cm) high.
**£80–100** *DFA*

A pine table, with a draw in one end, cut down,
48in (122cm) wide.
**£110–125** *SA*

An Irish rustic pine table, with 3 drawers, c1800,
30in (76cm) high.
**£250–300** *DFA*

A pine table, c1870, 94in
(238cm) diam extended.
**£200–250** *DFA*

A pine drop-leaf table, c1850, 52in (132cm) wide.
**£200–250** *DFA*

An Irish pine cricket table, c1860,
27in (69cm) high.
**£150–180** *DFA*

A small pine table, early
18thC, 26in (66cm) wide.
**£600–800**  *Al*

An early pegged straight
leg pine table, c1830, 26½in
(67cm) wide.
**£200–300**  *AL*

A Georgian pine side table,
with original swan neck
handles, 34in (86cm) wide.
**£300–400**  *OA*

A Victorian pine side table
with a frieze drawer, 27½in
(70cm) wide.
**£200–300**  *OA*

A Victorian one-flap table,
with 2 frieze drawers, 48in
(122cm) wide.
**£450–600**  *OA*

A Georgian pine side
table, 32in (81cm) wide.
**£300–400**  *OA*

A Victorian pine side table,
36in (91.5cm) wide.
**£300–400**  *OA*

A pine gateleg table, c1840,
47½in (120cm) wide.
**£450–600**  *AL*

A mid-Victorian pine side
table, 36in (91.5cm) wide.
**£300–400**  *OA*

A Victorian three-plank pine
farmhouse kitchen table,
c1870s, 96in (243.5cm) wide.
**£225–275**  *OA*

A Victorian pine serving table,
44in (111.5cm) wide.
**£300–450**  *OA*

A pine side table,
30½in (76cm) wide.
**£70–80**  *AL*

A pine farmhouse kitchen table,
c1870, 84in (213cm) long.
**£225–275**  *OA*

A baker's table, with a marble
top, 19thC, 37in (94cm) long.
**£400–500**  *BR*

*l.* A Victorian extending
pine dining table, with a
single leaf, 60in (152cm)
long extended.
**£600–750**  *OA*

*l.* A sycamore and pine cricket table, mid-18thC, 30in (76cm) diam.
**£450–600** *CHA*

A pine drop leaf table, with a drawer under, 59½in (150cm) long.
**£350–450** *CHA*

*l.* A pine work bench, c1840, 46in (117cm) long.
**£200–250** *AL*

A pine cricket table, c1840, 26in (66cm) diam.
**£250–350** *AL*

*l.* A picnic table and 4 folding chairs, c1930.
**£300–350** *MCA*

A French pine side table, c1890.
**£150–200** *TPF*

A pine bench table,
19thC, 84in (213cm) long.
**£120–130** *MS*

A Victorian pine desk, with a
mahogany top and 3 frieze
drawers, 80in (203cm) wide.
**£500–700** *AL*

A pine work table, with an applewood top, 19thC,
78in (198cm) long. **£850–1,200** *AL*

An Irish pine country table,
with a double rail, c1850,
25in (64cm) wide.
**£500–700** *CC*

A pine table, c1860, 96in (243.5cm) long.
**£1,000–1,200** *Sca*

A Regency pine side table, with
original handles, 32in (80cm) wide.
**£300–400** *AL*

An octagonal pine table, c1880, 47½in (118cm) diam.
**£750–950** *AL*

A pine table, c1840,
35in (89cm) long.
**£350–400** *Sca*

A Victorian pine table,
c1880, 43in (109cm) wide.
**£200–350** *Far*

A Regency pine side table, with
'bamboo' legs, original handles,
c1820, 36in (91.5cm) wide.
**£200–350** *AL*

A pine cricket table, c1810,
30in (76cm) diam.
**£400–500** *AL*

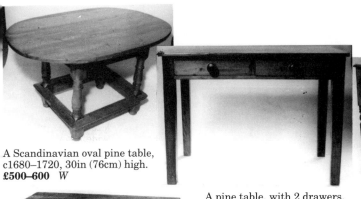

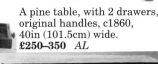

A Scandinavian oval pine table,
c1680–1720, 30in (76cm) high.
**£500–600** *W*

A pine table, with 2 drawers,
original handles, c1860,
40in (101.5cm) wide.
**£250–350** *AL*

A pine side table, c1860, 35½in
(91cm) wide.
**£150–200** *AL*

A pine two-drawer single leaf
table, 55in (139cm) wide.
**£300–400** *AL*

A pine table, with turned legs,
c1870, 28in (71cm) high.
**£100–150** *AL*

*l.* An Edwardian pine writing
table, with 3 drawers, 48in
(122cm) wide.
**600–800** *W*

A pine single flap table with
drawer, original porcelain
handles, c1850, 28in
(71cm) high.
**£200–300** *AL*

A pine serving table, c1840.
**£300–350** *CPA*

A pine farmhouse table, with
a sycamore top, c1880.
**£650–700** *CPA*

A pine serving table, from the North of England, with original handles, c1800, 74in (188cm) wide.
**£600–800** *BH*

A pine console table, 58in (147.5cm) wide.
**£1,000–1,300** *PH*

A pine table, reduced in height, c1800, 36in (91.5cm) wide.
**£150–200** *AL*

A pine table, c1720, 36in (91.5cm) wide.
**£400–500** *W*

An adjustable pine bed table, 23½in (59cm) wide.
**£120–200** *AL*

A pine gateleg table, c1850, 29in (74cm) high.
**£350–400** *AL*

A pine bench table, c1860, 26in (66cm) wide.
**£80–100** *AL*

A pair of pine potboard bases, c1880, 46in (117cm) wide.
**£900–1,000** *AL*

A pine writing table, with carved supports, c1860, 50in (127cm) wide.
**£650–750** *BH*

A pine side table, c1880, 60in (152cm) wide.
**£600–800** *UP*

A pine drop-leaf table, with a drawer, c1860, 35in (89cm) wide open.
**£250–300** *AL*

*l.* A pine hunt table, American, used for cutting up game after hunting, 74in (187cm) wide.
**£400–500** *PAC*

*l.* A pine gateleg table, with drawer under, 48in (122cm) wide.
**£500–550** *AL*

A Victorian pine lyre-ended library table, 36in (91.5cm) wide.
**£400–500** *AH*

A pine table, c1850, 82in (208cm) long.
**£400–450** *DFA*

A pine drop-leaf table, with drawers, c1880, 35in (89cm) wide.
**£300–325** *AL*

A pine table, with turned legs, c1880, 47in (119cm) wide.
**£350–425** *AL*

An Irish pine farmhouse table, c1880, 34in (86cm) long.
**£150–180** *DFA*

A pine side table, with 2 drawers, c1870, 36in (91.5cm) wide.
**£200–300** *AL*

A pine cricket table, on turned legs, c1860, 29½in (75cm) diam.
**£350–450** *AL*

A pine side table, with one long drawer, on turned legs, c1870, 33in (84cm) wide.
**£200–300** *AL*

A pine cricket table, c1860, 34½in (87cm) diam.
**£300–400** *AL*

A low pine table, with two-way drawer, on turned legs, c1890, 27in (69cm) wide.
**£150–220** *AL*

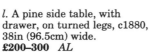

*l.* A pine side table, with drawer, on turned legs, c1880, 38in (96.5cm) wide.
**£200–300** *AL*

A pine press table, c1870, 18½in (47cm) wide.
**£200–250** *AL*

A pine cricket table, c1860, 30in (76cm) diam. **£550–600** *AL*

A Danish pine side table, c1890, 31in (79cm) high.
**£200–250** *RK*

*l.* A pine cricket table, with bobbin turned legs, c1870, 27in (69cm) diam.
**£200–300** *AL*

A pine cricket table, c1840, 24in (60cm) diam.
**£200–300** *AL*

A pine table, 52in (132cm) wide.
**£200–250** *CHA*

A North Wales baker's pine table, with lift-off lid revealing a dough trough, 56in (142cm) wide.
**£300–400** *CHA*

A pine work table, c1860, 60in (152cm) long.
**£250–300** *AL*

A pine table, with a single drop leaf, c1860, 35in (89cm) wide.
**£200–250** *AL*

An Irish pine wine table, with an unusual carved Celtic design, 1820–40, 21in (52.5cm) diam.
**£175–300** *PIN*

A pine table, c1860.
**£200–250** *AL*

A pine drop-leaf table, c1860, 50in (127cm) wide extended. **£250–350** *AL*

A pine writing table, c1860, 42½in (107cm) wide.
**£250–350** *AL*

A pine writing table, c1860, 36in (91.5cm) wide.
**£250–300** *AL*

An Irish pine bobbin leg three-tier cake table, c1860, 27in (69cm) high. **£300–400** *BH*

A pine serving table, with shelf, c1870,
87in (221cm) long.
**£400–500** *AL*

A pine side table, with drawer,
c1870, 36in (91.5cm) wide.
**£170–230** *AL*

A pine cricket table, with
turned legs, burn mark
to top, c1870, 20in
(51cm) diam.
**£200–250** *AL*

A pine stretcher table, with
three-plank top, c1860, 81in
(205.5cm) long.
**£500–600** *HON*

An Irish pine drop-leaf table,
on square legs, c1870, 42in
(106.5cm) diam.
**£175–250** *Byl*

A pine dairy table, with single drawer,
c1850, 24in (61cm) wide.
**£125–175** *SA*

A harbour commissioner's pine boardroom table,
with 6 turned legs and 2 side drawers, c1850s,
53in (134.5cm) wide.
**£900–1,100** *SA*

A pine coffee table, cut-down to size, on square legs
and stretchers, c1805, 60in (152cm) wide.
**£110–135** *SA*

A pine coffee table, cut-down to size, with
turned legs, c1890, 48in (122cm) diam.
**£110–125** *SA*

A pine cupboard, c1850,
72½in (183cm) wide.
**£650–850** *AL*

A Co. Galway pine
cupboard, c1840.
**£1,100–1,500** *HON*

A Victorian housekeeper's
pine cupboard, on a nine-
drawer base, c1840, 78in
(197.5cm) high.
**£2,000–3,000** *PIN*

A German pine cupboard,
with interior shelves.
**£375–400** *CPA*

An Irish pine food cupboard, 18thC,
63in (160cm) wide.
**£3,000–4,500** *Ad*

A Victorian pine pantry
cupboard, 75in (190.5cm) high.
**£3,000–4,000** *OA*

A Victorian pine
press/cupboard, doors
enclosing shelves, 48in
(122cm) wide.
**£1,200–2,000** *OA*

A pine huffer, c1840,
31½in (79.5cm) high.
**£600–750** *AL*

A two-door pine
cupboard, c1850,
83½in (212cm) high.
**£1,200–1,500** *AL*

An Irish cupboard,
with drawers, 72in
(182cm) high.
**£1,700–2,000** *RK*

A pine cupboard, c1840,
21in (53cm) high.
**£300–350** *AL*

A pine unit, the centre
cupboard with shelves,
19thC, 55½in (139cm) wide.
**£300–500** *AL*

An Irish pine food
cupboard, 58in (147cm)
high. **£1,400–1,800** *RK*

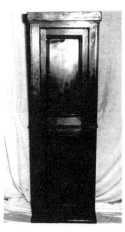

A narrow pine cupboard,
with 2 doors, c1840,
22½in (57cm) high.
**£850–1,000** *AL*

A Gothic pine cupboard,
53½in (135cm) wide.
**£1,200–1,500** *PH*

A Northern Irish panelled pine food
cupboard, c1800, 58in (145cm) wide.
**£1,100–1,500** *HG*

An Irish pine food
cupboard, c1850, 54in
(137cm) high.
**£1,500–2,000** *PH*

A pine fielded panelled food
cupboard, c1800, 56in
(142cm) wide.
**£2,000–3,000** *UP*

An Irish pine food cupboard,
c1870, 46in (116cm) wide.
**£1,100–1,500** *UP*

An Irish pine food cupboard,
58in (147cm) high.
**£1,500–2,500** *PH*

A French pine display
cupboard, c1890.
**£250–300** *TPF*

*l.* An Irish rustic pine
food cupboard, with
oak and pine frame,
early 18thC, 51in
(127.5cm) high.
**£1,200–1,500** *PIN*

A Welsh pine food cupboard,
18thC, 40in (101.5cm) wide.
**£2,000–2,500** *PH*

A pair of Continental pine waxed bedside cupboards, c1920. **£200–220** *TRU*

A pine food cupboard, 50in (127cm) wide. **£1,000–1,500** *Far*

A Victorian housemaid's pine cupboard, c1860, 44in (111.5cm) high. **£1,100–1,300** *PIN*

A pine cupboard, 84in (213cm) high. **£300–350** *SAn*

A small pine cupboard, c1870, 13in (33cm) wide. **£65–75** *AL*

A pine cupboard, with a shaped door, shelf inside, c1860, 50in (127cm) high. **£250–350** *AL*

An Irish pine food cupboard, with a knife drawer, c1820, 76½in (194cm) high. **£3,000–4,000** *W*

A pine wall cupboard, c1860, 29in (72.5cm) wide. **£150–200** *AL*

A twelve-door food cupboard, with original escutcheons, 19thC, 87in (222cm) wide. **£1,200–2,000** *AL*

A pine cupboard, with 4 shelves and shaped mahogany base, c1800, 71in (180cm) high. **£800–1,000** *AL*

A pine warming cupboard, c1830, 43in (109cm) wide. **£600–750** *AL*

A pine cupboard, c1850, 24in (61cm) high. **£200–250** *AL*

A pine cupboard, 20in (51cm) high. **£100–150** *LAM*

A pine huffer, c1840, 39in (99cm) wide. **£600–750** *AL*

A Georgian two-door pine cupboard, with raised and fielded panels, shelved interior, c1780, 58in (147cm) wide.
**£1,400–1,600** *TPC*

A pine cupboard, with canted sides and pigeonhole fitted interior, 19thC, 48in (122cm) wide.
**£600–800** *TPC*

An Irish pine four-door panelled cupboard, with dentil mouldings, c1850, 60in (152cm) wide.
**£700–800** *HON*

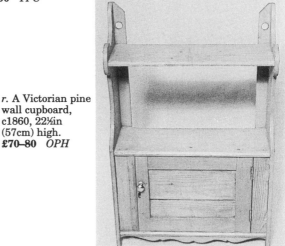

*r*. A Victorian pine wall cupboard, c1860, 22½in (57cm) high.
**£70–80** *OPH*

A Victorian pine farmhouse cupboard, c1885, 30in (76cm) wide.
**£90–110** *OPH*

An Irish pine cupboard, with breakfront top, panelled sides and 4 fielded panelled doors, c1820, 58in (147cm) wide.
**£1,500–2,000** *HON*

A pine tack cupboard, late 19thC, 30in (76cm) wide.
**£500–600** *CUL*

A pine wall cupboard, 19thC, 43in (109cm) high.
**£200–300** *LIB*

A pine cupboard, 52in (132cm) high.
**£950–1,200** *SAn*

A pine cupboard, with shelves and a drawer in base, c1800, 74in (188cm) high.
**£800–1,000** *AL*

An Irish panelled pine food cupboard, c1780, 50in (127cm) high.
**£900–1,100** *UP*

A panelled pine cupboard, c1840, 75½in (191cm) high.
**£550–600** *AL*

A pine wall cupboard.
**£80–100** *WEL*

A pine cupboard, with shelves inside, 40in (101.5cm) high.
**£2,000–2,500** *AL*

A pine wall cupboard, 15in (38cm) wide.
**£120–160** *AL*

An Irish food cupboard, with fitted interior, c1800, 51in (129.5cm) high.
**£1,200–1,600** *UP*

An Irish pine food cupboard, 49in (124cm) wide.
**£2,000–2,500** *PH*

A pine wall cupboard, c1860, 37in (92.5cm) wide.
**£200–250** *AL*

A pine cupboard, with 4 doors and 2 drawers, c1850.
**£1,000–1,500** *HON*

A Welsh pine hanging cupboard, 18thC, 52in (133cm) high.
**£1,500–2,000** *PH*

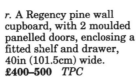

*r.* A Regency pine wall cupboard, with 2 moulded panelled doors, enclosing a fitted shelf and drawer, 40in (101.5cm) wide.
**£400–500** *TPC*

A Spanish pine food cupboard, with 2 doors, c1780, 40in (101.5cm) wide.
**£2,000–2,500** *Ced*

*r.* An Irish pine food cupboard, late 19thC, 60in (152cm) wide.
**£900–1,000** *CUL*

*l.* An Irish pine food cupboard, c1780, 48in (122cm) wide.
**£750–850** *CUL*

An Irish pine food cupboard, with 4 doors and 3 centre drawers, painted interior, late 19thC, 60in (152cm) wide.
**£1,100–1,200** *HeR*

A pine food cupboard,
c1850, 58in (147cm) high.
**£1,100–1,300** *UP*

A Georgian pine cupboard, with
arch panelled doors, standing on
bracket feet, 57in (144.5cm) wide.
**£3,000–4,000** *Ad*

An Edwardian pine hanging
bookcase, 36in (92cm) wide.
**£120–200** *OA*

A Danish pine cupboard,
with a fall front, 40in
(101cm) wide.
**£650–700** *RK*

A pitch pine cupboard, c1900,
71in (180cm) wide.
**£600–800** *PCL*

A pine two-door cupboard, with
adjustable shelves, c1880, 60in
(152cm) wide.
**£200–300** *AL*

A pine livery cupboard,
with 3 short and 2 long
drawers, 19thC.
**£900–1,200** *ARK*

A pine wall cupboard, c1880, 21in
(53cm) wide.
**£100–150** *AHL*

A pine estate cupboard, c1820,
96in (244cm) wide.
**£2,500–3,000** *SPA*

An Irish pine food cupboard,
c1800. **£2,000–3,000** *UP*

An Irish pine fielded panelled food
cupboard, c1800, 50in (125cm) high.
**£1,500–2,500** *UP*

An Irish pine food cupboard,
18thC, 56in (142cm) wide.
**£3,000–4,000** *Ad*

*l*. A Georgian pine panelled cupboard, with 2 doors, 48in (122cm) wide.
**£400–600** *TPC*

*r*. A Victorian pine wall cupboard, with panelled door, c1880, 26½in (67cm) high.
**£125–150** *COT*

*r*. An Irish pine butler's pantry cupboard, with panelled doors, c1850, 54in (137cm) wide.
**£2,500–3,000** *UC*

A Welsh pine harness cupboard, c1790, 58in (147cm) wide.
**£2,800–3,250** *UC*

A German pine cupboard, with one single drawer, beech turned legs and carvings, mid-19thC, 74in (188cm) high.
**£550–700** *HGN*

*l*. A pine wall hanging kitchen cupboard, original iron hinges, c1820, 36in (91.5cm) wide.
**£250–350** *HGN*

A Victorian pine floor standing cupboard, with 4 doors, replacement chicken wire panels, new handles, 35in (89cm) high.
**£450–650** *HGN*

An Irish pine food cupboard,
c1780, 57in (144cm) high.
**£2,000–3,000** *UP*

An architectural pine cupboard,
c1780, 50in (127cm) high.
**£900–1,100** *UP*

An Irish panelled pine food
cupboard, c1790, 53in
(135cm) high.
**£2,500–3,500** *UP*

A Scottish panelled pine
cupboard, c1800, 73in
(185cm) high.
**£900–1,100** *HG*

A pine cupboard, 39½in
(100cm) wide.
**£100–150** *WHA*

An Irish pine food cupboard, 18thC,
78in (198cm) high.
**£2,500–4,000** *Ad*

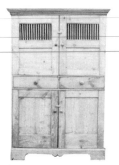

A pine food cupboard,
19thC, 50in (127cm) high.
**£800–850** *RK*

A pine proving cupboard, c1840,
46in (116.5cm) high.
**£500–800** *AL*

A pine proving cupboard, tin
lined, c1840, 44in (111.5cm) wide.
**£500–800** *AL*

A Dutch pine kitchen cupboard,
with decorative cornice, 19thC,
35in (89cm) wide.
**£400–500** *CI*

An Irish pine food cupboard,
with panelled doors and sides
and fantail moulding to cupboard
doors, c1850, 80in (203cm) high.
**£3,000–4,500** *CC*

A pine two-door cupboard, c1860,
36½in (92cm) high. **£200–300** *AL*

A pine single door cupboard, with false press front, c1840, 33in (84cm) wide.
£680–720 *GD*

*r.* A set of 3 pine stacking campaign cupboards, each with 2 doors and lifting handles, 19thC, 48in (122cm) wide.
£900–1,200 *TPC*

*l.* A pine cupboard, with shelves, 18thC, 57in (144.5cm) wide.
£950–1,150 *WV*

*r.* A German pine cupboard, with beech carvings and feet, original escutcheons and lock, replacement knob handles, c1870, 32in (81cm) high.
£400–550 *HGN*

A Czechoslovakian pine food cupboard, with original ribbed china knobs, 19thC, 34in (86cm) wide.
£375–400 *ERA*

A Continental pine food cupboard, c1860, 40in (101.5cm) wide.
£500–550 *GD*

A small pine cupboard, with 2 drawers and 2 cupboards, early 19thC, 48in (122cm) wide.
**£780–850** *GD*

A pine cupboard, with 2 drawers at top, c1885, 38in (96.5cm) wide.
**£150–180** *DFA*

A Georgian Irish pine food cupboard, with dentil cornice, raised and fielded panelled doors, bracket feet, c1770, 80in (203cm) wide.
**£2,500–3,000** *AF*

A pine food cupboard, in 2 sections, the top with 2 doors, the base with 2 drawers and 2 doors, c1830, 49in (124.5cm) wide.
**£1,000–1,500** *UC*

An Irish pine food cupboard, c1860, 82in (208cm) high.
**£1,200–1,500** *AF*

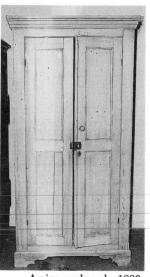

A pine cupboard, c1880, 37in (94cm) wide.
**£200–270** *DFA*

*l.* A pine press cupboard, with hinged top, two panelled doors enclosing shelving and 13 small drawers with brass ring handles, panelled sides and plinth base, 18thC, 43½in (110cm) wide.
**£1,000–1,400** *AH*

A Continental pine hanging cupboard, late 19thC, 69in (175cm) high.
**£500–600** *HGN*

A pine two door food cupboard, with lift-up shoe press above, dated '1829', 83in (210.5cm) high.
**£1,200–1,800**  *OCP*

A pine cupboard, c1840, 45in (114cm) wide.
**£150–180**  *DFA*

A pine cupboard, c1870, 37½in (95cm) wide.
**£130–150**  *DFA*

A pine linen cupboard, in 2 parts, c1870, 42½in (107cm) wide.
**£450–500**  *DFA*

An Irish pine cupboard, with 2 centre drawers and 4 panelled cupboard doors, c1860, 53in (134.5cm) wide.
**£800–900**  *HON*

A pine wall cupboard, c1880, 36in (91.5cm) wide.
**£150–175**  *AL*

A pine wall cupboard, with adjustable shelves, c1880, 36in (91.5cm) wide.
**£250–300**  *AL*

An Irish pine architectural cupboard, with 4 doors and sunburst decoration, c1840, 57½in (146cm) wide.
**£1,000–1,400**  *HON*

An Irish pine cupboard, with breakfront top, 2 panelled doors, with rope-twist columns to either side and panelled sides, c1820, 61in (155cm) wide.
**£2,000–2,200**  *HON*

A pine cupboard, with dentil moulded top and 2 panelled doors, c1850, 57in (144.5cm) wide.
**£750–820**  *HON*

A pine cupboard, with 2 doors, one side of interior with shelves, c1875, 48in (122cm) wide.
**£300–400** *Byl*

A pine cupboard, with single four-panel door, c1875, 38in (96.5cm) wide.
**£275–375** *Byl*

A pitch pine school cupboard, with 3 doors, the interior fitted with shelves, c1880, 54in (137cm) wide.
**£300–450** *Byl*

A pine cupboard, with 2 panelled doors, c1870, 55in (139.5cm) wide.
**£400–500** *Byl*

A pine cupboard, with 4 panelled doors and 2 centre drawers, c1880, 48in (122cm) wide.
**£500–800** *Byl*

A pine food cupboard, with 4 doors and decorated surround, c1860, 64in (162.5cm) wide.
**£550–750** *Byl*

An Irish pine food cupboard, with 2 glazed doors to top and 2 panelled doors to base, c1865, 49in (124.5cm) wide.
**£650–850** *Byl*

A Georgian pine wall cupboard, with single glazed door, c1790.
**£300–400** *SA*

A pine cupboard, with 2 panelled doors and 2 drawers to base, c1875, 50in (127cm) wide.
**£350–450** *Byl*

A pine cupboard, with
4 panelled doors, c1860,
48in (122cm) wide.
**£500–550** *SA*

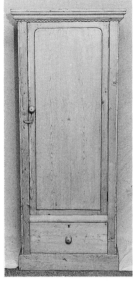

A pine cupboard, with
single door and drawer
beneath, late 19thC,
27in (69cm) wide.
**£285–325** *SA*

A pine cupboard, with glazed top, c1860,
54in (137cm) wide.
**£600–800** *TPC*

A Victorian pine china cupboard,
with 2 astragal glazed doors
above 2 blind panelled doors,
50in (127cm) wide.
**£800–1,200** *TPC*

A Continental pine cupboard,
with glazed doors to top, 42in
(106.5cm) wide.
**£620** *LIB*

A Continental pine medicine
cupboard, 19thC, 18in
(46cm) high.
**£50–60** *Cou*

A pine wall cabinet, with glazed
doors, c1880, 23½in (60cm) high.
**£120–130** *OPH*

*r.* A European pine
wall cabinet, c1900,
18in (45.5cm) high.
**£90–120** *OPH*

An Irish pine glazed cupboard, c1820, 77in (195.5cm) high.
**£3,000–4,000** *Ad*

An Irish pine pantry cupboard, late 19thC, 51in (129.5cm) wide.
**£2,500–3,000** *Ad*

A Georgian Irish pine cupboard, 48in (122cm) wide.
**£400–500** *Ad*

An Irish pine corner cupboard, c1800, 52in (130cm) wide.
**£2,000–2,500** *UP*

A pine two-door glazed cupboard, originally with metal mesh, c1825, 72½in (183cm) high.
**£900–1,000** *AL*

A pine glazed cupboard, with an arched top, 36in (91.5cm) wide.
**£300–350** *CHA*

*l.* A pine glazed cupboard, with adjustable shelves, c1860, 39½in (99cm) high.
**£250–400** *AL*

A pine food cupboard, c1880, 39in (99cm) wide.
**£1,500–2,000** *W*

A pine glazed cupboard with enclosed drawers, c1870, 15in (38cm) high.
**£280–350** *AL*

A pine glazed cupboard, 26in (66cm) wide.
**£200–350** *PH*

An Irish pine glazed cupboard, c1780, 56in (142cm) wide.
**£1,100–1,300** *UP*

A pine glazed cupboard, unrestored, c1840.
**£1,200–1,600** *CPA*

A pair of South German pine bedside cupboards, c1900.
**£120–150 each** *TPF*

A German pine bedside cupboard, c1900.
**£100–150** *CPA*

A German pine bedside cupboard. **£100–150** *CPA*

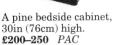

A pine bedside cabinet, 30in (76cm) high.
**£200–250** *PAC*

A pair of pine bedside cupboards, with one drawer and cupboard below, 20thC, 24in (61cm) wide.
**£150–200** *PC*

*l.* A Victorian pine bedside cupboard, 16in (41cm) wide.
**£200–300** *OA*

A Danish pine bedside cupboard, c1870, 25in (64cm) wide. **£175–200** *RK*

*l.* A Victorian pine bedside cupboard, c1880, 15in (38cm) wide.
**£200–300** *OA*

A Regency tambour-fronted bedside cupboard, c1820, 18in (46cm) wide.
**£250–350** *OL*

A pine bedside cabinet, 15in (38cm) wide.
**£200–300** *AL*

A pine pot cupboard,
c1850 15½in (40cm) wide.
**£200–300** *W*

A deep two-door pine
cupboard, c1840, 34in
(86cm) wide.
**£300–400** *AL*

A pine pot cupboard,
c1900, 30½in (77cm) high.
**£175–250** *W*

A pine drum-shaped
pot cupboard, with
marble top, c1840,
15½in (38cm) diam.
**£200–250** *LAM*

A Victorian pine
cupboard on stand,
19in (48cm) wide.
**£150–200** *AL*

A pine cupboard with
drawer, c1840, 22in
(56cm) wide.
**£150–200** *AL*

A late Victorian pine pot
cupboard, 15in (38cm) wide.
**£200–300** *W*

A pine pot cupboard,
with original
porcelain handle,
14in (36cm) wide.
**£175–250** *AL*

A pine cupboard, with
adjustable shelves, original
lock and key, c1840, 51in
(129.5cm) high.
**£110–130** *AL*

A pine pot cupboard,
19thC, 15in (37.5cm) wide
**£200–250** *AL*

A central European pine
pot cupboard, c1920,
12in (31cm) wide.
**£100–150** *SPA*

A pine pot cupboard,
with gesso
decoration, c1880,
15in (37.5cm) wide.
**£200–250** *AL*

A Swedish pine pot cupboard,
c1910, 24½in (62cm) wide.
**£140–180** *BEL*

*l.* A Regency pine
pot cupboard,
with tapered legs,
32in (81cm) high.
**£130–150** *AL*

*r.* A mid-European
pot cupboard,
17in (43cm) wide.
**£120–150** *RK*

A pine food cupboard, on bracket feet, c1820, 45in (114cm) wide.
**£600–700** *POT*

*r.* A pine glazed food cupboard, with 2 drawers and pillar sides, c1880, 74in (188cm) wide.
**£750–950** *OCP*

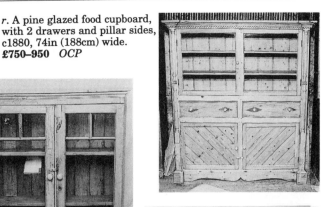

An Irish pine cupboard, with 2 glazed doors above 2 small doors, c1880, 36in (91.5cm) wide.
**£280–320** *SA*

*r.* A pine vitrine, original lock and key, late 19thC, 66in (167.5cm) high.
**£600–750** *HGN*

*l.* A Dutch pine corner cupboard, c1865, 20in (51cm) wide.
**£225–275** *AnD*

A pine cupboard, with 2 glazed doors to top and 2 panelled doors to base, c1875, 56in (142cm) wide.
**£500–560** *SA*

A pine bowfronted corner cupboard, c1780, 34in (86cm) wide.
**£950–1,200**  *UP*

A pine bowfronted barrel back corner cupboard, with carved shelves and a slide, c1740.
**£3,000–5,000**  *LAM*

A mid-Georgian corner cupboard, with a breakfront moulded cornice above a recess with open shelves and semi-domed top, flanked by moulded uprights, 48in (122cm) wide.
**£850–900**  *CSK*

A George III Cumbrian pine corner cupboard, 76in (193cm) high.
**£850–950**  *UP*

A pine corner cupboard, with barrel back and shaped shelves, c1840, 79in (200.5cm) high.
**£2,000–3,000**  *Ad*

A pine two-piece corner cupboard, c1780, 44in (112cm) wide.
**£1,000–1,300**  *UP*

An astragal glazed, barrel-backed pine corner cupboard, c1840, 80in (203cm) high.
**£1,500–2,500**  *AL*

A pine corner cupboard, 18thC.
**£800–1,000**  *ARK*

A George III pine corner cupboard, on moulded apron and block feet, 41½in (105cm) wide.
**£2,500–3,500**  *P(L)*

*l.* A pine corner cupboard, 80in (203cm) high.
**£700–800**  *RK*

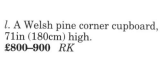

*l.* A Welsh pine corner cupboard, 71in (180cm) high.
**£800–900**  *RK*

*r.* A late George III pine standing corner cupboard, the moulded cornice with a foliate carved frieze above a central lion's head and spandrels with paterae and trailing husks, a single arched astragal glazed door between reeded uprights, with a panelled door below between similar uprights, 32½in (82cm) wide.
**£2,000–2,500**  *CSK*

A Georgian pine corner cabinet, the upper cupboards with shaped shelves, 50in (127cm) wide.
**£1,500–2,500** *Ad*

A pine corner cupboard, c1860, 46in (116.5cm) wide.
**£550–650** *WHA*

A late Georgian full length pine standing corner cabinet, 39in (99cm) wide.
**£1,500–2,500** *OA*

A pine corner cupboard, 19thC.
**£2,000–3,000** *PH*

A pine corner cupboard, 43in (109cm) wide.
**£1,200–1,500** *LAM*

*r.* An astragal glazed pine corner cupboard, 39in (99cm) wide.
**£1,500–2,500** *PH*

*l.* A Scandinavian pine corner cupboard dated 1731, 72in (182.5cm) high.
**£800–1,000** *W*

A Georgian stripped pine corner cabinet, 86½in (220cm) high.
**£1,500–2,000** *AG*

A Victorian Cornish pine corner cupboard, 33in (84cm) wide.
**£400–600** *Ad*

*r.* A pine glazed corner cupboard, c1860, on a new base, 84in (213cm) high.
**£700–750** *AL*

A pine architectural corner
cupboard, with barrel-back
and shaped interior display
shelves, early 19thC, 90in
(228.5cm) high.
**£2,500–3,500** *Ced*

A Victorian pine wall corner cupboard,
36in (91.5cm) high.
**£175–225** *WaH*

A Victorian pine hanging corner
cupboard, 30in (76cm) wide.
**£175–200** *ERA*

A pine corner cupboard,
the panelled doors with
original hinges,
enclosing shaped
shelved interior, 18thC,
40in (101.5cm) wide.
**£1,200–1,400** *TPC*

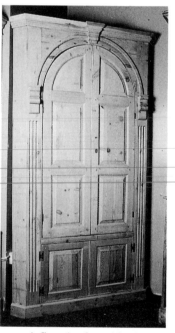

A Georgian barrel-back
corner cupboard, c1740,
51in (129.5cm) wide.
**£1,200–1,500** *COT*

A pine corner cupboard,
with glazed door, early
19thC, 31in (79cm) wide.
**£375–475** *POT*

*l.* A pine hanging
corner cupboard,
with single glazed
door, c1900, 29in
(74cm) wide.
**£160–185** *SA*

*r.* A pine corner
cupboard, the top with
2 panelled doors, the
base with 3 small
drawers and 2 panelled
doors, c1830, 36in
(91.5cm) wide.
**£1,150–1,250** *HeR*

A pine corner cupboard, with raised and fielded panelled doors, enclosing shaped shelves, bull's-eye and column mouldings to sides, 18thC, 42in (106.5cm).
**£1,400–1,800** *TPC*

A pine corner cupboard, with 2 glazed and 2 panelled doors, original blue painted interior, c1810, 46in (116.5cm) wide.
**£2,800–3,250** *UC*

A pine corner cupboard, with glazed cupboard doors, on bracket feet, c1860.
**£1,100–1,275** *POT*

A pine corner cupboard, with glazed top section, c1880, 51in (129.5cm) wide.
**£700–900** *OCP*

A Georgian barrel-back pine recess cupboard, with domed hood and shaped shelves, 37in (94cm) wide.
**£1,000–1,300** *ERA*

A pine glazed corner cupboard, the 2 upper doors with carved decoration and cut-outs, c1880, 54in (137cm) wide.
**£950–1,150** *OCP*

*l.* A Georgian pine barrel-back corner cupboard, with arched interior and shaped shelves, 2 raised and fielded panel doors with original iron work, by T. Greer, N. Ireland, c1811, 74in (188cm) high.
**£1,500–2,000** *AF*

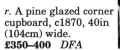

*r.* A pine glazed corner cupboard, c1870, 40in (104cm) wide.
**£350–400** *DFA*

A pine corner cupboard, with key, c1830, 41in (104cm) high.
**£450–500** *AL*

A bowfronted pine corner cupboard, with original handles, 12½in (32cm) high.
**£120–150** *AL*

A pine corner cupboard, c1870, 27in (69cm) wide.
**£275–300** *RK*

A Georgian bowfront pine cupboard, 35in (89cm) high.
**£300–350** *JAC*

A Scottish pine corner cupboard, 16in (41cm) wide.
**£70–100** *BH*

A pine hanging corner cupboard, c1790, 37in (94cm) wide.
**£500–600** *UP*

A Victorian pine corner cabinet, 25in (63cm) wide.
**£300–400** *AL*

A Victorian pine corner cabinet, with a single locking door, 18in (46cm) wide.
**£300–400** *AL*

A Georgian pine corner cupboard, with shaped shelves inside, 41in (104cm) high.
**£400–500** *AL*

A pine corner cupboard, c1840, 27in (69cm) wide.
**£300–400** *W*

A two-door pine hanging corner cupboard, c1850, 32in (81cm) high.
**£450–500** *AL*

A pine hanging corner cupboard, c1840, 36in (92cm) high.
**£250–350** *AL*

An Austrian pine corner cupboard, with 3 coloured glass panels in the single door, 31½in (80cm) high.
**£300–400** *CHA*

A pine corner cupboard with semi-arched moulded panelled doors, 19thC, 31in (79cm) wide.
**£400–600** *OK*

A pine hanging corner cupboard, 19thC, 28in (71cm) wide.
**£400–500** *CHA*

A late Georgian pine corner cupboard, with a panelled and moulded door, 31in (79cm) wide.
**£400–600** *OA*

An astragal glazed pine corner cupboard, c1800, 39in (99cm) wide.
**£350–400** *UP*

A pine corner cupboard, c1800, 55½in (139.5cm) high.
**£450–550** *AL*

*l.* A bowfront pine corner cupboard, 32in (81cm) high.
**£500–600** *PH*

*r.* A pine corner cupboard, with handmade butterfly hinges, c1800, 21in (54cm) high.
**£300–350** *AL*

*l.* A mid-Georgian pine hanging corner cabinet, the fielded panel door flanked by reeded and moulded sides, 28in (71cm) wide.
**£400–600** *OA*

A late Victorian pine bedside cabinet, with shaped shelf beneath, on tapered legs, 16in (41cm) wide.
**£125–175**  *TPC*

A Continental pine pot cupboard, c1890, 29in (74cm) high.
**£100–125**  *ASP*

A pine bedside locker, c1880, 29in (74cm) high.
**£90–120**  *Byl*

A pine bedside locker, c1880, 31½in (80cm) high.
**£90–120**  *Byl*

A pine bedside locker, c1880, 30in (76cm) high.
**£90–120**  *Byl*

A pine pot cupboard, with 2 doors, c1870, 30in (76cm) high.
**£150–220**  *AL*

A pine pot cupboard, c1870, 30in (76cm) high.
**£100–200**  *AL*

A pine pot cupboard, c1870, 30in (76cm) high.
**£100–200**  *AL*

A pine pot cupboard, with single drawer, replacement handles, early 20thC, 16in (41cm) wide.
**£50–70**  *HNG*

An Eastern European pine
chest of 3 drawers, with half-
cut pillars 1860s, 39in
(100cm) wide.
**£325–375** *NWE*

An Eastern European pine
chest of drawers, 1880–1900,
23in (59cm) wide.
**£200–250** *NWE*

An Eastern European chest
of 3 drawers, 1880, 42½in
(107cm) wide.
**£225–275** *NWE*

A pine chest of 2 short and
2 long drawers, 19thC,
36in (91.5cm) wide.
**£250–350** *TPC*

*r.* A pitch pine ship's chest of
4 long drawers, with tray top,
late 19thC, 36in (92cm) wide.
**£350–500** *TPC*

A Shaker pine chest of drawers,
the moulded cornice above 5
graduated moulded drawers, on
bracket feet, Havard Community,
Massachusetts, c1840, 60in
(152cm) high.
**£1,600–2,000** *S(NY)*

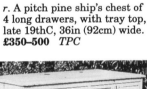

*r.* A Victorian pine chest
of 2 short and 3 long
drawers, with white
ceramic knobs, on plinth,
44in (111.5cm) wide.
**£400–600** *TPC*

*l.* A pine chest of
2 short and 3 long
drawers, with
carved mouldings to
fronts, on solid
plinth base, 19thC,
48in (122cm) wide.
**£400–600** *TPC*

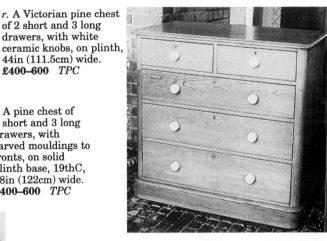

*r.* A Georgian pine
Winchester chest of
2 short and 3 long
drawers, with original
brass handles, on bracket
feet, 54in (137cm) wide.
**£700–900** *TPC*

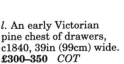

*l.* An early Victorian
pine chest of drawers,
c1840, 39in (99cm) wide.
**£300–350** *COT*

A miniature pine chest of drawers, c1880, 14in (35.5cm) wide.
**£160–200** *UP*

A pine bowfronted chest of drawers, c1860.
**£600–650** *PIN*

A pine chest of drawers, c1860, 42in (106.5cm) wide.
**£250–350** *SPA*

A pine chest of drawers, with original knobs and bracket feet, c1830, 34in (86cm) wide.
**£400–500** *SPA*

A Federal pine bowfronted chest of drawers, painted and grained all-over in brown and ochre to simulate mahogany, New England, c1810, 40in (102cm) wide.
**£1,200–1,500** *S(NY)*

A pine chest of drawers, with new brass handles, c1890, 36in (92cm) wide.
**£200–300** *SPA*

A small pine chest of drawers, 14in (36cm) wide.
**£90–100** *AL*

A German pine chest of drawers, with turned columns, original handles and fittings, c1850, 43in (109cm) wide.
**£400–450** *Sca*

A box-shaped pine chest of drawers, with locking fall front, c1860, 31in (78.5cm) wide.
**£420–500** *AL*

A pine chest of drawers, c1870, 36in (92cm) wide.
**£300–400** *SPA*

A late Georgian pine chest, 34in (85cm) wide.
**£200–240** *UP*

A Victorian pine chest of drawers.
**£350–500** *PIN*

A pine chest of drawers, c1860, 34in (86cm) wide.
**£350–450** *AL*

A Georgian pine chest of 3 long drawers, on bracket feet, 36in (92cm) wide.
**£400–600**   *TPC*

A pine chest of 2 short and 2 long drawers, c1920, 35½in (90cm) wide.
**£100–185**   *BEL*

A mid-Victorian pine chest of 5 drawers, 39in (99cm) wide.
**£250–285**   *ERA*

A pine chest of 4 drawers, flanked by columns, c1870, 37½in (95cm) wide.
**£250–320**   *BEL*

A pine chest of 3 drawers, c1920, 37½in (95cm) wide.
**£150–225**   *BEL*

*r.* A pine bowfront chest of drawers, c1860, 38½in (98cm) wide.
**£300–360**   *BEL*

A Scandinavian pine chest of 5 drawers, c1840, 39in (99cm) wide.
**£350–450**   *BEL*

A pine chest of 3 long drawers, c1900, 36in (92cm) wide.
**£250–300**   *FAG*

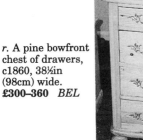

*r.* A Victorian pine chest of 5 drawers, 1875, 41in (104cm) wide.
**£340–360**   *OPH*

A Victorian pine chest of drawers, with original handles, 34in (86cm) wide.
**£350–500** *OA*

A chemist's shop pine flight of drawers, with original knobs, 19thC.
**£350–500** *AF*

A pine five-drawer narrow chest, the top drawer containing 3 secret drawers, Lincolnshire, c1850, 41½in (105cm) high.
**£800–900** *UC*

A Victorian pine chest of drawers, with original handles, 34in (86cm) wide.
**£350–500** *OA*

A Victorian pine chest of drawers, c1840, 45in (114cm) wide.
**£250–270** *Sca*

A pine chest of drawers, unrestored, c1835.
**£800–1,000** *CPA*

A Scottish pine chest of drawers, with bobbin turning at the sides, c1850, 49in (124.5cm) high.
**£700–800** *AL*

A pine chest of drawers, with new handles, 19thC, 40in (100cm) wide.
**£400–500** *AL*

A pine bowfronted chest, with graduated drawers, 18thC, 36in (90cm) wide.
**£500–700** *RdeR*

A pine chest of drawers, 19thC, 27in (67.6cm) high.
**£400–500** *AL*

A Georgian pine chest of drawers, with high bracket feet and original brass handles, 39in (97.5cm) high.
**£600–800** *AF*

*l*. A three-piece pine bedroom suite, comprising: a chest of drawers, 45in (112.5cm) wide, a wardrobe, 49in (122.5cm) wide, and a dressing table, 50in (125cm) wide.
**£3,000–4,000** *Sca*

A pine chest of drawers,
with original handles,
36in (91.5cm) wide
**£200–280** *ASP*

A mid-Victorian pine chest of
4 drawers, with porcelain knob
handles, 34in (86cm) wide.
**£250–280** *ERA*

An pine chest of
drawers, c1860,
41in (104cm) wide.
**£285–350** *ASP*

*r*. A Victorian pine
chest of 2 short
and 3 long
drawers, c1880,
37in (94cm) wide.
**£325–350** *WaH*

*l*. A Victorian pine
chest of 2 short and
2 long drawers,
33in (84cm) wide.
**£250–275** *WaH*

A pine chest of 4 graduated drawers,
on plinth base, 35in (89cm) wide.
**£325–375** *CCP*

A Victorian pine chest of
drawers, c1850, 38in
(96.5cm) wide.
**£200–300** *DMe*

A Continental pine chest,
with 5 drawers, c1880,
37in (94cm) wide.
**£285–325** *ASP*

A Victorian pine chest of 2 short and
3 long drawers, on plinth base, pine
knob handles, 41in (104cm) wide.
**£350–400** *CCP*

A Scandinavian pine chest, with 4 drawers and
1 cupboard, c1900, 37in (94cm) wide.
**£200–275** *BEL*

A Scottish pine chest of drawers, with one deep top drawer made to appear as 5 small drawers, 44in (111.5cm) wide.
**£650–750** *PF*

A pine chest of drawers, with 3 drawers and mahogany handles, 19thC, 40in (101.5cm) wide.
**£400–600** *PD*

A Scandinavian pitch pine chest of drawers, with split turned decorations to the side and original small brass handles, 19thC, 36in (91.5cm) wide.
**£500–700** *CC*

A pair of Victorian pine chests of drawers, one on legs, 44in (111.5cm) wide.
**£600–900** *AL*

A Georgian pine chest of drawers, 42in (106.5cm) wide.
**£600–800** *AL*

A serpentine fronted chest of drawers, with splashback and applied split turnings, late 19thC, 39in (99cm) wide.
**£600–800** *PF*

A pine plan chest, c1880, 48in (122cm) wide.
**£500–600** *RK*

A pine chest of drawers, c1890, 36in (92cm) wide.
**£300–350** *RK*

A pine chest of drawers, c1840.
**£450–500** *CPA*

A pine chest of drawers, c1820.
**£550–650** *CPA*

A miniature waxed pine chest of drawers, 11in (28cm) wide.
**£100–120** *TRU*

A pine chest of drawers, 1880, 36in (92cm) wide.
**£300–350** *TRU*

A Continental pine chest, the 4 drawers, with beech and rosewood mouldings, replaced handles, late 19thC, 43in (109cm) wide.
**£375–500**   *HNG*

A late Victorian pine chest, with 2 long drawers at top and bottom and 2 small in the middle, original glass handles, replacement feet, 46in (116.5cm) wide.
**£275–400**   *HNG*

*r.* A German pine chest of drawers, with 2 small and 3 long drawers, original brass handles, new feet, c1840, 31½in (80cm) wide.
**£400–600**   *HGN*

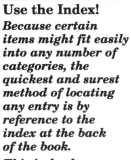

An Eastern European pine chest, with 4 drawers, replacement handles and escutcheons, late 19thC, 39in (99cm) wide.
**£375–500**   *HNG*

**Use the Index!**

*Because certain items might fit easily into any number of categories, the quickest and surest method of locating any entry is by reference to the index at the back of the book.*

*This index has been fully cross-referenced for absolute simplicity.*

A North country chest of drawers, with splashback and shelf, 19thC, 36in (91.5cm) wide.
**£400–475**   *WV*

A pine chest of drawers, with splashback, 19thC, 28in (71cm) wide.
**£300–350**   *WV*

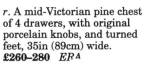

*r.* A mid-Victorian pine chest of 4 drawers, with original porcelain knobs, and turned feet, 35in (89cm) wide.
**£260–280**   *ERA*

*l.* A mid-Victorian, pine chest of 4 drawers, with original ebonised handles and feet, c1870, 36in (91.5cm) wide.
**£260–280**   *ERA*

A pine chest of drawers, with 2 short and 3 long drawers, c1870, 45in (114cm) wide.
**£650–750** *SSD*

A Victorian pine chest of drawers, 36in (91.5cm) wide.
**£350–450** *FP*

A pine chest of 2 short and 3 long drawers, c1860, 45in (111cm) wide.
**£300–350** *SSD*

A pine chest of drawers, with replacement handles, c1850, 46in (116.5cm) wide.
**£500–600** *AL*

A pine chest of drawers, with 3 long drawers, c1890, 39in (99cm) wide.
**£300–400** *SSD*

A Victorian pine chest of drawers, with a shaped back and scrolled ends, 31in (79cm) wide.
**£350–500** *AH*

A pine chest of 2 short and 2 long drawers, c1890, 39in (99cm) wide.
**£300–350** *SSD*

A pine chest of drawers, with 2 short and 3 long drawers, c1860, 45in (114cm) wide.
**£450–600** *SSD*

A pine chest of drawers, with bracket feet, c1820, 36in (91.5cm) wide.
**£650–700** *AL*

A Yorkshire pine chest-on-chest, with original ebonised handles, c1860, 40in (101.5cm) wide.
**£1,500–2,500** *UC*

A Scottish pine chest of drawers, with original cockbeading and handles, c1830, 42½in (108cm) wide.
**£700–900** *AL*

A pine chest of drawers, with a splash back, 41⅛in (104cm) wide.
**£600–700** *PH*

A Regency Suffolk pine and sycamore chest of drawers, with original feet and brass, c1810, 37in (94cm) wide.
**£1,100–1,300** *UC*

*r.* A Victorian pine 5 drawer chest, with original knobs, on turned feet, c1880, 42in (106.5cm) wide.
**£200–300** *POT*

*l.* A late Victorian pine chest, with 2 short and 2 long drawers, 35in (89cm) wide.
**£180–300** *HNG*

A pine chest of drawers, with gallery, c1845, 36in (91.5cm) wide.
**£300–350** *DMe*

A large Victorian pine chest of drawers, with original knobs, on original elm bun feet, c1860, 47in (119cm) wide.
**£400–440** *POT*

A pine chest of drawers, with 2 small above 2 long drawers, on turned feet, c1880, 38in (96.5cm) wide.
**£265–300** *SA*

A pine chest of drawers, with 2 short and 2 long drawers, c1880, 40in (101.5cm) wide.
**£200–240** *OCP*

A pine breakfront side cabinet, c1875, 54in (137cm) wide.
**£350–400** *DFA*

*r.* A pine chest, with
2 short and 3 long
drawers, c1860,
39½in (100cm) wide.
**£500–580** *AL*

*l.* A pine chest of
drawers, with
2 small above 2 long
drawers, c1810,
32½in (82cm) wide.
**£350–450** *AL*

A pine chest of drawers, the
2 small and 2 long drawers
with glass knob handles,
38in (96.5cm) wide.
**£370–430** *AL*

A Welsh pine chest of 3 drawers,
c1870, 36in (91.5cm) wide.
**£370–430** *AL*

A pine chest of drawers, with
shaped back above, 2 small
and 2 long drawers, c1880,
40in (101.5cm) wide.
**£265–300** *SA*

A pine chest of drawers, on bun
feet, c1840, 46in (116.5cm) wide.
**£300–360** *DMe*

---

### Make the most of Miller's

*In* Miller's Pine &
Country Buyer's
Guide *we do NOT
just reprint saleroom
estimates. Our
consultants work from
realised prices and
then calculate a price
range for similar
items, avoiding
uncharacteristic 'one
off' high or low results.*

---

A Continental pine chest of 3
drawers, with carved corbels, brass
handles, c1870, 49½in
(125cm) wide.
**£500–600** *AF*

*r.* An Irish chest-
on-chest, all
original, c1800,
50in (127cm) wide.
**£600–700** *COT*

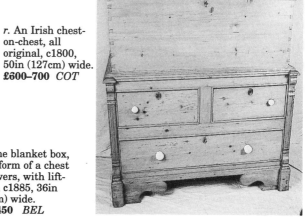

*l.* A pine blanket box,
in the form of a chest
of drawers, with lift-
up top, c1885, 36in
(91.5cm) wide.
**£350–450** *BEL*

A pine drop-leaf table, with a drawer at one end, on turned legs, c1880, 44⅛in (112cm) wide.
**£280–320** *AL*

A pine drop-leaf table, with a drawer at each end, on turned legs, c1850, 42in (106.5cm) wide.
**£200–230** *DAM*

A pine draw-leaf table, c1880, 37in (94cm) wide, extended.
**£270–330** *AL*

A Victorian pine drop-leaf table, with one drawer, on turned legs, c1850, 47in (119cm) wide.
**£250–300** *DMA*

A pine drop-leaf table, with a drawer, c1880, 36in (91.5cm) wide. **£250–280** *AL*

A pine washstand, with gallery back, c1880, 24in (61.5cm) wide. **£180–220** *AL*

A pine table, with turned legs, and shelf beneath, c1880, 30in (76.5cm) wide. **£130–170** *AL*

A pine table, with a drawer, c1870, 55in (139.5cm) wide. **£400–435** *AL*

A French pine dough bin, lid missing, c1870, 72in (182.5cm) wide. **£500–535** *AL*

A pine side table, with 2 drawers, c1870, 45in (114cm) wide. **£350–400** *AL*

A pine table, with one leaf, c1880, 40in (101.5cm) wide. **£200–245** *AL*

A pine serving table, with one small and 2 large drawers, c1850, 57in (144.5cm) wide. **£750–800** *AL*

A pine side table, with 2 drawers, and turned legs, 38in (96.5cm) wide. **£200–240** *LIB*

A pine tray-top washstand, c1870, 26in (66cm) wide.
**£250–270** *AL*

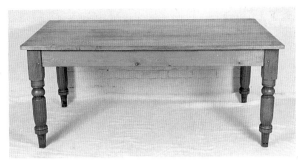

A pine table, with turned legs, c1880, 72in (182.5cm) wide.
**£700–735** *AL*

A pine writing table, with new leather top, c1880, 36in (91.5cm) wide.
**£350–400** *AL*

A pine side table, with one drawer, on turned legs, 28½in (72.5cm) wide.
**£165–185** *AL*

A pine refectory table, with 3 drawers, on turned legs with stretchers, 19thC, 60in (152cm) long.
**£400–500**  *TPC*

A Victorian pine table, with drawers, on turned legs, c1840, 36in (91.5cm) long.
**£350–375**  *DMA*

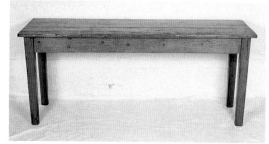

A pine side table, c1870, 67in (170cm) long.
**£300–335**  *AL*

A pine farmhouse table, with one long end drawer with a wooden knob, c1820, 66in (167.5cm) long.
**£260–300**  *DMA*

A pine farmhouse table, on turned legs, c1835, 84in (213cm) long.
**£440–460**  *DMA*

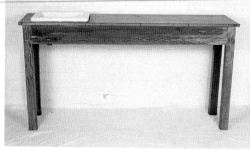

A pine table, with an inset sink, c1890, 72in (182.5cm) long.
**£435–465**  *AL*

A pine farmhouse table, with 2 drawers, on turned legs, c1850, 85½in (217cm) long.
**£650–700**  *DMA*

A pine table, on 6 turned legs, 19thC, 96in (243.5cm) long.
**£600–800**  *TPC*

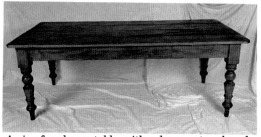

A pine farmhouse table, with a drawer at each end, on turned legs, c1830, 82in (208cm) long.
**£600–650**  *DMA*

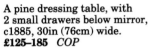

A pine dressing table, with
2 small drawers below mirror,
c1885, 30in (76cm) wide.
**£125–185** *COP*

A Victorian pine dressing table,
c1865, 60in (152cm) wide.
**£750–900** *AnD*

A pine dressing table, with
spindle galleries, 19thC, 38in
(96.5cm) wide.
**£300–350** *TPC*

A pine dressing table, with
2 small and one long drawer,
on turned legs, c1900, 39in
(99cm) wide.
**£250–350** *CCP*

A pine dressing chest,
with 2 long drawers below
2 small drawers, c1880,
33in (83.5cm) wide.
**£250–300** *DMA*

A pine dressing table, with oval
mirror, c1880, 48in (122cm) wide.
**£375–425** *COP*

A Victorian pine four-drawer
dressing chest, on bun feet, handles
replaced, 42in (106.5cm) wide.
**£350–450** *CCP*

A pine dressing chest, with
carved mirror supports,
19thC, 42in (106.5cm) wide.
**£500–600** *TPC*

A pine dressing table, on casters,
c1880, 48in (122cm) wide.
**£1,000–1,300** *AL*

A pine compactum wardrobe, with gesso decoration, 19thC, 68in (172.5cm) wide.
**£750–850** *TPC*

A pine 2 door 'knock down' wardrobe, c1875, 42in (106.5cm) wide.
**£450–475** *AnD*

A pine collapsible wardrobe, with 3 drawers, c1880, 60in (152cm) wide.
**£550–600** *AnD*

A pine wardrobe, with 2 doors and one long drawer, c1880, 43in (109cm) wide.
**£400–450** *AnD*

A German pine cupboard, c1860, 34in (86cm) wide.
**£425–475** *AnD*

A Victorian Gothic style pine press cabinet, c1860, 53in (134.5cm) wide.
**£625–675** *AnD*

A pine wardrobe, with 2 doors and 2 drawers, 41in (104cm) wide.
**£425–475** *AnD*

A collapsible pine armoire, the 2 doors with raised and fielded panels, c1880, 53in (134.5cm) wide.
**£600–625** *AnD*

A eastern European pine wardrobe, with glazed panels, and one drawer, early 20thC, 75in (190.5cm) wide.
**£425–475** *AnD*

A beech and ash butcher's block, on original pine base, with trademark 'Herbert & Sons Ltd., West Smithfields, London', 24in (61cm) wide.
**£400–500** *CCP*

A beech butcher's block, with a galleried knife back, on a pine base with a drawer, raised on casters, early 19thC, 42in (106.5cm) wide.
**£800–1,200** *CCP*

A pine chopping block, c1880, 18in (46cm) wide.
**£240–280** *MIL*

A beech and maple butcher's block, on beech legs, early 19thC, top 18in (46cm) thick.
**£1,500–2,000** *CCP*

A sycamore coffee table, on a pine trestle base, early 19thC, 56in (142cm) wide.
**£700–900** *CCP*

A Dutch pine washstand, with
replaced decoration, 38in
(96.5cm) wide.
**£250–300** *AnD*

A German pine
washstand, with brass
knob and handle, c1890,
24in (61cm) wide.
**£175–275** *AnD*

A Czechoslovakian pine washstand,
with 2 small drawers above
2 cupboard doors, the splashback
with a narrow shelf, c1865, 36in
(91.5cm) wide.
**£350–400** *AnD*

A Victorian pine washstand,
with metal towel rails on each
side, a drawer with 2 wooden
knobs, on turned legs, c1845,
30in (76cm) long.
**£100–140** *DMA*

A Victorian pine washstand,
the drawer with a wooden
knob, on turned legs, c1890,
24in (61cm) wide.
**£150–225** *AnD*

A Victorian pine washstand, with
2 small drawers, on shaped end
supports joined by a shaped
stretcher, c1850, 39in (99cm) wide.
**£250–280** *DMA*

A Victorian pine washstand, with
3 drawers and 2 cupboard doors,
on turned feet, c1850, 44½in
(113cm) wide.
**£550–575** *DMA*

A Victorian pine washstand,
with elaborately turned legs,
36in (91.5cm) wide.
**£275–375** *AnD*

A pine corner washstand,
with a shelf below, c1860,
28in (71cm) wide.
**£450–480** *MIL*

A pine washstand, with a gallery top, turned legs, shaped under shelf, early 19thC, 42in (106.5cm) wide.
**£250–350** *TPC*

A Victorian pine washstand, with a drawer under, on turned legs, 35in (89cm) wide.
**£175–225** *WaH*

A Victorian pine washstand, with spindled gallery back, on turned legs with a shaped undershelf, 36ins (92cm) wide.
**£300–400** *TPC*

A two-door pine washstand, with a gallery top, and a marble worktop, c1870, 29⅚in (75cm) wide.
**£250–300** *CCP*

A pine washstand, with a marble top, on turned legs, c1880, 30in (76cm) wide.
**£125–145** *AnD*

A pine washstand, with slab ends, one drawer and a shaped stretcher, c1870, 34in (86cm) wide.
**£200–300** *MIL*

A pine washstand, with a marble top, on straight legs, c1885, 36in (91.5cm) wide.
**£150–185** *AnD*

A Victorian pine washstand, with a marble top, and one drawer, on turned front legs joined by a shaped stretcher.
**£300–350** *WaH*

A pine washstand, with 3 drawers, on turned legs, c1870, 38in (96.5cm) wide.
**£250–280** *MIL*

A Victorian pine washstand, with a shaped gallery top, and one drawer below, on turned legs, c1880, 33in (84cm) wide.
**£300–350** *WaH*

A pine washstand cupboard, with a lift-up top, c1890, 30½in (78cm) wide.
**£150–200** *HeR*

A French Henry II pine buffet, 59in (149.5cm) wide.
**£1,500–2,000** *AnD*

A pine 2 door corner cupboard, c1865, 47in (119cm) wide.
**£750–800** *AnD*

A pine panelled food cupboard, early 19thC, 48in (122cm) wide.
**£800–900** *TPC*

A French Provincial pine armoire, c1840, 59in (149.5cm) wide.
**£925–975** *AnD*

A pine linen press, with 8 short drawers, c1880, 58in (147cm) wide.
**£800–1,200** *AnD*

A pine hanging corner cupboard, late 19thC, 47in (119cm) wide.
**£450–500** *AnD*

A pine dresser, with glazed top cupboard doors, 2 drawers and 2 cupboards beneath, c1870, 41in (104cm) wide.
**£450–500** *AnD*

A Dutch pine kitchen dresser, with spice drawers, c1865, 37½in (95cm) wide.
**£500–525** *AnD*

A pine dresser, with glazed top cupboard doors, 2 short drawers and 3 internal drawers, c1870, 43in (109cm) wide.
**£550–575** *AnD*

A housemaid's pine press cupboard, with 4 cupboard doors, and 2 drawers, on bun feet, c1855, 51in (129.5cm) wide.
**£850–950**  *DMA*

A pine linen press, with 2 short and 2 long drawers, below 2 cupboard doors, 46in (116.5cm) wide.
**£850–875**  *DMA*

A Cumbrian pine linen press, with fitted interior slides, 18thC, 62in (157cm) wide.
**£700–900**  *BOA*

A pine linen press, with 2 short and 2 long drawers, below 2 cupboard doors, on bracket feet, c1840, 48½in wide.
**£750–1,000**  *DMA*

A pine linen press, with interior slides, and carved corbels, c1850.
**£800–900**  *BOA*

A pine linen press, with a fitted interior, on bracket feet, c1850.
**£800–900**  *BOA*

A Regency pine linen press, with fitted interior slides, on splayed feet, c1830, 48in (122cm) wide.
**£900–1,100**  *BOA*

A Yorkshire pine linen press, with fitted interior slides, c1850, 48in (122cm) wide.
**£900–1,100**  *BOA*

A Scottish pine linen press, with bonnet and glove drawers, c1840, 48in (122cm) wide.
**£900–1,000**  *BOA*

A George III pine standing corner cupboard, the moulded cornice above an astragal door, enclosing painted shaped shelves, 35½in (90cm) wide.
**£1,200–1,400** *S(S)*

A pine corner cupboard, with one door, c1880, 34in (86cm) wide.
**£200–225** *LIB*

A Victorian pine glazed corner cupboard, c1860, 37in (94cm) wide.
**£750–850** *DMA*

A Victorian pine corner cabinet, with shaped shelves and barrel back, 1865, 42in (106.5cm) wide.
**£1,000–1,250** *AnD*

An Irish pine corner cupboard, with astragal glazed doors above 2 cupboard doors, c1810, 46in (116.5cm) wide.
**£1,500–1,800** *TPC*

An Austrian painted pine food cupboard, with original paint finish, c1870, 36in (91.5cm) wide.
**£675–725** *UC*

A pine corner cabinet, with a glazed door and 2 shelves, c1870, 17in (43cm) wide.
**£150–200** *AnD*

A Dutch pine corner cupboard, on bun feet, c1880, 28in (71cm) wide.
**£300–400** *AnD*

A bowfronted pine corner cupboard, with a panelled door, c1850, 39½in (100cm) wide.
**£380–420** *DMA*

An Irish pine food cupboard, with panelled doors, c1850, 78in (198cm) high.
**£1,000–1,200** *RK*

A pine wardrobe, with turned pillars, c1880, 50in (127cm) wide.
**£650–850** *UP*

A Danish pine wardrobe, c1880, 40in (101.5cm) wide.
**£450–550** *UP*

A pine food safe, c1900, 25½in (65cm) high.
**£80–100** *AHL*

An Irish food cupboard, with glazed doors, c1870, 50in (127cm) wide.
**£1,500–2,000** *UP*

An Irish pine cupboard, c1820, 50in (127cm) wide.
**£1,000–1,500** *RK*

A pine display cabinet, with 3 glazed doors above 3 drawers, c1840, 78in (198cm) wide.
**£1,400–1,600** *UP*

A pine linen press, c1860, 46in (116.5cm) wide.
**£800–1,000** *SA*

*r*. A Georgian country pine corner cupboard, with shaped open shelves, 26in (66cm) wide.
**£800–1,000** *TPC*

A French pine buffet, with 2 drawers, and 2 cupboard doors, c1850, 52in (132cm) wide.
**£800–1,000** *UP*

An Irish pine cupboard, with 2 cupboard doors, and 6 drawers below, c1820, 54in (137cm) wide.
**£1,000–1,200** *RK*

A pine press cupboard, with 3 panelled cupboard doors, above 2 short and 2 long drawers, c1840, 88in (223.5cm) high.
**£1,000–1,200** *RK*

A French pine buffet base, c1880, 44in (111.5cm) wide.
**£500–600** *UP*

A pine single wardrobe, c1850, 40in (101.5cm) wide.
**£800–1,000** *UP*

A Danish pine single wardrobe, c1870, 40in (101.5cm) wide.
**£500–600** *RK*

An Irish pine cupboard, with 4 panelled doors, c1850, 65in (165cm) wide.
**£1,000–1,200** *RK*

A pine double wardrobe, with an elaborately carved cornice, c1890, 48in (122cm) wide.
**£600–800** *UP*

A Southern Irish pine corner cupboard, with astragal glazed doors above, decorated with shamrocks, c1850, 45in (114cm) wide.
**£1,200–1,400** *RK*

A pine chest of 5 drawers, c1880, 42in (107cm) wide. **£500–800** *UP*

A Irish pine bed, from County Clare, c1820, 66in (168cm) wide. **£1,800–2,000** *UP*

A pine harness cupboard, c1820, 60in (152cm) wide. **£1,500–2,000** *UP*

A pine linen press, with a brushing slide, c1790, 48in (122cm) wide. **£1,500–2,000** *UP*

A housemaid's pine cupboard, c1890, 96in (244cm) high. **£1,500–1,750** *UP*

A pine bureau, c1780, 42in (107cm) wide. **£1,500–1,750** *UP*

A French pine glazed cupboard, c1870. **£1,000–1,500** *UP*

A French pine cupboard, c1870, 76in (193cm) high. **£1,400–1,600** *UP*

A pine corner cupboard, c1770. **£700–1,000** *RK*

A Scandinavian pine chest of drawers, c1860, 48in (122cm) wide. **£700–900** *RK*

A pine breakfront bookcase, c1820, 168in (427cm) wide. **£2,400–2,600** *UP*

An Irish pine food cupboard, c1850, 58in (147cm) wide. **£1,400–1,600** *UP*

An Irish pine glazed cupboard, c1850, 82in (208cm) high. **£1,400–1,600** *UP*

A pine panelled sideboard, with 3 cockbeaded drawers on both sides of central cupboard doors, 19thC, 96in (243.5cm) wide. **£1,000–1,500** *TPC*

A pine sideboard, with panelled ends, 7 drawers, and a recessed cupboard, 19thC, 70in (177.5cm) wide. **£800–1,100** *TPC*

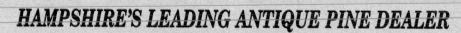

A pine high backed panelled settle, with 2 drawers under, solid sides with arms, on sledge feet, 18thC, 48in (122cm) wide. **£700–900** *TPC*

*l.* A pine serpentine sideboard, with carved back, 19thC, 66in (167.5cm) wide. **£1,000–1,500** *TPC*

A Welsh pine high backed settle, with 2 drawers under, early 18thC, 52in (132cm) wide. **£600–800** *TPC*

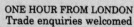

A pine chest of drawers, with 2 short and 4 long drawers, and original handles, c1860, 32in (81cm) wide.
**£650–750** *SSD*

A Victorian pine chest of drawers, 30in (76cm) wide.
**£400–500** *OA*

A South German pine chest of 4 long drawers, c1880.
**£200–265** *TPF*

A pine chest of drawers, with 2 short and 4 long drawers, c1860.
**£650–750** *SSD*

*l.* A Scandinavian bowfronted pine chest of drawers, 38in (96.5cm) wide.
**£300–350** *BEL*

A Scottish pine chest, c1850, 48in (120cm) wide.
**£350–500** *UP*

A pine chest of 2 short and 2 long drawers, with a gallery back, c1865, 42in (106.5cm) wide.
**£550–650** *SSD*

A Victorian pine chest of 2 short and 2 long drawers, 26in (66cm) wide.
**£400–500** *AL*

A mid-European pine chest of drawers, 37in (94cm) wide.
**£300–360** *RK*

A pine specimen chest, c1880, 40in (101.5cm) wide.
**£650–750** *UP*

A Victorian bowfront veneered chest of drawers, c1850, later painted with East Coast maritime theme, 42in (106.5cm) wide.
**£500–700** *PIN*

A pine chest of 3 long drawers, c1820, 37in (94cm) wide.
**£500–600** *UP*

*l.* An Irish pine mule chest, with mock drawer fronts and original knobs, c1850, 42in (106.5cm) wide.
**£400–600** *PIN*

A Victorian pine chest of drawers, with a shaped gallery back, 33in (82.5cm) wide.
**£450–550** *AF*

A pine chest, with lift-up lid and 2 opening drawers, c1830, 42in (107cm) wide.
**£400–450** *AL*

A serpentine front pine chest of drawers, with an apron, original crystal knobs and mahogany feet, c1860. **£220–260** *PIN*

A pine chest of drawers, c1870, 32in (81cm) high.
**£250–280** *AL*

A pine chest of drawers, with scroll decoration, c1850, 36in (91.5cm) wide.
**£300–350** *AL*

A Scandinavian or South German pine chest of drawers, 44in (112cm) wide.
**£250–350** *CHA*

A bowfronted pine chest of drawers, 34in (86cm) wide.
**£600–700** *PH*

A pine chest of drawers, with plywood drawer bottoms, c1900, 45in (114cm) high.
**£600–650** *AL*

A pine chest of drawers, c1820, 42in (104cm) wide.
**£550–750** *PH*

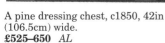

A pine dressing chest, c1850, 42in (106.5cm) wide.
**£525–650** *AL*

A pine chest of drawers, c1880, 33in (84cm) wide.
**£425–550** *PAC*

A pine combination chest of drawers, c1860, 40in (101.5cm) wide. **£600–700** *AL*

A Victorian pine chest of drawers, with a splashback, c1840, 39in (99cm) wide. **£375–500** *W*

A pine chest of drawers, with original brass escutcheons, on turned feet, c1840, 37in (94cm) wide. **£300–400** *W*

A Regency pine chest of drawers, with original handles, c1835, 33in (84cm) wide. **£500–750** *AL*

A pine flour barrel, made to resemble a chest of drawers, c1850, 26in (66cm) high. **£200–300** *AL*

A pine chest of drawers, c1860, 33in (84cm) wide. **£350–500** *W*

A pine chest of drawers, c1880, 18in (46cm) wide. **£100–150** *AL*

A low pine chest of drawers, c1860, 41in (104cm) wide. **£350–500** *W*

*l.* A pine chest of drawers, 49½in (126cm) wide. **£600–700** *PH*

*l.* A pine chest of drawers, with original handles and escutcheons, c1840, 34½in (86cm) wide. **£400–500** *Sca*

A Regency pine two-door wardrobe, with applied hardwood mouldings, on shaped bracket feet, 54in (137cm) wide.
**£800–1,200** *TPC*

A pine single wardrobe, with panelled door and one long drawer to base, 19thC, 30in (76cm) wide.
**£300–500** *TPC*

A pine two-door wardrobe, 19thC, 54in (137cm) wide.
**£500–700** *TPC*

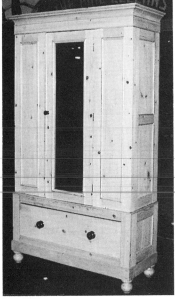

A pine panelled wardrobe, with mirrored door and long drawer to base, on bun feet, 19thC, 52in (132cm) wide.
**£600–800** *TPC*

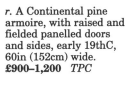

A mid-Victorian pine wardrobe, with 2 long drawers to base, all original, c1860, 48in (122cm) wide.
**£650–750** *COT*

A late Victorian pine wardrobe, with applied gesso urn decoration to 2 small upper doors, 50in (127cm) wide.
**£600–800** *TPC*

*r.* A Continental pine armoire, with raised and fielded panelled doors and sides, early 19thC, 60in (152cm) wide.
**£900–1,200** *TPC*

*l.* A Continental pine three-door wardrobe, c1890, 66in (167.5cm) wide.
**£600–800** *AnD*

*l.* A Continental pine armoire, with columns flanking moulded and fielded panelled door, 19thC, 42in (106.5cm) wide. **£600–800** *TPC*

*r.* A Dutch pine wardrobe, with 3 drawers to base, c1890, 66in (167.5cm) wide. **£600–800** *AnD*

A Dutch armoire, with 2 doors and one drawer to base, c1920, 42in (106.5cm) wide. **£450–500** *AnD*

A Continental pine wardrobe, with 2 doors, c1865, 40in (101.5cm) wide. **£450–500** *AnD*

A Spanish pine armoire, with double fielded panels to sides and doors, 18thC, 50in (127cm) wide. **£800–1,200** *TPC*

*l.* A Dutch pine armoire, c1920, 42in (106.5cm) wide. **£450–500** *AnD*

*r.* A Continental pine wardrobe, c1890, 34in (86cm) wide. **£350–450** *AnD*

A German pine wardrobe, c1900,
42in (106.5cm) wide.
**£425–500** *AnD*

A pine wardrobe, c1890,
41½in (105cm) wide.
**£200–300** *BEL*

A Continental pine armoire, with
2 doors and 2 drawers to base,
late 19thC, 54in (137cm) wide.
**£600–800** *TPC*

A Dutch pine armoire, c1810,
42in (106.5cm) wide.
**£950–1,250** *AnD*

A pine single wardrobe,
c1890, 41½in (105cm) wide.
**£250–350** *BEL*

A pine wardrobe, with
2 panelled doors and
drawer to base, c1820,
51½in (130cm) wide.
**£550–650** *BEL*

*r*. A pine wardrobe, with
2 doors, flanked by
columns, and 2 drawers
to base, c1820, 59½in
(150cm) wide.
**£900–1,000** *BEL*

*l*. A Continental pine
armoire, with 2 panelled
doors flanked by turned
columns, 19thC, 54in
(137cm) wide.
**£500–700** *TPC*

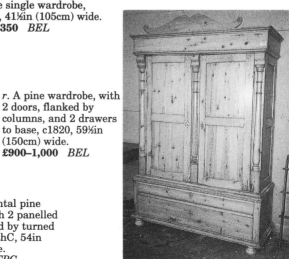

A pine double wardrobe, 96in (243.5cm) wide.
**£2,000–3,000**  *SAn*

A pine wardrobe, with rounded corners, c1880, 36in (92cm) wide.**£450–650**  *SPA*

A French pine armoire, c1780, 50in (127cm) wide.
**£1,500–2,000**  *MCA*

*r.* An Edwardian pine wardrobe, with fielded panels flanking a central door, 48in (122cm) wide.
**£175–200**  *OA*

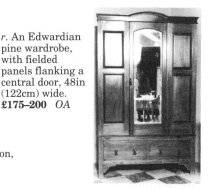

A Scottish pine two-door wardrobe, with carved decoration, 45in (114cm) wide.
**£650–750**  *LAM*

A pine wardrobe, 19thC, 35in (89cm) wide.
**£400–600**  *Ad*

A Scandinavian pine wardrobe, with 2 drawers under, c170, 55in (140cm) wide.
**£700–900**  *AHL*

A two-door cupboard, with 9 drawers, c1860, 78in (198cm) high.
**£1,200–1,500**  *AL*

A pine mirror door wardrobe, with brass fittings, c1890, 42in (106.5cm) wide.
**£600–1,000**  *SPA*

*l.* A hazel pine combination wardrobe, with feature panels in East Indian satinwood, dated 1891, 72in (182.5cm) wide.
**£1,500–2,000**  *SSD*

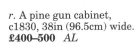

*r.* A pine gun cabinet, c1830, 38in (96.5cm) wide.
**£400–500**  *AL*

A pine wardrobe with 2 drawers under, c1880, 48in (147cm) wide.
**£400–500** *SSD*

A Danish pine wardrobe, with pagoda top, c1880, 38in (97cm) wide.
**£400–500** *RK*

A pine wardrobe, 44in (137cm) wide.
**£400–500** *PH*

A German pine wardrobe, with 2 panelled doors.
**£450–500** *CPA*

A pine wardrobe, c1875, 84½in (214cm) high.
**£500–550** *BEL*

A Danish pine wardrobe, with one door and one drawer, c1860, 37in (94cm) wide.
**£375–400** *R*

*l.* A pitch pine and pine wardrobe, c1880, 46in (142cm) wide.
**£400–450** *CPA*

A Continental pine wardrobe/armoire, 19thC, 78in (198cm) high.
**£600–700** *CHA*

*l.* A pine wardrobe, 41½in (108cm) wide.
**£500–600** *PH*

A Danish pine wardrobe, c1860, 37in (94cm) wide.
**£300–400** *BEL*

A hazel pine wardrobe, c1890, 54in (137cm) wide.
**£450–550** *SSD*

A European pine armoire, c1910, 60in (152cm) wide.
**£500–600** *AnD*

A pine wardrobe, c1880, 43½in (110cm) wide.
**£300–350** *NWE*

An Eastern European pine wardrobe, with carved arched top, c1880, 41in (104cm) wide.
**£400–500** *NWE*

An Eastern European pine two-door wardrobe, with arched top and dummy drawers, 19thC, 55½in (140cm) wide.
**£500–600** *NWE*

An Eastern European pine wardrobe, with arched top, 2 doors and one drawer, late 19thC, 40½in (102cm) wide.
**£450–500** *NWE*

An Eastern European carved pine wardrobe, c1860, 41½in (105cm) wide.
**£400–450** *NWE*

An Eastern European pine wardrobe, with a single door, one drawer and decorative moulding, c1880, 43½in (110cm) wide.
**£350–400** *NWE*

*r.* A pine wardrobe, with bowed doors, flanked by columns, c1820, 59½in (150cm) wide.
**£750–850** *BEL*

An Edwardian pitch pine wardrobe, with deep drawer to base and porcelain handles, 32in (81cm) wide.
**£400–500** *MM*

A Scandinavian pine wardrobe with 2 fielded panelled doors, interior fitted with swivel pegs and a drop well in the base, 19thC, 79in (200.5cm) high.
**£400–500** *CC*

A pine wardrobe and washstand, with 2 drawers and cupboard with panelled doors, 19thC, 77in (195.5cm) wide.
**£1,000–1,500** *AL*

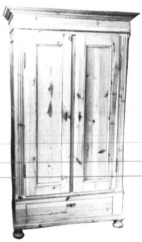

A Scandinavian seven-piece pine wardrobe, with panelled doors, one drawer in base, standing on bun feet, 19thC, 76in (193cm) high.
**£1,000–1,500** *CC*

A pine wardrobe, with shelves and hanging space in the upper part, c1850, 57in (144.5cm) high.
**£1,000–1,300** *AL*

A pine wardrobe, with astragal glazed insets, 48in (122cm) high.
**£550–600** *LAM*

A pine wardrobe, with marked Wedgwood insets, carved top and garland decoration, 46in (116.5cm) high.
**£500–600** *LAM*

A gentleman's pine wardrobe, c1740, 165in (419cm) high.
**£1,500–2,000** *UP*

*l.* A German pine wardrobe, 37in (94cm) wide.
**£180–220** *BEL*

*r.* A pine wardrobe, with panelled doors, early 19thC, 78in (198cm) high.
**£325–375** *BEL*

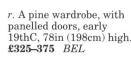

A pitch pine wardrobe, early 20thC, 46in (116.5cm) wide.
**£575–750**   *HNG*

A pine single wardrobe, c1870, 35in (89cm) wide.
**£500–600**   *AL*

A German wardrobe, with single drawer and original fittings, some beech carvings, early 20thC, 45in (114cm) wide.
**£550–750**   *HNG*

A pine carved 2 door Bed press/TV cupboard, with 2 upper drawers, 77in (195.5cm) high.
**£550–750**   *OCP*

A 'knock down' armoire, with rounded fielded panels, rounded cornice, on bun feet, c1890, 61in (155cm) wide.
**£900–1,100**   *POT*

A Continental pine double wardrobe, c1880, 72in (182.5cm) high.
**£575–675**   *ASP*

A late 19thC 'knock down' pine armoire, with fielded panelled doors, 56in (142cm) wide.
**£900–1,100**   *POT*

A mid-Victorian pine wardrobe, with removable cornice, panelled doors and bun feet, c1870, 57in (144.5cm) wide.
**£550–650**   *POT*

A pine cupboard, with fielded panelled doors, originally with 6 drawers inside, mid-19thC, 48in (122cm) wide.
**£550–625**   *POT*

A pine wardrobe, with
drawers under, 76in
(193cm) high.
**£550–575** *AL*

A pine wardrobe, c1860,
81in (205.5cm) high.
**£570–600** *AL*

A pine wardrobe, 77in
(195.5cm) high.
**£350–450** *AL*

A pine wardrobe,
with arched doors and
shelves on one side, 54in
(135cm) wide.
**£850–1,200** *AF*

A Hungarian pine
wardrobe, c1885.
**£450–550** *TPF*

A Danish pine single
door wardrobe, 72in
(182cm) wide.
**£350–400** *RK*

A pine wardrobe,
67in (170cm) wide.
**£850–1,200** *PH*

A Danish pine wardrobe,
76in (193cm) wide.
**£750–800** *RK*

A Georgian bachelor's pine
wardrobe/press.
**£1,200–1,500** *DM*

A pine three-section wardrobe,
c1880, 83in (210.5cm) high.
**£1,400–2,000** *W*

A Victorian pine wardrobe
with reeded decoration,
54in (137cm) wide.
**£175–225** *OA*

A Danish two-door pine
wardrobe, 69in (175cm) high.
**£400–500** *BR*

A combination pine wardrobe,
c1870, 79in (200.5cm) high.
**£1,200–1,350** *AL*

A pine wardrobe, the drawer
with ceramic handles,
c1890, 45in (114cm) high.
**£350–450** *SPA*

A 'knock down' armoire, with hanging space and storage drawers below, early 20thC, c1910, 63in (160cm) wide.
**£800–900** *POT*

An Eastern European pine wardrobe, with arched top and single door, c1860, 37½in (95cm) wide.
**£400–450** *NWE*

A Continental pine single door wardrobe, with single drawer, carved outside leg decoration, steel barrel hinges, original escutcheons, c1860, 72in (182.5cm) high.
**£300–600** *AF*

A Victorian three-piece pine wardrobe, with bevelled mirror door and fielded panelled doors, 43in (109cm) wide.
**£350–425** *POT*

A pine wardrobe, with 2 doors, c1880, 38½in (98cm) wide.
**£250–350** *Byl*

An Edwardian pine single door mirror wardrobe, with a drawer in base, 75½in (191cm) high.
**£250–350** *AF*

A pine wardrobe, with 2 doors and interior drawer, c1896, 45in (114cm) wide.
**£425–465** *SA*

A European pine wardrobe, with decorated cornice, c1860, 82½in (209cm) high.
**£750–950** *AF*

A pine wardrobe, with chamfered panelled doors and sides, c1895, 44in (111.5cm) wide.
**£475–520** *SA*

A pine press cupboard, 50in (127cm) wide. **£1,100–1,300** *SAn*

A pine linen press with slides, in 2 sections, c1860, 50in (127cm) wide. **£1,200–2,000** *AL*

A Danish pine panelled double armoire, with 2 drawers to base, c1870, 73½in (186cm) high. **£1,000–1,200** *UC*

A butler's pine cupboard, c1870, 106in (269cm) wide. **£1,500–2,500** *UP*

A small Victorian pine linen press with shelves, 40in (101.5cm) wide. **£1,200–2,500** *AL*

A housekeeper's breakfront pine cupboard, 19thC. **£2,500–3,500** *PH*

A Scottish pine linen press, with 2 interior drawers and a secret drawer, c1780, 72in (182.5cm) high. **£900–1,100** *BH*

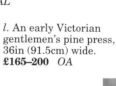

*l.* An early Victorian gentlemen's pine press, 36in (91.5cm) wide. **£165–200** *OA*

A North Wales housekeeper's pine cupboard, 75in (190.5cm) wide. **£2,000–3,000** *PH*

A pine linen press, c1840, 47½in (120cm) wide. **£1,100–1,200** *AL*

A press cupboard, with panelled sides, 44in (111.5cm) wide. **£1,100–1,300** *PH*

A mid-Victorian pine linen press, with arched, moulded panelled doors, enclosing 5 linen slides, original white ceramic handles, 48in (122cm) wide.
**£800–1,200  TPC**

A pine linen press on chest, early 19thC, 48in (122cm) wide.
**£800–1,200  TPC**

A housekeeper's cupboard, with 2 short and 2 long drawers in base, 44in (111.5cm) wide.
**£750–850  ASP**

A late Georgian pine linen press, on bracket feet, c1830, 50in (127cm) wide.
**£750–850  POT**

A Georgian pine linen press, with unusual drawer arrangement, on original bracket legs, c1830, 47in (119cm) wide.
**£1,200–1,400  POT**

An early Victorian pine linen press, with original knobs, c1850, 50½in wide.
**£700–825  POT**

r. A pine livery cupboard, with sunburst design, in 2 pieces, c1835, 58in (147cm) wide.
**£1,300–1,500  DMe**

l. A pine housekeeper's cupboard, with unusual cornice, original turned feet, c1850, 62in (157cm) wide.
**£1,000–1,200  POT**

A pine linen press, feet replaced, c1860, 78½in (199cm) high. **£800–1,000**  *AL*

A Cumberland pine press, c1850, 58in (147cm) wide. **£1,100–1,500**  *UP*

A pine linen press, 35in (89cm) wide. **£800–1,000**  *AL*

An Irish pine food press, c1840, 72in (182.5cm) high. **£1,100–1,500**  *BH*

A pine linen press, by Heal & Co., London, porcelain handles, c1850, 43in (107.5cm) wide. **£1,100–1,500**  *AL*

A Dutch carved pine linen press, 93in (236cm) high. **£2,300–2,700**  *RK*

A Victorian pine linen press, c1800, 49in (124.5cm) wide. **£1.000–1,300**  *PIN*

A Georgian linen press, 47½in (120cm) wide. **£1,200–1,500**  *PH*

A pine linen press, 19thC, 49in (122.5cm) wide. **£1,000–1,250**  *AL*

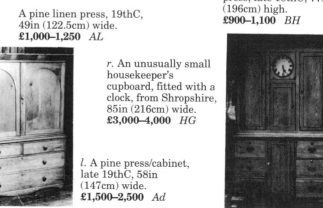

*r.* An unusually small housekeeper's cupboard, fitted with a clock, from Shropshire, 85in (216cm) wide. **£3,000–4,000**  *HG*

A Scottish pine linen press, late 18thC, 77½in (196cm) high. **£900–1,100**  *BH*

A pine press, c1840, 51in (127.5cm) wide. **£1,500–2,000**  *UP*

*l.* A pine press/cabinet, late 19thC, 58in (147cm) wide. **£1,500–2,500**  *Ad*

A pine 2 door wardrobe, with
decorative linen drawer, c1900,
74in (188cm) high.
**£280–350** *OCP*

An Irish pine linen
cupboard, on bracket feet,
restored, c1800, 52in
(157cm) wide.
**£900–950** *DFA*

An Irish pine linen cupboard,
with panelled sides,
Co. Donegal, restored, c1830,
49in (124.5cm) wide.
**£850–950** *DFA*

A pine linen press, with shelved
interior, c1800, 65in (165cm) wide.
**£800–900** *DFA*

A pine housekeeper's cupboard, with
original interior paint, c1860,
97in (246cm) wide.
**£1,200–1,500** *OCP*

**Use the Index!**

*Because certain items might fit
easily into any number of
categories, the quickest and
surest method of locating any
entry is by reference to the index
at the back of the book.*

*This index has been fully cross-
referenced for absolute simplicity.*

*l.* A stripped pine bookcase on cupboard, 84in (212.5cm) high.
**£1,500–2,000**
*Wor*

*Above and left.* A Victorian glazed secrétaire pine bookcase, with etched glass doors, and fitted interior, c1820.
**£2,500–3,000** *PIN*

A glazed pine bookcase, with broken pediment, 50in (127cm) wide.
**£1,500–2,000** *RK*

A pine bookcase, 83in (211cm) wide.
**£1,500–2,000** *PH*

*l.* A William IV pine bookcase, with false drawers, 50in (127cm) wide.
**£800–1,000** *UP*

An Austrian pine bookcase, the upper tier with cupboard with original frosted glass doors, 19thC, 48in (122cm) wide.
**£1,000–1,500** *Ad*

An Irish pine bookcase, 18thC, 54in (137cm) wide.
**£2,000–3,500** *AD*

A pine secrétaire bookcase, c1820, 39½in (99cm) wide.
**£1,250–1,500** *W*

A Victorian pine bookcase, c1860, 44in (111.5cm) wide.
**£1,000–1,500** *AL*

A pine bookcase, 71in (180cm) wide.
**£1,500–2,000** *LAM*

*r.* A pine open bookcase, early 19thC, 46in (116cm) high.
**£800–1,000** *DN*

A pine bookcase, with adjustable shelves, original handles, c1860, 76½in (194cm) high.
**£1,200–1,500** *AL*

A Victorian pine bookcase, with carved moulding to the top of glazed doors, and cushion moulded drawers, 48in (122cm) wide.
**£2,000–3,000** *OA*

A pine bookcase, 46in (116.5cm) wide.
**£750–1,000** *UP*

A William IV pine bookcase, 47in (119cm) wide.
**£1,000–1,300** *UP*

A Victorian pine bookcase, 50in (127cm) wide.
**£2,000–3,000** *OA*

A late Georgian pine bookcase, 42in (105cm) wide.
**£1,200–1,500** *UP*

*r.* A Continental pine bookcase, c1860, 43in (109cm) wide.
**£500–1,000** *UP*

*r.* A George III style pine breakfront bookcase, 74in (188cm) wide.
**£3,000–3,500** *Bon*

*l.* A Georgian bookcase, with astragal glazing, on bracket feet, 54in (137cm) wide.
**£2,000–3,000** *Ad*

A pine bookcase, with glazed top cupboards, c1880, 36in (92cm) wide.
**£250–350** *SPA*

*l.* An Edwardian pine bookshelf, 36in (91.5cm) wide.
**£250–350** *OA*

*l.* A pine bookcase in 2 parts, the 2 doors carved with shield design panels, c1870, 44in (111.5cm) wide.
**£300–400** *Byl*

A pitch pine bookcase, on plinth base, c1880, 48in (122cm) wide.
**£475–575** *POT*

A pine country bureau bookcase, with astragal glazed door, over two-door cupboard fronted desk, fall revealing fitted interior, 19thC, 38in (96.5cm) wide.
**£900–1,200** *TPC*

A pine bookcase, with glazed door to top enclosing shelves, and cupboard base, c1900, 39in (100cm) wide.
**£400–480** *BEL*

A pine bookcase, with glazed door, arched top and single drawer, 1860s, 32½in (83cm) wide.
**£500–600** *NWE*

An East European pine bookcase, with glazed doors, originally a wood panelled wardrobe, c1810, 35½in (90cm) wide.
**£250–300** *NWE*

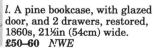

*l.* A pine bookcase, with glazed door, and 2 drawers, restored, 1860s, 21½in (54cm) wide.
**£50–60** *NWE*

A Victorian pine open bookcase, with tray top and solid plinth base, 54in (137cm) wide.
**£300–350** *TPC*

A George II pine bookcase cabinet, some damage, 118in (300cm) wide.
**£32,000–35,000**  *S(NY)*

A George II style pine bookcase, the pierced broken scroll pediment with acanthus ornament and central urn above a pair of astragal glazed doors and a pair of panelled cupboard doors, on plinth base, 50in (127cm) wide.
**£2,500–3,000**  *C*

*r.* A George III style pine bookcase, on a stiff-leaf carved plinth base, some carving 18thC, 78½in (199cm) wide.
**£7,000–8,000**  *C*

*l.* A pine wall bookcase, c1880, 24in (61cm) wide.
**£150–250**  *SPA*

A George III style pine bookcase, with breakfront stiff-leaf egg-and-dart and dentil moulded cornice, on a plinth base, some carving 18thC, 90in (229cm) wide.
**£4,000–5,000**  *C*

A Victorian pine
bookcase, c1860,
82in (208cm) high.
**£800–1,000**  *BH*

A pine bookcase, early
18thC, 90in (229cm) wide.
**£2,000–2,500**  *PCL*

A pine glazed top
bookcase, 19thC,
43in (107.5cm) wide.
**£1,200–1,500**  *SV*

A pine glazed bookcase,
39in (97.5cm) wide.
**£250–350**  *AL*

An Irish pine glazed
dresser/bookcase, c1840,
80in (203cm) high.
**£1,000–1,200**  *BH*

An Edwardian pine
bookcase, with original
doors and brasswork,
95in (241cm) wide.
**£3,500–4,500**  *OA*

A pine bookcase, with
frieze drawer, late 19thC,
45in (114cm) wide.
**£1,500–2,500**  *Ad*

A two-piece double arch door
pine bookcase, c1820.
**£1,200–1,500**  *PIN*

A Victorian Gothic pedestal
bookcase, with adjustable
shelves, 74in (188cm) wide.
**£1,000–1,150**  *OA*

A Welsh pine glazed
bookcase, with 2 bowfront
drawers, 2 cupboards
below with raised panel
doors, on ball feet, c1840,
55in (139.5cm) wide.
**£2,000–2,500**  *Sca*

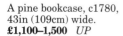

A pine bookcase, c1780,
43in (109cm) wide.
**£1,100–1,500**  *UP*

A pine bookcase, the doors with coloured
glass borders, c1880, 42in (106.5cm) wide.
**£600–800**  *SSD*

A pine breakfront bookcase,
made from old timber, 90in
(228cm) wide.
**£2,000–2,500**  *UP*

An Irish pine glazed cabinet, c1840, 51in (130cm) wide.
**£900–1,100** *UP*

A German pine kitchen cabinet, with original ceramic spice drawers, c1900s, 71in (180cm) high.
**£250–350** *WHA*

A Victorian collector's pine cabinet, with pigeonholes, 24in (61cm) wide.
**£350–700** *Ad*

A pine display cabinet, c1780, 27½in (70cm) wide.
**£250–400** *W*

A Georgian pine filing cabinet, 54in (137cm) wide.
**£1,500–2,000** *AL*

A bedside cabinet with gallery top, c1900, 31in (79cm) wide.
**£200–300** *LAM*

A Regency pine display cabinet, 49in (124.5cm) wide.
**£2,000–3,000** *W*

*l.* An Irish astragal glazed pine cabinet, c1800, 49in (124.5cm) wide.
**£1,100–1,300** *UP*

A European pine cabinet, c1860, 32in (81cm) wide.
**£300–500** *UP*

A pine corner cabinet, with astragal glazed upper doors, 41in (104cm) wide.
**£600–700** *PH*

*r.* A Quicksey pine kitchen cabinet, with original fittings, glass storage jars and drawers, spice rack, flour bin, and memoranda panels inside top doors, enamel work top, 48in (122cm) wide.
**£1,150–1,350** *OC*

*l.* A mid-European pine draper's cabinet, 71in (180cm) wide.
**£1,500–2,000** *MofC*

A Continental floor standing kitchen
cabinet with 3 shelves, replacement
bottom frieze, early 20thC, 35in
(89cm) high.
**£120–200** *HGN*

*r.* A pine china cabinet
with specimen drawers,
and two glazed side doors,
c1860, 45in (114cm) wide.
**£375–425** *ASP*

A Victorian pine collector's
cabinet, c1870, 37½in
(95cm) wide.
**£450–500** *MofC*

A Continental pine bedside
cabinet, with one door, 1890,
18in (46cm) high.
**£75–85** *ASP*

A pine sewing cabinet,
15in (38cm) wide.
**£65–85** *ASP*

*r.* A pine wall pipe
rack wall cabinet,
17½in (44cm) high.
**£20–30** *ASP*

A pitch pine wall cabinet, c1880,
20in (51cm) high.
**£75–85** *ASP*

*l.* A Victorian
entomologist's, ten-
drawer pine cabinet,
with original stain
on inside, 29in
(74cm) wide.
**£700–900** *CCP*

A Georgian pine mule chest, with bracket feet,
c1780, 44in (111.5cm) wide.
**£200–300**  *COT*

A Georgian pine mule chest,
restored, c1800.
**£200–300**  *COT*

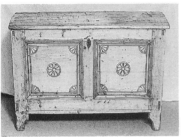

A Baltic region pine coffer, c1800,
51½in (131cm) wide.
**£650–750**  *HeR*

A panelled pine coffer on shaped bracket feet,
18thC, 48in (122cm) wide.
**£300–400**  *TPC*

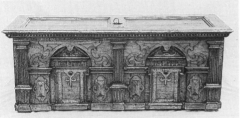

A German pine marriage chest, with carved
front, dated '1614', 68in (172.5cm) wide.
**£1,500–1,800**  *CCP*

A pine mule chest, with long base
drawer with key, on bracket feet,
19thC, 33in (84cm) wide.
**£350–450**  *CCP*

A pine mule chest, with
2 drawers, fitted internal candle
box and original lock and key,
37in (94cm) wide.
**£375–750**  *CCP*

A Victorian pine carpenter's tool box,
38in (96.5cm) wide.
**£140–160**  *WaH*

*l.* A Victorian pine trunk, 36in (92cm) wide.
**£150–175**  *CCP*

A Welsh pine mule chest, c1820, 35in (87.5cm) wide.
**£350–500** *HG*

A pine box on stand, 19thC, 27½in (69cm) wide.
**£100–150** *AL*

A pine box, 22in (55cm) wide.
**£120–200** *AL*

*r.* An Austrian pine chest, dated '1861'.
**£300–350** *TPF*

*l.* A pine two-drawer mule chest, c1860.
**£300–350** *PIN*

*r.* A pine mule chest, c1840, 42½in (107cm) wide.
**£350–500** *AL*

*l.* A pine sea chest, with fitted tray, c1880, 27in (69cm) wide.
**£200–250** *AL*

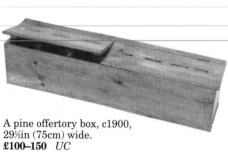

A pine offertory box, c1900, 29½in (75cm) wide.
**£100–150** *UC*

A pine box, c1860, 35in (89cm) wide.
**£200–300** *AL*

A pine box, c1880, 24in (62cm).
**£100–150** *SPA*

A mid-Victorian pine chest, with side carrying handles, fitted interior, 43½in (110cm) wide.
**£225–300** *OA*

A mid-Victorian pine trunk, with side handles, 33in (84cm) wide.
**£225–300** *OA*

A pine box, c1900, 36in (92cm) wide.
**£100–150** *SPA*

A pine box, with iron hinges, 26½in (66cm) wide.
**£100–150** *AL*

A Continental pine dome topped box, 43in (109cm) wide.
**£150–200** *CPA*

A pine dome-top box, restored,
1860, 31in (79cm) wide.
**£130–160** *NWE*

A Continental pine box, with dome top
and original iron furnishings, dated
'1868', 39in (99cm) wide.
**£150–300** *HNG*

A Continental pine blanket box, with original
furnishings, c1900, 35in (89cm) wide.
**£90–200** *HNG*

An pine carpenter's chest,
with fitted interior, c1860,
31in (79cm) wide.
**£250–300** *ASP*

A pitch pine and elm coffer, with original candle
box and fittings, mid-19thC, 43in (109cm) wide.
**£200–300** *HNG*

A Continental pine box, with dome top, c1870,
41in (104cm) wide.
**£150–300** *HNG*

An Austrian pine dome-topped coffer, 18thC,
48in (122cm) wide.
**£520–580** *GD*

A German pine blanket box, with original
iron fittings and original lock and key,
47in (119cm) wide.
**£250–400** *HGN*

An English pine linen chest, with candle box, 1850, 36½in (92cm) wide.
**£140–170** *ASP*

A pine mule chest, with fitted interior, drawers and candle box, all original, 45in (114cm)wide.
**£225–300** *ASP*

A pine deed box, c1900, 21in (53cm) long.
**£50–60** *ASP*

A Continental pine trunk, with dome top and metal bands, c1880, 32in (81cm) wide.
**£125–175** *ASP*

A Victorian pine blanket box, c1880, 34½in (87cm) wide.
**£100–150** *POT*

*l.* A pine grain/flour bin, c1890, 48in (122cm) wide.
**£285–325** *OCP*

A pine rug chest/mule chest, with candle box, c1835, 41½in (105cm) wide.
**£200–300** *DMe*

A European carved pine mule chest, the single drawer with original handles, c1840, 45in (114cm) wide.
**£450–500** *AF*

A pine grain/flour bin, c1840, 31in (79cm) wide.
**£300–360** *DMe*

A European pine dome-topped linen chest, with iron hinges, c1860, 34in (86cm) wide.
**£130–150** *DMe*

*r.* A pine box, with domed top, c1880, 27½in (70cm) wide.
**£100–120** *DFA*

A pine box, with nameplate, c1850, 26in (66cm) wide.
**£100–140** *DFA*

A pine box, c 1870, 42in (106.5cm) wide.
**£110–130** *DFA*

A pine iron bound box, c1870, 30in (76cm) wide.
**£50–100** *AL*

A small pine blanket box, with original handles, c1850, 31in (79cm) wide.
**£95–125** *SA*

An Austrian pine linen box, with handles, c1880, 44in (111.5cm) wide.
**£80–120** *Byl*

A pine sea chest, with rope handles, c1860, 38½in (97cm) wide.
**£250–300** *AL*

*l.* An Irish pine metal bound document box, c1880, 28in (71cm) wide.
**£90–100** *Byl*

A pine blanket box, c1850, 36in (91.5cm) wide.
**£110–145** *SA*

A pine box, with handles, c1880, 47in (119cm) wide.
**£250–300**  *AL*

A pine box, c1880, 47in (119cm) wide.
**£150–200**  *AL*

Two sailors' pine diddy boxes, c1890,
12in (31cm) wide.
**£40–50 each**  *AL*

A pine box, with one drawer and a candle box,
c1860, 40in (101.5cm) wide.
**£250–300**  *AL*

A pine fishing rod box, c1890, 45in (114cm) wide.
**£50–55**  *AL*

A pine box, with a tray, c1880, 15in (38cm) wide.
**£35–45**  *AL*

A pine box, c1890, 32in (81cm) wide.
**£45–55**  *AL*

An iron-bound pine box, c1890, 26in (66cm) wide.
**£95–115**  *AL*

*l.* A pine box, with a candle box, c1870,
42in (106.5cm) wide.
**£200–260**  *AL*

# A Michelangelo. Only in Florence.

# A Van der Tol. Only in Almere.

We carry one of the world's finest collections of antique pine furniture.

Available in unstripped, stripped and finished & painted versions. Plus pine

reproductions and decorative items. We offer quality, quantity & profit and

full packing service. Please visit our 65.000 sq.ft. warehouse

in Almere and enjoy the personal and friendly service.

## Jacques van der Tol
### unique antique pine furniture

A pine blanket chest, with dovetail joints, c1875.
**£100–150**  *PIN*

A Danish pine dome-topped box, c1860, 43in (109cm) wide.
**£160–180**  *RK*

A pine chest, with a divided top, original locks, 48in (122cm) wide.
**£600–800**  *AL*

A Scandinavian pine dome-topped coffer, all original iron, c1800.
**£145–200**  *W*

A pine chest, some damage to mouldings, c1750, 46in (116.5cm) wide.
**£400–500**  *AL*

A small pine box, c1890, 29in (74cm) wide.
**£90–100**  *PAC*

A pine chest, with original ironwork, c1850, 24in (61cm) wide.
**£75–120**  *W*

A pine box, 20in (50cm) wide.
**£40–60**  *AL*

A pine dome-topped child's box, with original ironwork, c1860, 18½in (47cm) long. **£75–125**  *MPA*

A pitch pine box, 44in (111.5cm) wide. **£150–200**  *LAM*

A pine mule chest with wooden hinges to lid, c1790, 39in (99cm) wide.
**£300–400**  *W*

A pine chest, 19thC, 38in (96.5cm) wide. **£225–300**  *WHA*

A pine mule chest, with rising top and 2 drawers under, 19thC, 28in (71cm) wide.
**£400–600**  *PM*

A pine box, with a trim round base, 29in (74cm) wide.
**£120–200**  *AL*

A pine box, with a candle box, c1860, 42in (107cm) long.
**£250–350**  *AL*

A pine chest, with dovetail joints and original brass handles, c1880, 44in (111.5cm) wide.
**£150–200**  *Sca*

*r.* A pine mule chest, with a drawer, c1840, 42½in (107cm) wide. **£350–500** *AL*

A pine box, c1880, 42in (106.5cm) wide. **£100–150** *SPA*

*l.* A pine panelled coffer, 51½in (130cm) wide. **£200–300** *PH*

A pine box, c1860, 24in (61cm) wide. **£100–150** *AL*

A pine box, 36in (91.5cm) wide. **£90–100** *PAC*

A pine box, c1850, 20in (53cm) wide. **£150–250** *AL*

A pine coffer, c1800, 66in (167.5cm) wide. **£300–450** *SSD*

A pine coffer, carved 'In this chest are the books and maps belonging to the Commission of Severs for the Eastern park of the County of Kent, 1715', with original escutcheons, feet replaced, 78in (198cm) long. **£950–1,100** *LAM*

A small pine box, 15in (38cm) wide. **£100–120** *LAM*

A pine trunk, with side carrying handles, 18thC, 25in (63.5cm) wide. **£250–350** *OA*

A pine fitted box, c1880, 39in (99cm) wide. **£250–350** *AL*

A German pine domed top box. **£150–200** *CPA*

A pine tool chest, with two trays, c1860, 36in (92cm) wide. **£250–300** *AL*

A pine dome-topped box, with iron straps, c1840, 41in (104cm) wide.
**£150–200** *AL*

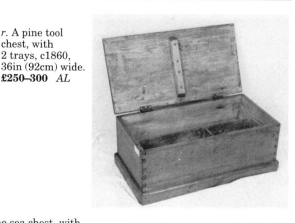

*r.* A pine tool chest, with 2 trays, c1860, 36in (92cm) wide.
**£250–300** *AL*

*l.* A pine sea chest, with a fitted tray, c1880, 27in (69cm) wide.
**£200–250** *AL*

A pine fitted tool box, c1850, 33in (84cm) wide.
**£300–400** *AL*

A pine mule chest, with a hinged top and two drawers beneath, 19thC, 36in (91.5cm) wide.
**£400–600** *CC*

*r.* A pitch pine coffer, with interior candle box, 19thC, 36in (91.5cm) wide.
**£200–300** *SSP*

A pine chest, with well concealed secret drawers, c1860, 35in (89cm) wide.
**£250–350** *Far*

*l.* A Victorian pine workbox, with a sectioned tray, 20in (51cm) wide.
**£40–50** *CI*

A pine box, with padlock and key, 21in (53cm) wide.
**£100–150** *AL*

*r.* A pine deed box, with original iron handles and spearhead hinges, pegged sides to lid, date on exterior added later, 3 earlier dates inside, 18thC.
**£100–150** *PF*

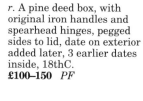

A pine box, with original fittings, c1820, 45in (114cm) wide.
**£300–400** *AL*

A German pine dome-topped box.
**£150–200** *CPA*

A Spanish pine coffer, with original ironwork, c1840, 43in (109cm) wide. **£275–350** *UC*

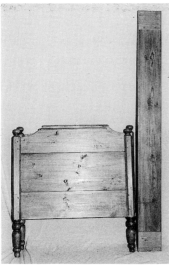

A pine single bed with knob
finials, c1890, 39in (99cm) wide.
**£175–200** *ASP*

A Continental pine single bed,
with decorative headboard,
carved corbels and turned legs,
c1860, 76in (193cm) long.
**£200–450** *AF*

A pine sleigh bed, c1870,
74in (188cm) wide.
**£800–1,100** *AnD*

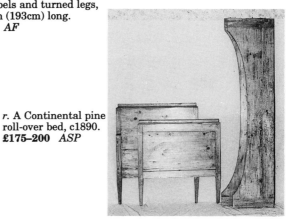

*r.* A Continental pine
roll-over bed, c1890.
**£175–200** *ASP*

**Did you know?**
*MILLER'S* **Antiques
Price Guide** *builds up
year-by-year to form the
most comprehensive
antiques photo-reference
library available.*

A Victorian Crib, c1860,
40in (101.5cm) long.
**£200–250** *COT*

A child's pine extending bed, c1910,
51in (130cm) long before extended.
**£280–310** *BEL*

A pine bed, c1890,
36in (91.5cm) wide.
**£200–250** *AL*

A cane and carved pine bed head
and foot, 66in (167.5cm) wide.
**£500–550** *LAM*

A two-door Irish pine bed
cupboard, with panelled sides,
c1840, 48in (122cm) wide.
**£550–600** *LC*

A pine Victorian bed, with oak posts
and legs, and close boarded base,
c1850, 78in (198cm) long.
**£400–500** *CC*

An Irish pine settle/
bed, c1840, 72in
(182.5cm) long.
**£600–800** *LC*

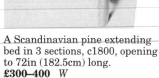

A Scandinavian pine extending
bed in 3 sections, c1800, opening
to 72in (182.5cm) long.
**£300–400** *W*

A German pine bed, c1890,
75½in (191cm) long.
**£200–250** *Sca*

A pine single bed head and foot,
from an Austrian sleigh bed,
75in (190cm) long.
**£200–250** *CHA*

A pine bed, *(head only
shown),* with original
sides and slats, 54in
(137cm) wide.
**£450–600** *AL*

*r.* A pine sleigh bed,
c1880. **£200–250** *TPF*

*l.* A pine bedstead, with high ship's
sides, 19thC, 72in (180cm) long.
**£200–250** *AF*

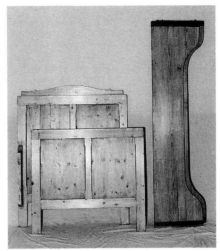

A Texan yellow pine daybed, with outward flared ends, each with horizontal slats, on square tapering chamfered legs ,retains traces of original blue paint, mid-19thC, 77½in (196cm) long.
**£350–450** *CNY*

A Continental pine bed, c1890.
**£175–200** *ASP*

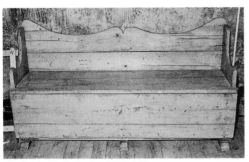

An Irish settle bed, c1870, 72in (182.5cm) wide.
**£350–400** *AF*

An Eastern European pine sleigh bed, early 20thC, 76in (193cm) long.
**£150–250** *HNG*

*l.* A German sleigh bed, c1890, 78in (198cm) long.
**£225–300** *AnD*

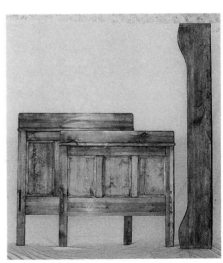

A Welsh pine bed, c1870, 64in (162.5cm) wide.
**£550–600** *AL*

A Continental pine bed, c1890.
**£175–200** *ASP*

A Dutch pine sideboard, c1870,
48in (122cm) wide.
**£650–700**  *FAG*

A pine buffet, c1900,
49½in (126cm) wide.
**£250–320**  *BEL*

A carved pine sideboard, with
3 drawers and 2 doors, c1890,
54in (137cm) wide.
**£850–950**  *OCP*

*r.* A pine side
serving table, with
8 drawers, c1900,
108in (274cm) wide.
**£400–500**  *OCP*

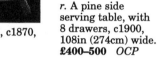

A French pine serving table, with 2 drawers, c1850,
49in (124.5cm) wide.
**£400–470**  *GD*

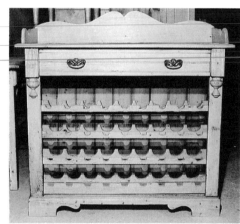

A pine wine rack, converted from a buffet,
c1880, 45in (114cm) wide.
**£285–350**  *OCP*

A Danish pine sideboard, with
mirrored back, c1870, 50in
(127cm) wide.
**£900–950**  *UC*

*r.* A pine side server,
c1880, 37in (94cm) wide.
**£225–275**  *OCP*

A Victorian pine chiffonier,
64in (162.5cm) wide.
**£1,500–2,500** *Ad*

A Regency pine chiffonier, c1820,
46in (116.5cm) wide.
**£950–1,200** *AL*

A Welsh chiffonier, c1830, 68in
(172.5cm) wide.
**£1,250–1,500** *Sca*

A pine chiffonier, 33½in
(85cm) wide.
**£500–600** *PH*

A pine chiffonier, c1860, 42in
(106.5cm) wide.
**£700–900** *AL*

An Austrian pine chiffonier, 19thC,
36in (91.5cm) wide.
**£700–900** *Ad*

*l.* A pine chiffonier,
with brass
escutcheons, c1850,
34½in (87cm) wide.
**£800–1,000** *AL*

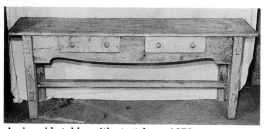

A pine side table, with stretcher, c1870, 28½in (72cm) high.
**£200–300** *DFA*

*l.* A pine side table, with single drawer and stretcher, c1840, 60½in (153cm) wide.
**£200–250** *DFA*

A pine buffet, from Co. Laois, c1845, 36in (91.5cm) wide.
**£230–260** *DMe*

A pine side cabinet, c1870, 45in (114cm) wide.
**£200–240** *DFA*

A pine side serving table, with glass knobs, c1870, 69in (175cm) wide.
**£750–850** *AL*

A pine breakfront sideboard, with 3 central drawers flanked by 2 cupboard doors, c1870, 71in (180cm) wide.
**£400–450** *DFA*

A pine sideboard with single frieze drawer, c1865, 45½in (115cm) wide.
**£200–240** *DFA*

A pine side serving table, c1870, 42½in (107cm) wide.
**£250–300** *AL*

A pine sideboard, with bull's-eye decoration on doors, c1870, 48in (122cm) wide.
**£700–800** *AL*

A pine sideboard, c1880, 50in (127cm) wide.
**£200–240** *DFA*

A North Country pine sideboard, c1880, 58in (147cm) wide.
**£1,000–1,150**  *Sca*

A mid-Victorian gallery backed sideboard, c1860, 78in (198cm) wide.
**£900–1,000**  *PIN*

A carved pine sideboard, with original handles, 35in (89cm) wide.
**£850–1,000**  *AL*

A pine sideboard, with arched panel doors, c1860, 54in (137cm) wide.
**£650–800**  *UP*

A Victorian sideboard, with 6 small drawers above, 3 large drawers each side of a central cupboard and central drawer, c1860, 74in (188cm) wide.
**£1,200–1,500**  *PH*

A pine sideboard, 47in (119cm) wide.
**£700–900**  *SAn*

*l.* A pine sideboard, with Gothic panelled doors, 70in (177.5cm) wide.
**£2,000–2,500**  *PH*

*l.* A pine sideboard, with beaded and panelled doors and carved side pillars, 19thC, 49in (124.5cm) wide.
**£600–700**  *MS*

A Regency pine sideboard, 54in (135cm) wide.
**£950–1,200**  *UP*

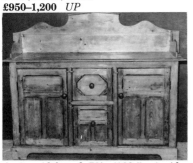

A pine sideboard, 72in (182.5cm) wide.
**£700–900**  *SAn*

A pine sideboard, with gallery,
2 drawers and 2 panelled doors,
c1870, 48in (122cm) wide.
**£200–300** *Byl*

A pine sideboard, with
shaped back, 2 drawers,
2 panelled doors and
pillars to sides, c1875,
39in (99cm) wide.
**£175–275** *Byl*

A Victorian pine sideboard,
carved in relief with ribbon
and bow decoration, 50in
(127cm) wide.
**£400–500** *SA*

## 'Antique' Pine

Made today out of
antique or reclaimed
wood, 'antique' pine is
often made in
contemporary styles,
and both accurate and
inaccurate copies of
original pieces.

A pine server, with gallery
and 2 doors, c1900, 45in
(114cm) wide.
**£280–300** *SA*

A pine sideboard, with gallery,
one drawer and 2 panelled doors,
42in (106.5cm) wide.
**£225–265** *SA*

A pine sideboard, with
gallery back, 2 drawers and
2 cupboard doors, c1880,
42in (106.5cm) wide.
**£175–275** *Byl*

An Edwardian sideboard,
with one drawer and
2 carved doors, c1910,
41in (104cm) wide.
**£220–260** *SA*

A pitch pine chiffonier, c1885,
49in (124.5cm) wide.
**£325–375** *ASP*

*l.* A pine chiffonier, with
raised shelf on turned
column supports, early
19thC, 48in (122cm) wide.
**£600–800** *TPC*

A Victorian pine chiffonier,
48in (122cm) wide.
**£550–650** *WV*

A pine bureau bookcase, with glazed doors to top, 3 drawers, and pigeonhole interior base, early 19thC, 38in (96.5cm) wide.
**£800–1,200** *TPC*

A pine filing chest, with 2 fitted drawers, c1910, 29in (75cm) high.
**£400–485** *BEL*

A pine desk with 4 drawers, c1890, 22½in (57cm) wide.
**£200–280** *BEL*

A pine school desk, lift-up top, c1910, 20in (51cm) wide.
**£80–90** *DMe*

A pine clerks' chest, with slope top above 7 graduated drawers, 19thC, 30in (76cm) wide.
**£400–600** *TPC*

A Welsh pine clerk's desk, c1880, 20in (51cm) wide.
**£125–150** *ASP*

*l.* A Victorian pine writing slope, c1860, 22in (56cm) wide.
**£35–45** *SA*

A pine pedestal desk, c1900, 55in (140cm) wide.
**£400–450** *BEL*

A pine kneehole desk, with 18 drawers, c1830, 46½in (117cm) wide.
**£750–850** *GD*

A pine escritoire, c1890, 37in (94cm) wide.
**£2,000–3,000** *W*

A pine desk.
**£70–80** *AL*

A pine writing desk, 74in (188cm) wide.
**£700–800** *RK*

A German Biedermeier style pine secrétaire, late 19thC, 37in (94cm) wide.
**£900–1,150** *CPA*

A clerk's pine desk, with a slide, pegged construction, c1860, 43½in (110cm) high.
**£200–300** *AL*

A pine desk, with later leathered slope, c1860, 53in (134.5cm) wide.
**£850–1,150** *AL*

A pine desk, fitted with pigeonholes, 22½in (56cm) wide.
**£100–120** *AL*

A pine desk, with new leather and handles, 19thC, 49in (122.5cm) wide.
**£850–1,200** *AL*

A glazed pine bureau bookcase, with 6 interior drawers and 2 drawers below, 19thC, 42in (106.5cm) wide.
**£2,500–4,000** *CC*

*r.* A kneehole desk, 47in (119cm) wide.
**£800–1,000** *RK*

A Queen Anne pine bureau, with fitted interior, 35in (89cm) wide.
**£1,100–1,300** *GC*

A pine secrétaire, 40in (101.5cm) wide.
**£1,200–1,500** *W*

A clerk's pine desk, with cupboards at the back, 2 shelves, and a china ink well with brass cover, c1850, 47in (119cm) high.
**£350–450** *AL*

A Danish pine secrétaire, c1880, 38in (96.5cm). **£1,00–1,250** *UP*

A pine pedestal desk, 61in (155cm) wide. **£650–700** *PH*

A pine desk/cupboard, mid-19thC, 34in (86cm) wide. **£110–150** *WHA*

A pine desk, with cupboards under, 44⅖in (113cm) wide. **£900–1,100** *AL*

A Georgian lady's pine work box, fitted with a sliding shelf, 30½in (76cm) wide. **£500–700** *LAM*

A pine writing table, with 3 drawers, c1820, 31½in (79cm) high. **£600–650** *AL*

A carved pine desk, with cabriole legs, c1880, 72in (182.5cm) wide. **£2,500–3,500** *PH*

A Victorian pine desk, 47in (119cm) wide. **£950–1,500** *AL*

A pine pedestal desk, with one central drawer, and 4 drawers each side, 36in (91.5cm) wide. **£800–1,200** *PC*

A Scandinavian pine desk, with an oak top, c1910, 51in (130cm) wide.
**£450–550**  *BEL*

A twin pedestal pine desk, c1880, 57in (145cm) wide.
**£700–800**  *RK*

A three-piece pine partners' desk, 51in (130cm) wide.
**£900–1,000**  *AL*

A Regency simulated bamboo pine desk, with new leather top, c1820, 45in (114cm) wide.
**£1,200–1,400**  *AL*

A pine fitted desk, with new sledge feet, c1870, 48in (122cm) high.
**£1,000–1.200**  *AL*

A pine desk, with black china knob handles, new leather top, c1860, 47in (119cm) wide.
**£2,000–2,500**  *AL*

A pine desk, c1870, 59in (150cm) wide.
**£500–600**  *AL*

A pine desk, 26in (66cm) wide.
**£800–1,000**  *PH*

A pine bureau, c1840, 43in (135cm) wide.  **£1,000–1,500**  *UP*

A pine knee-hole desk, with gallery back and original knobs, c1880, 50in (127cm) wide.
**£600–650**  *SSD*

A pine bureau/estate desk, with turned gallery and legs, the interior with pigeon holes, early 19thC, with later gallery, 24in (61cm) wide.
**£750–1,000**  *OA*

A pine pedestal desk, with new leather top and handles, c1860, 54in (137cm) wide.
**£1,500–2,000**  *AL*

*l*. A Victorian pedestal pine partners' desk, c1880, 60in (152cm) wide.
**£2,500–3,500**  *DDS*

A Victorian pine pedestal desk, 48in (122cm) wide.
**£1,000–1,500**  *PM*

A Victorian pine school desk with slot for slate, c1880, 29in (74cm) high.
**£100–150** *COT*

A pine cupboard, with writing slope, c1860, 23½in (60cm) wide.
**£230–250** *DMe*

An Irish pine shopkeeper's desk, c1880, 24in (61cm) wide.
**£70–100** *Byl*

A Continental pine two-seater school desk, with original inkwell, c1900, 46in (116.5cm) wide.
**£150–175** *ASP*

A pine single drawer lady's writing table, c1900, 36in (91.5cm) wide.
**£140–185** *OCP*

A pine clerk's desk, with lift-up lid, c1900, 44in (111.5cm) wide.
**£300–400** *OCP*

A French pine desk, with split fall and kneehole, 3 drawers one side and cupboard the other, panelled back, c1880, 47in (119cm) wide.
**£680–760** *GD*

An Irish pitch pine desk, 2 doors, with book shelves, c1900, 41in (104cm) wide.
**£300–400** *Byl*

A pine kneehole desk, with 7 drawers, c1860, 50in (127cm) wide.
**£450–500** *DFA*

An pine kneehole desk, with waxed finish, c1890, 55in (139.5cm) wide.
**£400–500** *DFA*

A Victorian pine desk, with a hinged top, the doors hiding 2 sets of sliding trays, 48in (122cm) wide.
**£500–700** *AL*

A breakfront kneehole pine desk, c1860, 47in (119cm) wide.
**£1,200–1,500** *AL*

A Georgian double teller's pine desk, with spindle gallery, c1780.
**£650–700** *PIN*

A Georgian pine estate desk on stand, the interior with 3 drawers, 24in (61cm) wide.
**£750–900** *OA*

A pitch pine desk, c1860, 42in (105cm) wide.
**£1,000–1,200** *SSD*

A pine flat topped desk, c1850, 19in (48cm) wide.
**£60–75** *AL*

A Georgian pine estate desk, 26in (66cm) wide.
**£750–1,000** *OA*

A late Georgian slope-top estate desk, with a bank of drawers, c1800–30.
**£300–400** *PIN*

A Georgian pine bureau, the top drawer acts as a support for the writing leaf, oak interior, c1800.
**£1,500–2,000** *PIN*

A pine desk, c1850, 29in (74cm) wide.
**£300–500** *AL*

A pine bureau, c1830, 41in (104cm) wide.
**£1,500–2,000** *W*

A Victorian pine desk, leather top renewed, 49in (124.5cm) wide.
**£250–300** *Far*

A Victorian pitch pine school teacher's desk, with rising lid and cupboard below.
**£200–300** *PM*

A pine bowfronted kneehole writing table, with a leather top, on turned legs with brass casters, 19thC, 42in (106.5cm) wide.
**£500–600** *TPC*

A pine pedestal desk, with 9 drawers, leather top renewed, c1840, 54in (137cm) wide.
**£500–700** *DMA*

A Victorian pine partners' desk, with 32 drawers, 1875, 102in (259cm) wide.
**£750–1,000** *AnD*

A Danish pine kneehole desk, with 5 drawers, on turned legs, c1870, 44in (111.5cm) wide.
**£800–1,200** *UC*

A late Victorian clerk's pine desk, with a tooled leather sloping top, 52in (132cm) wide.
**£500–600** *WAT*

A Victorian pine writing table, with 5 drawers, and original brass handles, on turned legs, c1845, 54in (137cm) wide.
**£500–600** *DMA*

A pine partners' desk, one side with 3 pedestal drawers and one cupboard, the other side with 2 cupboards and a centre drawer, c1860, 60in (152cm) wide.
**£700–900** *HOA*

An architect's pine flight of drawers, c1875, 42in (106.5cm) wide.
**£300–350** *AnD*

A mid-Victorian pine pedestal partners' desk, 54in (137cm) wide.
**£800–1,000** *TPC*

An eastern European pine kneehole desk, with 7 drawers, on turned feet, the date '1867' carved under the left pedestal, 49in (124.5cm) wide.
**£750–800** *HeR*

A Victorian pitch pine desk, with a cupboard and one drawer to the right side, a central drawer, and 4 drawers to the left side, the drawers with scallop-shaped handles, c1860, 49in (124.5cm) wide.
**£400–500** *COT*

A Victorian pine pedestal desk, with 3 drawers above 2 cupboard doors each concealed as 3 false drawers, 48in (122cm) wide.
**£550–650** *CCP*

An eastern European pine kneehole desk, with a leather top, 3 drawers, and 2 cupboard doors, c1900, 53in (134.5cm) wide.
**£700–800** *HeR*

A pine kneehole desk, with one central drawer and 4 drawers to each pedestal, 54in (137cm) wide.
**£1,400–1,600** *TPC*

A Victorian pine kneehole desk, with a shaped frieze below a central drawer, and 4 drawers to each pedestal, 47in (119cm) wide.
**£850–950** *HeR*

A Victorian pine davenport, leather top replaced, c1880, 26½in (68cm) wide.
**£400–450** *OPH*

A panelled pine coffer, c1820, 46in (116.5cm) long.
**£400–450** *DMA*

A German seaman's pine chest, c1890,
45in (114cm) long.
**£175–225** *AnD*

An Austrian pine chest, originally painted with naïve
decoration, c1860, 40in (101.5cm) long.
**£225–275** *AnD*

A pine mule chest, with 2 drawers,
c1780, 45in (114cm) long.
**£440–480** *MIL*

A Bavarian pine chest, c1860, 72in (182.5cm) long.
**£350–450** *AnD*

*This chest was made to collapse, to enable it to get
through chapel doors. It was used to store heavily
embroidered ceremonial religious garments.*

A pine mule chest, with original bale handles,
45in (114cm) long.
**£460–500** *DMA*

A German pine box, c1870, 48in (122cm) long.
**£165–245** *AnD*

A Continental seaman's pine chest,
c1880, 36in (91.5cm) long.
**£150–250** *AnD*

A pine box, fitted with a tray, c1870, 37in (94cm) wide.
**£225–250** *AL*

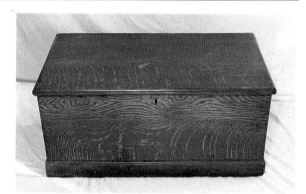

A pine blanket box, with original finish, c1870, 38in (96.5cm) wide.
**£150–170** *MIL*

A pine box, with a domed top, c1870, 42in (106.5cm) long.
**£150–200** *AnD*

A pine blanket box, with a domed top, fitted with a candle box, c1890, 36in (91.5cm) wide.
**£150–160** *MIL*

A pine box, with a dome top, fitted with a candle box, c1880, 33in (83.5cm) wide.
**£150–200** *AnD*

A pine box, c1880, 45in (114cm) wide.
**£150–200** *AnD*

A carpenter's pine tool chest, c1870, 35in (89cm) wide.
**£300–350** *AnD*

A pine box, c1870, 27in (68.5cm) wide.
**£150–200** *AnD*

A pine curved settle, c1820,
55in (139.5cm) wide.
£500–550 *MIL*

An elm and pine curved settle,
with a panelled back, and
3 drawers, 64in (162.5cm) wide.
£750–1,000 *DMA*

A pine barrel back settle, c1850,
84in (213cm) high.
£900–1,100 *COP*

A pine settle, with open arms and turned
spindle back, c1860, 72in (182.5cm) wide.
£325–375 *COP*

A pine settle, with solid back and slatted
arms, c1860, 72in (182.5cm) wide.
£325–375 *COP*

A Czechoslovakian pine
buffet dresser, c1880,
38in (96.5cm) wide.
**£550–650** *AnD*

A pine dresser, with
2 glazed cupboard doors,
above 2 drawers and
cupboards, 40in
(101.5cm) wide.
**£580–650** *MIL*

A Welsh pine dresser, with 6 drawers,
c1820, 64in (162.5cm) wide.
**£3,500–3,850** *UC*

A Continental pine dresser,
c1900, 60in (152cm) wide.
**£500–600** *AnD*

A Czechoslovakian dresser,
the top with glazed doors,
c1860, 60in (152cm) wide.
**£600–750** *AnD*

A Cornish pine dresser, with
3 glazed doors, 3 drawers
with 3 cupboards beneath,
and applied split turnings,
59in (149.5cm) wide.
**£900–950** *MIL*

An Irish pine and elm farmhouse
dresser, with fretted frieze, c1850,
59in (149.5cm) wide.
**£2,000–2,500** *UC*

A Dutch pine dresser, with
3 glazed doors, 60in
(152cm) wide.
**£600–700** *AnD*

A West Country pine dresser,
with turned moulding to
doors, 46in (116.5cm) wide.
**£850–900** *MIL*

A Victorian seven-drawer dresser base, with central 'dog kennel', and original brass handles, 113in (287cm) wide.
**£800–1,200** *CCP*

An eastern European pine dresser base, with carved panel motifs, c1880, 41½in (105cm) wide.
**£250–300** *NWE*

A Continental pine kitchen cupboard, with carved panel motifs, c1910, 44in (111.5cm) wide.
**£300–400** *WAT*

A Victorian pine dresser base, with 3 serpentine drawers, above 4 cockbeaded drawers, with original glass handles, and solid mahogany worktop, 78in (198cm) wide.
**£800–900** *CCP*

An eastern European dresser base, with a serpentine front, 2 panelled doors below 2 drawers, c1860, 40in (101cm) wide.
**£325–375** *NWE*

An eastern European pine cupboard, with one small drawer above 2 panelled doors, c1830, 58½in (148.5cm) wide.
**£750–850** *HeR*

An ornate Victorian four drawer pine dresser base, with later marble galleried top, 50in (127cm) wide.
**£450–500** *CCP*

A pine dresser base, with 3 drawers above open shelving, and one side cupboard, mid-19thC, 70in (177.5cm) wide.
**£500–600** *CCP*

An Irish pine and elm farmhouse dresser, with a fretted frieze, c1850, 59in (149.5cm) wide.
**£2,000–2,500** *UC*

A Sussex pine dresser, with an open rack, c1830, 59in (149.5cm) wide.
**£2,000–2,500** *UC*

A Suffolk pine cottage dresser, with an open rack, c1830, 56in (142cm) wide.
**£1,500–2,000** *UC*

A pine Welsh dresser, with 2 narrow glazed cupboards, above 3 freize drawers and 2 lower cupboards, c1860, 63in (160cm) wide.
**£900–1,200** *BOA*

A pine dresser, with open shelves above 2 drawers and 2 cupboards, 18½in (47cm) wide.
**£1,200–1,400** *AL*

A Georgian pine Welsh dresser, with 6 drawers, c1820, 64in (162.5cm) wide.
**£3,450–3,850** *UC*

*l.* A mid-Victorian pine dresser, in original condition, 61in (155cm) wide.
**£1,200–1,600** *CCP*

A North Country pine dresser, restored, c1780, 98in (249cm) wide.
**£1,200–1,400** *BOA*

A pine Welsh dresser, c1820,
58in (147cm) wide.
**£1,200–1,400** *RK*

An Irish pine fiddle front dresser,
c1820, 50in (127cm) wide.
**£1,400–1,800** *UP*

A Scottish pine dresser, c1860,
52in (132cm) wide.
**£800–1,000** *RK*

An Irish pine dresser, c1840,
78in (198cm) high.
**£800–1,000** *RK*

An Irish pine dresser,
c1850, 49in (124.5cm) wide.
**£800–1,000** *RK*

An Irish pine dresser, c1880,
80in (203cm) wide.
**£800–1,000** *RK*

A Scottish pine dresser, c1860,
55in (139.5cm) high.
**£800–1,000** *RK*

An Irish pine dresser,
c1860, 80in (203cm) high.
**£800–1,000** *RK*

An Irish pine dresser, c1860,
60in (152cm) wide.
**£1,800–2,000** *UP*

*l.* An Irish pine dresser,
c1880, 52in (132cm) wide.
**£1,000–1,200** *UP*

An Irish pine settle, c1880, 75in
(190.5cm) wide.  **£500–600** *UP*

A pine bowfront chest of drawers, with a shaped frieze, 2 short and 3 long drawers, on squat ball feet, 19thC. **£500–800** *TPC*

A Danish pine bureau bookcase, c1860, 84in (213cm) high. **£2,000–2,500** *RK*

A pine bureau bookcase, c1790, 42in (106.5cm) wide. **£2,250–2,750** *UP*

A pine chest of drawers, with 2 short and 2 long gesso decorated drawers, 19thC, 101.5cm) wide. **£800–1,000** *TPC*

A Scandinavian chest of drawers, c1880, 52in (132cm) wide. **£600–800** *RK*

An Irish pine glazed bookcase, c1830, 84in (213cm) high. **£1,000–1,500** *RK*

A pine chest of 5 drawers, 41in (104cm) wide. **£500–700** *AL*

A painted pine chest, with a serpentine fronted top and 8 drawers, early 19thC, 30in (77cm) wide. **£1,500–2,000** *DN*

A pine sideboard, c1850, 96in (244cm) wide.
**£900–1,200** *SAn*

*l.* A pine cupboard base, c1800, with a later breakfront display plate rack, 60in (152cm) wide.
**£1,100–1,300** *PC*

A pitch pine single wardrobe, c1870, 48in (122cm) wide.
**£550–650** *PC*

A pine delft rack, c1840, 60in (152cm) wide.
**£500–700** *AL*

*r.* A hazel pine wardrobe, c1890, 39in (99cm) wide.
**£450–600** *PC*

A pine dresser base, with a gallery back, c1860, 66in (168cm) wide.
**£850–1,100** *PC*

A Yorkshire serpentine front pine dresser base, with original spice drawers, c1860, later plate rack, 54in (137cm) wide.
**£1,500–2,500** *PC*

A pine and elm dresser base, c1850, with a later plate rack, 72in (182cm) wide.
**£2,000–3,000** *PC*

A pitch pine dresser base, c1900, with a later plate rack, 42in (107cm) wide.
**£800–1,000** *PC*

A pine stool, c1880, 16in (40.5cm) wide.
**£30–40** *AL*

A pine stool, c1890, 16in (40.5cm) wide.
**£30–35** *MIL*

An Austrian pine chair, with shaped back, c1890.
**£65–95** *AnD*

A pine folding chair, by Thornet, c1930.
**£35–40** *Ber*

A pine stool, c1890, 15in (38cm) wide.
**£35–40** *AL*

A pine milking stool, c1890, 11in (28cm) high.
**£30–35** *MIL*

A pine stool, with a saddle seat, c1890, 26in (66cm) high.
**£50–60** *AL*

A pine chair, with carved bar across the back.
**£40–50** *LIB*

A pine milking stool, c1880, 14in (35.5cm) high.
**£50–60** *MIL*

A tall stool, c1900, 29in (73.5cm) high.
**£40–50** *AL*

A German pine wardrobe, with 2 doors flanking a central oval mirror, above 2 long drawers, c1900, 60in (152cm) wide.
**£600–800** *AnD*

A Flemish pine armoire, c1870, 48in (122cm) wide.
**£400–500** *AnD*

A Continental pine wardrobe, with one arched door and arched top, 19thC, 44in (111.5cm) wide.
**£480–520** *LIB*

A pine 'break down' wardrobe, 19thC, 66in (167.5cm) wide.
**£550–580** *LIB*

A Continental pine wardrobe, with decorated cornice and door panels, 46½in (118cm) wide.
**£800–900** *WAT*

A Dutch pine armoire, with 2 doors above 2 drawers, c1840, 60in (152cm) wide.
**£700–900** *AnD*

A Danish pine armoire, with 2 doors above 2 drawers, c1850, 55in (139.5cm) wide.
**£800–1,200** *UC*

A Continental pine wardrobe, 19thC, 44in (111.5cm) wide.
**£480–520** *LIB*

A pine armoire, with 2 doors above one long drawer, c1880, 48in (122cm) wide.
**£400–500** *AnD*

A pine fire surround, 19thC,
48in (122cm) wide.
**£250–275** *AnD*

A pine door, with frame,
19thC, 36in (91.5cm) wide.
**£200–230** *WEL*

A pair of pine church doors, 19thC,
62in (157cm) wide.
**£400–450** *WEL*

A pair of pine chapel doors, of
heavy braced construction,
with decorative hand forged
strap hinges, 18thC, 52in
(132cm) wide.
**£500–600** *TPC*

A cast iron fireplace, with
Art Nouveau tiles, c1900,
40in (101.5cm) wide.
**£375–400** *WaH*

A Victorian pine bedroom
fireplace, with fluted
decoration, c1860.
**£200–250** *OPH*

A Canadian Adam style fire surround, carved
with pilasters and paterae, early 19thC, 59in
(149.5cm) high.
**£2,000–2,500** *RIT*

A carved pine fire surround, with a leaf and
flower decorated frieze flanked by urn top
fluted and reeded column sides, the opening
surrounded with egg-and-dart moulding,
18thC, 62in (157cm) wide.
**£800–1,000** *TPC*

A pitch pine dressing chest, c1870, 42in (106.5cm) wide.
**£600–700** *SSD*

A hazel pine dressing chest, c1890, 42in (106.5cm) wide.
**£400–500** *SSD*

A hazel pine dressing chest, c1890, 36in (92cm) wide.
**£400–500** *SSD*

A pine dressing table, c1870, 39in (99cm) wide.
**£500–600** *SSD*

A pine dressing table, with original paint, 36in (92cm) wide.
**£400–500** *AL*

A pine dressing table, with new handles, 36in (92cm) wide.
**£400–500** *AL*

A pine dressing table, c1890, 42in (106.5cm) wide.
**£450–600** *W*

An Edwardian pine dressing chest, 34in (86cm) wide.
**£350–400** *OA*

An Edwardian pine dressing table, 36in (92cm) wide.
**£350–550** *OA*

A pine dressing table, with new handles, 36in (92cm) wide.
**£350–400** *AL*

*l*. A Devonshire pitch pine glazed dresser, with quadriform moulding and fielded panelled drawers, 19thC, 52in (132cm) wide.
**£600–800** *PC*

A pine dressing chest, with mahogany handles, 19thC, 39in (99cm) wide.
**£400–600** *CC*

*l*. A pine dressing table, c1870, 39in (99cm) wide.
**£450–600** *W*

*l*. A Swedish pine dressing chest, with unusual carving, 32in (81cm) wide.
**£200–400** *BEL*

A pine dressing table, with an elm top, 34in (87cm) wide.
**£400–500** *AL*

A pitch pine dressing chest, with carved mirror supports and shaped brackets below, 19thC, 36in (91.5cm) wide.
**£450–600** *PF*

A pine washstand/ dressing table, c1860, 30in (76cm) wide.
**£550–600** *AL*

A pine dressing chest, with original handles and fittings, c1840, 44in (110cm) wide.
**£600–750** *Sca*

A pine dressing table, with original handles, c1860, 38in (96.5cm) wide.
**£450–600** *AL*

A Victorian pine dressing table, with a bevelled mirror, 36in (91.5cm) wide.
**£350–500** *AH*

A pitch pine dressing table, c1880, 39in (99cm) wide.
**£450–550** *SSD*

A pine dressing chest, with bevelled glass, and porcelain handles, late 19thC, 42in (106.5cm) wide.
**£450–650** *AL*

A pine dressing table, c1870, 30in (76cm) wide.
**350–450** *W*

A Victorian dressing chest, c1880, 42in (106.5cm) wide.
**£525–650** *Sca*

A late Victorian pine dressing chest, c1890, 43in (109cm) wide.
**£300–400** *COT*

A Victorian Gothic style pitch pine dressing table, c1860, 44in (111.5cm) wide.
**£200–300** *COT*

A late Victorian pitch pine dressing chest, 42in (106.5cm) wide.
**£350–400** *WaH*

A pine dressing chest, c1910, 47½in (120cm) wide.
**£435–485** *BEL*

A pine dressing chest, with drawers and cupboards, c1920, 57½in (145cm) wide.
**£435–485** *BEL*

*l*. A mid-Victorian pine breakfront kneehole dressing table, with arched top mirror on carved supports, 52in (132cm) wide.
**£600–800** *TPC*

*r*. A pine and elm dressing table, c1940, 43½in (110cm) wide.
**£230–280** *BEL*

A dressing chest, with galleried mirror, c1880, 41in (104cm) wide.
**£300–350** *ASP*

A late Victorian pine dressing chest, with gesso decoration, 2 short and 2 long drawers, on solid plinth base, 40in (101.5cm) wide.
**£400–500** *TPC*

A pine and satin walnut dressing chest, original brass handles and bevelled glass mirror in excelent condition, early 20thC, 37in (94cm) wide.
**£200–450** *HNG*

A late Victorian pine dressing chest, with gesso decoration, 42in (106.5cm) wide.
**£400–600** *TPC*

A Victorian pine dressing table, 41in (104cm) wide.
**£260–290** *GD*

*r.* A pine dressing chest, with 4 drawers in base, c1880, 38in (96.5cm) wide.
**£350–385** *ASP*

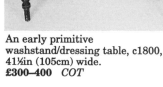

An early primitive washstand/dressing table, c1800, 41½in (105cm) wide.
**£300–400** *COT*

*r.* A late Victorian pine dressing table, with gesso decoration, on tapered legs, 40in (101.5cm) wide.
**£400–600** *TPC*

*l.* A pine dressing table, c1880, 36in (91.5cm) wide.
**£175–200**  *ASP*

A pine dressing table, with mirror, on turned legs, c1875, 41in (104cm) wide.
**£125–175**  *Byl*

A pine dressing table, with mirror and 2 drawers, c1940, 33in (84cm) wide.
**£185–220**  *OCP*

*l.* A pine dressing table, by Maples, c1880, 36in (92cm) wide.
**£360–460**  *AL*

## Old Pine

Old pine has often been restored, modified or customised, either because the piece had deteriorated beyond reasonable repair, or it is not suitable in its original state for modern use or taste.

# Clocks

A pine longcase clock, with 30 hour movement, arched dial, painted face, 82in (208cm) high.
**£750–850**  *MIL*

A French pine grandfather clock, 92in (233.5cm) high.
**£550–650**  *ASP*

*l.* A pine longcase clock, with 30 hour movement, c1810, 78in (198cm) high.
**£700–850**  *HOA*

An Irish pine grandfather clock, c1840.
**£1,200–1,400**  *HON*

A Victorian pine washstand, 36in (91.5cm) wide.
**£250–350** *OA*

A Victorian pine washstand, with a towel rail on either side, 41in (104cm) wide.
**£250–350** *OA*

A Victorian pine washstand, 39in (99cm) wide.
**£350–500** *OA*

A pine washstand, c1880s, 36in (91.5cm) wide.
**£250–400** *OA*

A pine washstand, with a marble top, the splashback with Art Deco tiles, 36in (91.5cm) wide.
**£200–300** *OA*

A Victorian pine washstand, with marble superstructure, 28in (71cm) wide.
**£300–500** *Ad*

A pine washstand, c1860, 43½in (110cm) wide.
**£300–500** *AL*

A Victorian pine washstand, with a marble top, and a pink tiled splashback, 36in (91.5cm) wide.
**£300–500** *OA*

A Victorian pine washstand, 24in (61cm) wide.
**£150–250** *OA*

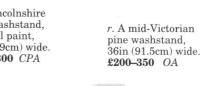

*l.* A Lincolnshire pine washstand, original paint, 35in (89cm) wide.
**£250–300** *CPA*

*r.* A mid-Victorian pine washstand, 36in (91.5cm) wide.
**£200–350** *OA*

A late Victorian pine marble topped washstand, 36in (91.5cm) wide.
**£300–500** *OA*

A late Victorian pine washstand, with a marble top and tiled splashback.
**£350–500** *OA*

A pine double washstand, 40½in (102cm) wide.
**£250–300** *AL*

A Georgian pine washstand,
14in (36cm) wide.
**£300–400** *W*

A pine washstand, with a drawer,
c1860, 23in (59cm) wide.
**£200–300** *W*

A marble topped pine washstand,
36in (91.5cm) wide.
**£300–450** *WHA*

A Victorian pine washstand,
37in (94cm) wide.
**£250–350** *AH*

A pine washstand,
c1850, 35in (89cm) wide.
**£120–145** *W*

A Swedish pine washstand/
side cabinet, c1890, 32½in
(82cm) wide.
**£160–185** *Far*

A pine washstand, c1900,
31in (84cm) wide.
**£200–300** *Ad*

A pine washstand, c1880,
28in (71cm) wide.
**£130–160** *WEL*

A Regency pine
washstand, 22in
(55.5cm) wide.
**£300–400** *W*

A pine washstand, with one door and
one drawer, c1880, 40in (102cm) high.
**£500–550** *AL*

A pine washstand, with a marble
top, c1880, 42in (107cm) wide.
**£350–450** *AL*

*r.* A pine dressing table/
washstand, c1870, 55in
(140cm) high.
**£450–550** *AL*

A single pine washstand, with a high splashback, and a drawer under the potboard, c1860.
**£200–250** *PIN*

A pine washstand, c1760, 13in (33cm) wide.
**£200–300** *UP*

A bowfront pine washstand, c1780, 35in (89cm) high.
**£300–400** *UP*

A pine washstand, c1850, 24in (61cm) wide.
**£200–300** *AL*

A pine cupboard/washstand, with a marble top, c1910, 42½in (107cm) high.
**£200–250** *BEL*

A pine washstand and shelf, c1860, 35in (89cm) high.
**£150–200** *AL*

A pine washstand, c1870, 21in (52.5cm) wide.
**£200–300** *AL*

A single pine washstand, c1860, 24in (61cm) wide.
**£250–300** *SSD*

A pine washstand, 30in (76cm) wide.
**£200–300** *AL*

A pine washstand, with a marble top, c1860, 30in (76cm) wide.
**£350–400** *AL*

A hazel pine washstand, with a marble top, c1890, 42in (106cm) wide.
**£350–400** *SSD*

A pine washstand, c1890, 31in (79cm) wide.
**£200–300** *W*

An Arts and Crafts style grained pine washstand c1880, 36in (91.5cm) wide.
**£200–250  COT**

A pine washstand, with square tapered legs, early 20thC, 36in (91.5cm) wide.
**£90–160  HNG**

A marble top washstand, with cupboard and drawers, 19thC.
**£350–400  WV**

*l.* A German pine washstand, c1880, 24in (61cm) wide.
**£175–225  AnD**

*r.* An early Victorian pine washstand, c1840, 36in (91.5cm) wide.
**£200–250  COT**

A pine washstand with gallery back, Essex, c1880, 37in (94cm) wide.
**£150–185  ASP**

A pine tiled back washstand, c1880, 35½in (90cm) wide.
**£160–190  ASP**

A Victorian pine washstand, 24in (61cm) wide.
**£175–250  ERA**

*r.* A pine marble topped washstand, with tiled splash-back, c1880, 42in (106.5cm) wide.
**£200–250  ASP**

*l.* A pine washstand, with marble top and side towel rails, c1880, 42in (106.5cm) wide.
**£175–200  ASP**

A marble topped pine washstand, with original green and white tiles, late 19thC, c1890, 36in (91.5cm) wide.
**£175–200** *POT*

A pine washstand, with gallery back, single drawer, shaped undertier and turned legs, c1855, 36in (91.5cm) wide.
**£120–200** *DMe*

A pine washstand, c1870, 33in (84cm) wide.
**£145–175** *ASP*

A pine washstand, with tiled back, original, c1880, 34in (86cm) wide.
**£150–200** *ASP*

A pine washstand, with gallery back, small single drawer and turned legs, c1845, 31½in (80cm) wide.
**£120–200** *DMe*

A pine washstand, c1880, 23in (59cm) wide.
**£40–60** *DFA*

An Irish pine single washstand, c1870, 23½in (60cm) wide.
**£60–80** *Byl*

A pine washstand, with single drawer and potboard, c1850, 42in (106.5cm) wide.
**£120–130** *SA*

A pine washstand, c1880, 34in (86cm) wide.
**£100–200** *AL*

r. A pine washstand, 19thC, 32in (81cm) wide.
**£175–200** *ERA*

## Use the Index!

*Because certain items might fit easily into any number of categories, the quickest and surest method of locating any entry is by reference to the index at the back of the book.*

*This index has been fully cross-referenced for absolute simplicity.*

A pine towel rail,
35in (87.5cm) high.
**£50–70** *AL*

A pine towel rail, c1880,
36in (91.5cm) wide.
**£60–100** *W*

A pine towel rail, c1900.
**£60–100** *W*

A pine towel rail, 25in
(63.5cm) wide.
**£60–80** *LAM*

A pine towel rail, 26½in
(67cm) wide.
**£75–95** *AL*

A pine towel rail, 29½in
(75cm) high.
**£80–100** *AL*

A pine towel rail, 19thC, 26in
(65cm) wide. **£60–100** *PCL*

A hoop towel rail, with
barley twist ends, 19thC.
**£80–130** *PF*

A pine towel rail, 28in (71cm) wide.
**£60–70** *TRU*

A pine towel rail, with barley
twist ends, c1870, 30in
(76cm) high.
**£60–100** *SPA*

A pine towel rail, 34in (87cm) high.
**£60–90** *AL*

A pine towel rail, all original,
c1880, 30in (76cm) high.
**£60–100** *SPA*

A pine nest of drawers, c1860, 54in (137cm) wide.
**£750–1,000** *UP*

A pine flight of 18 grocery drawers, 50in (127cm) wide.
**£750–900** *BEL*

A pine nest of drawers, c1820, 43in (109cm) high.
**£800–1,000** *UP*

*l.* A pine flight of drawers, c1850, 56½in (143cm) wide.
**£800–1,000** *AL*

A pine flight of drawers, with original handles, c1840, 51in (129.5cm) wide.
**£900–1,100** *AL*

A pine nest of drawers, 18in (45.5cm) wide.
**£300–350** *PH*

A pine flight of 6 drawers, c1860, 16in (40.5cm) high.
**£150–200** *BEL*

A pine flight of 38 drawers, 54in (137cm) high.
**£750–950** *AL*

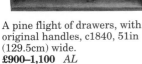

A pine flight of drawers, c1850, 56½in (143cm) wide.
**£800–1,000** *AL*

A pine flight of drawers, with original handles, c1850, 32in (81cm) wide.
**£150–200** *AL*

A miniature pine clock makers' chest of 36 drawers, with brass knob handles, early 19thC, 26in (66cm) wide.
**£300–350**  *TPC*

A pine drawer base, late 19thC, 108in (274cm) wide.
**£800–900**  *CUL*

A pine set of 9 drawers, c1870, 34in (86cm) long.
**£150–200**  *AL*

A pine Wellington chest, with original handles, c1880, 22in (56cm) wide.
**£425–500**  *ASP*

A Victorian pine bank of 4 drawers, 10in (25cm) wide.
**£70–80**  *OPH*

A Victorian pine specimen chest, with original brass handles, 46in (116.5cm) high.
**£300–350**  *ERA*

A pine military style flight of 10 drawers, with original handles, 19thC, 54in (137cm) wide.
**£375–400**  *ERA*

A flight of chestnut drawers, c1870, 38in (96.5cm) wide.
**£200–225**  *ASP*

A pine nest of drawers,
19in (48cm) wide.
**£400–450** *PH*

A bank of drawers, c1930,
24in (61cm) wide.
**£350–450** *SPA*

A pine shop counter, c1880,
109in (277cm) wide.
**£900–1,200** *UP*

A collector's pine cabinet,
29in (74cm) wide.
**£500–600** *PH*

*r.* A pine flight of
drawers, with
original brass
handles, c1860,
37in (94cm) wide.
**£200–350** *AL*

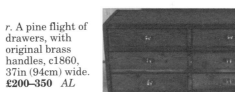

*l.* A pine bank
of drawers,
c1880, 89in
(226cm) wide.
**£800–900** *RK*

A pine tray-top commode,
c1840, 19in (48cm) wide.
**£450–550** *W*

A pine commode, c1850,
25in (63.5cm) wide.
**£300–400** *AL*

A pine commode, with pottery
liner, c1860, 19in (48cm) wide.
**£150–200** *AL*

A pine commode, 25in (64cm) wide.
**£250–400** *WHA*

*r.* A pine step commode,
new leather, c1850, 20in
(51cm) square.
**£300–400** *AL*

A pine commode, with liner,
18½in (47cm) high.
**£150–200** *AL*

A pine commode, with black
china handles, c1860, 26in
(66cm) wide.
**£250–400** *AL*

A Scandinavian pine commode
table, c1890, 18in (46cm) wide.
**£200–250** *W*

A pine commode, 19thC,
17in (42.5cm) wide.
**£160–200** *AL*

A Scandinavian commode, with lift-
up top, original fittings, c1890, 20in
(50.5cm) wide. **£200–250** *W*

A pine step commode, c1860,
18in (46cm) wide. **£150–250** *AL*

A pine commode, with
initials 'TD' on lid and
dated '1890'.
**£100–150** *CHA*

A Victorian pine bed cupboard,
with a dummy chest of drawers
front, 47in (119cm) wide.
**£300–500** *AL*

A pine commode
chair, c1850.
**£100–150** *AL*

A Scandinavian pine
commode, 19½in (49cm) wide.
**£100–130** *W*

A pine commode, with
a pottery liner, c1850,
19in (48cm) wide.
**£160–200** *AL*

A pine step commode,
26in (66cm) high.
**£300–350** *W*

A panel back settle, c1790,
76in (193cm) wide.
**£400–600** *UP*

A Dutch pine settle, c1880,
40in (100cm) wide.
**£500–600** *Sca*

A pine bed settle, c1740,
72in (183cm) wide.
**£600–700** *UP*

A carved pine rustic bench, the
back and arms in the form of
naturalistic branches, carved
with leaves and with a bear
seated in the branches, the plank
seat supported by carved
standing bears, probably Swiss,
c1860, 50½in (128cm) wide.
**£1,800–2,200** *S*

*r.* A pine church
pew, c1850, 64in
(160cm) wide.
**£250–350** *Sca*

A pine seat, 69in (175cm) long.
**£125–150** *AL*

An Austrian pine bench,
34in (86cm) long.
**£1,200–2,000** *MCA*

A pair of Georgian pine benches,
c1800, 91in (231cm) long.
**£550–650** *PIN*

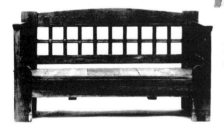

A pine bench, 68in
(172.5cm) long.
**£125–150** *AL*

A pine bench, with clover leaf and other
motifs carved into the back rail, c1900.
**£600–700** *LRG*

A pine bench
with pegged
back, c1840, 72in
(182.5cm) long.
**£400–500** *AL*

A pine bench, 68in
(172.5cm) long.
**£125–150** *AL*

A Dutch carved pine bench in the
baroque taste, on trestle end
supports, with blue squab, 18thC,
74in (188cm) wide.
**£2,000–2,500** *P*

*r.* A Cumbrian pine sheep shearing
bench, individually made for each
shearer, c1860, 44in (111.5cm) long.
**£200–250** *AL*

A pine settle, with lift-up seat, 19thC,
48in (122cm) wide.
**£250–300** *HeR*

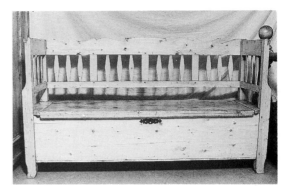

A Hungarian pine box settle, c1840,
65in (165cm) wide.
**£550–650** *HeR*

A pine church pew, early 20thC, 85in
(216cm) long.
**£150–280** *HGN*

A pine panelled box settle, 19thC,
54in (137cm) wide.
**£400–600** *TPC*

A pine barrel-back bench, c1880, 118in
(300cm) wide.
**£300–400** *AL*

A pine bench, c1870, 47¼in (120cm) long.
**£40–50** *ASP*

An Irish pine bed settle, with panelled
back, 72in (182.5cm) wide.
**£400–500** *TPC*

*l.* A pine bench, 78in (198cm) long.
**£50–75** *ASP*

A Georgian barrel back pine settle, with a cupboard, c1830, 81in (205.5cm) wide.
**£1,000–1,200** *BH*

A carved pine bench, 72in (182.5cm) wide.
**£450–500** *SAn*

A pine church pew c1880.
**£200–250** *WEL*

*l.* A Georgian barrel back pine settle, 69in (172.5cm) wide.
**£850–1,050** *JMW*

An early Victorian pine box settle, 50in (127cm) wide.
**£1,500–2,500** *W*

A pine settle, c1850, 39in (99cm) wide.
**£800–1,000** *AL*

An Irish high back pine settle, c1820, 74in (188cm) wide.
**£750–1,000** *UP*

A barrel back pine settle, c1840, 72in (182.5cm) wide.
**£325–375** *AL*

A Welsh pine box settle, c1840, 66in (167.5cm) wide.
**£750–850** *BH*

A pine bed-settle, in original condition, c1800.
**£700–800** *CPA*

A pine settle, c1840, 67in (170cm) high.
**£2,000–2,500** *W*

An Irish pine settle, 72in (182.5cm) wide.
**£600–800** *UP*

A concave wing-back pine settle, with a broad plank back, early 19thC, 66in (167.5cm) wide.
**£500–700** *S(S)*

A pine bench, c1880, 50in (127cm) long.
£150–175 *ASP*

A Continental pine bench, c1870,
73in (185cm) long.
£350–450 *ASP*

A pine country bench, 1870, 37½in (95cm) long.
£45–65 *ASP*

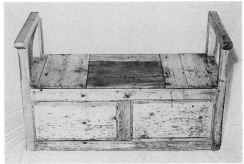

A late Georgian pine monk's bench,
with panelled base, c1830.
£500–600 *POT*

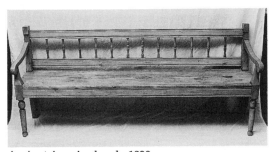

An Austrian pine bench, 1890,
78in (198cm) long.
£325–375 *ASP*

An early Victorian pine settle,
with high 5 panelled back, on
sledge feet, c1840, 55½in
(140cm) long.
£750–850 *POT*

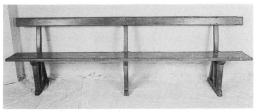

A pine bench, c1870, 97in
(246cm) long.
£170–230 *AL*

A pine settle/table, with worn
top, c1860, 63in (160cm) long.
£400–600 *OCP*

An early Victorian pine monk's
bench, with shaped back, 51in
(129.5cm) wide.
£600–800 *POT*

A pine bench, c1870, 36in
(91.5cm) wide.
£50–100 *AL*

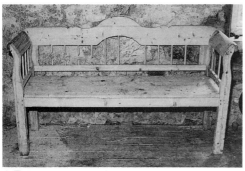

A European pine settle, c1870,
66in (167.5cm) wide.
**£500–700** *AF*

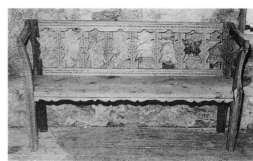

A European pine and oak settle, c1840,
61½in (156cm) wide.
**£500–700** *AF*

An Irish pine settle bed, c1875, 75in
(190.5cm) long.
**£300–400** *Byl*

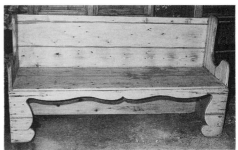

A pine settle, c1860, 72in (182.5cm) long.
**£300–350** *OCP*

An Irish pine settle, with drop down
front, c1840, 72in (182.5cm) long
**£350–450** *DFA*

A carved pine bench, c1870, 73in
(185cm) wide.
**£250–350** *DFA*

A pine settle, c1870, 66in
(167.5cm) long.
**£700–1,000** *AL*

A carved pine high back settle,
c1780, 74in (188cm) long.
**£1,500–1,800** *SA*

An Irish pine bench settle, with
panelled back, c1850, 69in
(175cm) long.
**£700–800** *HON*

A round stick back chair.
**£50–60** *AL*

A balloon back cane
seated chair.
**£50–60** *AL*

A pair of simulated
bamboo chairs, c1840.
**£150–200** *W*

A Regency cane seat
chair, 33in (84cm) high.
**£200–300** *W*

A scroll back kitchen
chair. **£50–60** *AL*

A set of 3 pine chairs, c1850.
**£200–300** *W*

A stick back chair.
**£60–70** *AL*

A rocking chair, c1860,
34in (85cm) high.
**£200–300** *AL*

A set of 4 pine chairs,
pegged, 34½in (87cm) high.
**£50–80 each** *AL*

A pine cane seated chair, and a rush
seated chair, c1860.
**£60–70 each** *AL*

An American pine
and bleached
mahogany rocking
chair, on original
casters, c1900, 42in
(105cm) high.
**£300–400** *LAM*

*l.* A pine chair, c1840.
**£120–170** *AL*

A set of 4 beech chairs, 32in (80cm) high.
**£150–180** *AL*

A beech chair,
new cane seat,
31½in (80cm) high.
**£70–100** *AL*

A reclining garden chair, c1880, 57in (144.5cm) wide.
**£50–100** *PEN*

A pine captain's chair.
**£175–200** *ASP*

A set of 4 pine slat back kitchen chairs, 1870s.
**£175–200** *ASP*

A Continental pine chair.
**£95–150** *AF*

One of a set of 4 Victorian pine bar-backed kitchen chairs, c1860.
**£175–225 the set** *ASP*

A Continental pine rocking chair, with 8 legs, late 19thC.
**£350–400** *ASP*

A primitive pine carver chair, with drawer under seat, c1880.
**£100–125** *OCP*

A Continental kitchen chair, with shaped back and pine seat, c1860.
**£55–95** *AF*

An Irish 'cock fighting' chair, 18thC.
**£100–150** *AF*

A pub stool, with elm seat and beech legs, c1870, 19½in (49cm) high.
**£30–40**  *OPH*

A pub stool, with elm seat and beech legs, c1870, 19in (48cm) high.
**£30–40**  *OPH*

A country pine stool, c1860, 23in (59cm) high.
**£30–40**  *OPH*

*l.* A pine stool, original, c1860, 20½in (52cm) high.
**£35–45**  *FAG*

A pine stool, c1880, 26in (66cm) wide.
**£50–60**  *AL*

A pine milking stool, with 4 legs, c1870, 18in (46cm) wide.
**£30–40**  *OPH*

A pine stool, c1870, 18½in (47cm) wide.
**£30–40**  *OPH*

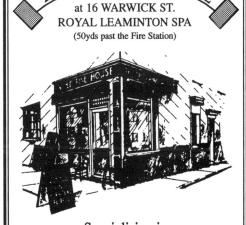

A round pine stool, c1880,
17½in (44cm) high.
**£45–50**  *CPA*

A pine stool.
**£30–40**  *SPA*

A pine stool, c1860, 12in
(32cm) high.
**£40–60**  *AL*

A pine stool.
**£30–50**  *WEL*

A set of pine steps, with
metal fittings, c1900, 55in
(140cm) high.
**£60–80**  *SPA*

A pine stool, 27in (67.5cm)
high.  **£40–70**  *AL*

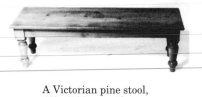

A Victorian pine stool,
48in (122cm) wide.
**£75–100**  *OA*

A pair of pine stools,
18in (45.5cm) high.
**£60–80**  *AL*

A pine sloping desk
stool, 29½in (73cm) high.
**£40–60**  *AL*

A pine stool, on turned legs,
28in (71cm) high.
**£55–75**  *AL*

A set of pine steps, early 20thC,
28in (71cm) high.  **40–60**  *AL*

A pine stool, 14in
(35.5cm) wide.
**?25–35**  *AL*

*r.* A set of pine
steps, 49in
(122.5cm) high.
**£60–80**  *AL*

A pine stool, c1880,
19in (48cm) high.
**£30–35** *FAG*

A pine country stool, c1880,
18in (46cm) wide.
**£25–30** *ASP*

A pine bar stool, c1890,
21in (53cm) high.
**£25–35** *ASP*

A pine bar stool, c1880,
18in (46cm) high.
**£25–35** *ASP*

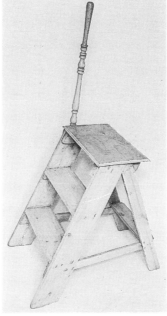

A set of pine library steps,
original, c1880, 28in (71cm) high.
**£160–200** *FAG*

A Victorian bar stool, c1870,
29in (74cm) high.
**£40–50** *OPH*

A pair of pine open-sided library
steps, c1900, 69in (175cm) high.
**£55–65** *ASP*

A pine step ladder, c1890,
59in (149.5cm) high.
**£45–55** *ASP*

A pine step ladder, c1900,
48in (122cm) high.
**£45–65** *ASP*

A pine stool, 10in (25cm) diam.
**£25–30** *AL*

A pine stool, 19thC,
12in (31cm) high.
**£35–50** *AL*

A stool, or small table, c1860,
15in (38cm) diam.
**£35–45** *AL*

A pine stool, 24in (61cm) long.
**£30–60** *AL*

A pine stool, 18in (45cm).
**£20–25** *AL*

A pine shoe cleaning stool,
15in (38cm) high. **£50–70** *AL*

A pine stool, c1880,
13in (33cm) wide.
**£45–60** *AL*

A pair of pine stools, 19thC,
18in (46cm) high.
**£60–80** *AL*

A pine stool, with hand
hole in top, c1860, 24in
(61cm) high.
**£30–50** *AL*

A rustic pine stool, c1840,
27in (69cm) long.
**£50–70** *AL*

A set of pine library steps,
restored, 18thC, 71in
(180cm) high.
**£800–1,000** *W*

A pine stool, c1880, 7in (17.5cm) high.
**£35–45** *AL*

A pine stool, 21in (53cm)
high. **£40–60** *AL*

A set of pine shelves,
21in (53cm) wide.
**£75–100** *AL*

A French decorated pine shelf,
Alsace, c1880, 19in (48cm) wide.
**£100–200** *MCA*

A pine pot rack,
37in (94cm) high.
**£75–100** *AL*

A set of pine hanging shelves,
17½in (44.5cm) wide.
**£90–100** *AL*

A set of pine hanging shelves,
38in (96.5cm) wide.
**£150–250** *AL*

A set of pine hanging shelves,
c1860, 22in (56cm) wide.
**£85–100** *AL*

A set of pine hanging
shelves, 23in (57.5cm) wide.
**£100–150** *AL*

A set of pine shelves, c1860,
34in (87cm) wide.
**£85–100** *AL*

A set of pine shelves, with
bobbin supports, c1850,
50in (127cm) high.
**£300–400** *AL*

A set of pine hanging shelves,
39in (97.5cm) wide.
**£250–300** *PCL*

A set of pine book shelves,
c1860, 27in (69cm) wide.
**£100–150** *AL*

A set of pine shelves,
19thC, 27in (67.5cm)
wide. **£150–200** *AL*

A pine corner unit, c1860,
31in (79cm) wide.
**£200–250** *AL*

A tall pine shelf unit, c1860,
41in (104cm) wide.
**£120–150** *AL*

A pair of George II style carved
pine open wall shelves, by Callow of
Mount Street, with egg-and-tongue
borders, each arched pediment
centred by a female mask, with
adjustable shelves, c1930, possibly
incorporating 18thC components,
38in (97cm) wide.
**£2,500–3,000** *S(S)*

A set of pine shelves,
c1860, 33in (84cm) wide.
**£250–300** *AL*

A pine hanging wall shelf,
c1860, 27½in (70cm) wide.
**£1,500–2,000** *AL*

A set of pine shelves,
36in (91.5cm) wide.
**£120–160** *AL*

An early Victorian pine hanging
delft rack, 43in (109cm) wide.
**£300–500** *OA*

A pine rack, unpolished, early
19thC, 60in (152cm) wide.
**£250–300** *CC*

A set of Liberty pine shelves,
c1890, 31in (79cm) high.
**£100–140** *AL*

A pine hanging rack,
30in (76cm) wide.
**£150–200** *PH*

A Victorian pine hanging
bookshelf, 30in (76cm) wide.
**£30–45** *OA*

A set of pine shelves, c1870,
30in (76cm) wide.
**£175–300** *AL*

*r.* A set of pine bookshelves,
48in (122cm) high.
**£200–300** *LAM*

A set of German pitch pine hanging shelves, with fielded panels, late 19thC, 24in (62cm) high.
**£50–90**  *HGN*

A pine shelf unit, with 'cotton reel' supports, 24in (61cm) wide.
**£40–50**  *FOX*

An Eastern European pine whatnot, 48in (122cm) wide.
**£125–200**  *AnD*

A pine wall shelf unit, c1890, 24in (61cm) wide.
**£50–100**  *AL*

A pine wall shelf unit, c1880, 36in (91.5cm) high.
**£145–200**  *AL*

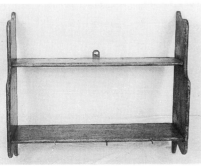

A Victorian pine delft rack restored back and cornice, c1890, 60in (152cm) wide.
**£275–375**  *POT*

A set of pine shelves, c1890, 29in (74cm) wide.
**£65–75**  *AL*

A pine dresser top, c1880, 44in (111.5cm) wide.
**£125–175**  *SA*

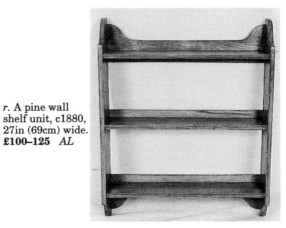

*r.* A pine wall shelf unit, c1880, 27in (69cm) wide.
**£100–125**  *AL*

A pine wall shelf unit, 30in (76cm) wide.
**£30–50**  *FOX*

A Victorian pine mirror
frame, 38in (96.5cm) high.
**£100–120** *Far*

A pine overmantel mirror, c1860,
44in (111.5cm) wide. **£100–150** *AL*

A pine framed mirror,
c1830, 34in (86cm) wide.
**£150–250** *Far*

Two pine framed mirrors, 14 and
16in (36 and 41cm) square.
**£25–35** *CPA*

A pine and elm dressing table
mirror, c1860, 24 by 22in
(60 by 55cm).
**£200–250** *SSD*

A pine frame, 16in (41cm) wide.
**£100–140** *AL*

A carved pine picture frame,
30 by 36in (76 by 92cm).
**£200–250** *LAM*

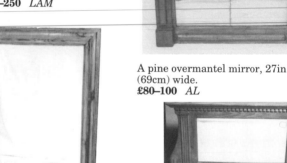

A pine overmantel mirror, 27in
(69cm) wide.
**£80–100** *AL*

A pine frame, c1860,
30 by 26½in (76 by 67cm).
**£120–170** *SSD*

A pine mirror, 30in (77cm) wide.
**£150–200** *AL*

A Victorian pine overmantel
mirror, 40in (101.5cm) wide.
**£100–200** *Far*

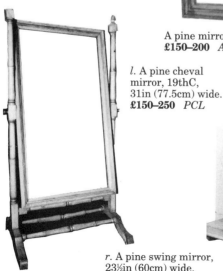

*l.* A pine cheval
mirror, 19thC,
31in (77.5cm) wide.
**£150–250** *PCL*

*r.* A pine swing mirror,
23½in (60cm) wide.
**£950–1,200** *AL*

A pine dressing mirror, c1850,
23½in (60cm) wide.
**£200–250** *AL*

A panelled pine fireplace, c1860.
**£200–300**  *AL*

A pair of French carved pine
fireplace surrounds, 19thC,
79in (200cm) wide.
**£6,000–6,500**  *PH*

A pine door, with brass letter
box, handle and finger plate,
26in (65cm) wide.
**£150–170**  *PCL*

A pine fireplace surround,
52in (132cm) high.
**£200–250**  *LAM*

A carved pine doorway,
59in (150cm) wide.
**£2,800–3,200**  *PH*

*l.* A pair of carved pine
pillars, 95in (241cm) high.
**£1,200–1,500**  *GRF*

A pine fireplace,
38in (95cm) wide.
**£200–250**  *AL*

A Victorian pine fire
surround, 40in
(101.5cm) wide.
**£200–250**  *AL*

A reeded pine fire surround,
51in (129.5cm) wide.
**£250–300**  *LAM*

*l.* A Colonial white painted pine room section, comprising a fireplace surround and two cupboard doors with surrounds, each section with moulded corners above a fluted frieze with raised panels below, 96in (243.5cm) high.
**£7,000–8,000** *S(NY)*

A pine and gesso fire surround, 18thC, 66in (167.5cm) wide.
**£2,000–2,500** *AF*

*l.* An Irish pine internal door, with carved Gothic panels, c1800, 78in (198cm) high.
**£200–300** *AF*

An pine architectural frame, c1880, 25in (64cm) wide.
**£100–125** *HON*

A glazed draper's display unit, with original handles and escutcheons, 75½in (191cm) wide.
**£850–1,050** *LAM*

A set of West Country stocks, mid-19thC.
**£700–800** *RP*

A hall stand, c1890, 71in (180cm) high.
**£200–300** *AL*

A pine luggage rack, c1880, 25in (64cm) wide.
**£90–100** *AL*

A pine plant stand, tin lined, c1900, 46in (116cm) wide.
**£100–200** *AL*

A brass gong, on a pine stand, c1860, 48in (122cm) high.
**£300–400** *AL*

A primitive plant stand, c1840, 25in (64cm) high.
**£60–65** *AL*

An elm wheelbarrow, with a wrought-iron wheel, c1860, 60in (152cm) long.
**£200–250** *AL*

A pine stick stand, 41in (104cm) wide.
**£250–350** *PH*

A Victorian pine screen, 70in (177.5cm) high.
**£150–200** *AL*

A small pine plant stand, 12in (31cm) wide.
**£75–100** *AL*

A pine, fruitwood and tôle food cage, 18thC, 34in (86cm) wide.
**£400–450** *MCA*

A pine game safe, with copper roof, for hanging 16 brace of game birds, 37in (94cm) high.
**£500–600** *AL*

A pine easel, 43in (109cm) high.
**£55–75** *AL*

A wheelbarrow, c1860, 26in (66cm) wide.
**£200–250** *UP*

A large rocking horse, 87in (220cm) long.
**£1,500–2,000** *PH*

*l.* An Irish rustic pearwood turf or peat box, Connemara, c1840, 36in (92cm) wide.
**£700–900** *UC*

A pine shop counter, with a panelled back, 76in (193cm) wide.
**£800–900** *RK*

A Victorian pine shop counter, c1870.
**£950–1,100** *WEL*

A carved bear, with a flower holder, 22in (56cm) high.
**£300–350** *PH*

A pine plant stand, c1910, 60in (152cm) high.
**£60–100** *SPA*

An iron bound oak wash tub on legs, Lincolnshire, c1890, 21in (53cm) diam.
**£250–350** *UC*

A pair of painted carved fairground horses.
**£1,500–2,000** *CSK*

A pine spinning wheel and spindle, late 19thC.
**£160–190** *W*

A Victorian two-fold screen, restored, c1870.
**£300–350**  *PIN*

A pair of mid-Victorian mahogany hanging shelves, with shaped toprails, the rectangular shelves divided by turned baluster columns, 39in (99cm) wide.
**£800–1,000**  *C(S)*

A pine tub, 27in (69cm) diam.
**£150–200**  *AL*

*r.* A Danish pine 8-day grandfather clock, with painted dial, c1862, 76in (192cm) high.
**£950–1,200**  *BEL*

*r.* A Danish pine 8-day grandfather clock, with later paint, c1860, 73in (186cm) high.
**£950–1,200**  *BEL*

*r.* A Scandinavian pine sledge, 14in (36cm) long.
**£75–100**  *W*

A pine frame, 23½in (60cm) wide.
**£75–100**  *LAM*

A pine torchère, 60in (152cm) high.
**£200–300**  *PH*

A pine croquet box, 35½in (90cm) wide.
**£100–150**  *PAC*

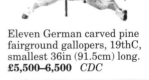

Eleven German carved pine fairground gallopers, 19thC, smallest 36in (91.5cm) long.
**£5,500–6,500**  *CDC*

A pine writing box, 14½in (37cm) wide.
**£100–150**  *PH*

A pine fireplace, with gesso applications.  **£750–800**  *EA*

An adjustable easel, on a trestle base, with casters, 92in (232.5cm) high.
**£950–1,000**  *CNY*

A pine box, on a later stand, c2880, 22in (56cm) high.
**£100–150**  *AL*

A pine hymn board.
**£30–40**  *WEL*

A set of pine pigeonholes,
37in (92.5cm) wide.
**£75–85**  *AL*

A pine standard
lamp, 64½in
(163cm) high.
**£120–150**  *LAM*

A set of coat pegs, on a
horseshoe-shaped frame,
c1920, 17½in (44cm) high.
**£75–85**  *AL*

A small pine stand, 19thC,
18in (45cm) high.
**£60–100**  *AL*

A carved and panelled pine mule
chest, c1680, 48in (101.5cm) wide.
**£800–1,200**  *PH*

A pine umbrella stand,
23in (57.5cm) wide.
**£70–100**  *AL*

A set of pine hat stands,
2 with original pads,
largest 38in (96.5cm) high.
**£20–30**  *PAC*

A pine cattle trough, c1860,
120in (304cm) wide.
**£300–400**  *AL*

An Edwardian pine coal box, with
an iron carrying handle and brass
side handles, 17in (43cm) wide.
**£85–125**  *OA*

A pine plant stand, c1850,
30in (76cm) high.
**£40–70**  *AL*

*l*. A pine hall stand, carved in the
form of a bear, 85in (216cm) high.
**£1,200–1,500**  *Wor*

A hatter's block, 8in (20cm) high.
**£30–40**  *LAM*

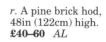

*r*. A pine brick hod,
48in (122cm) high.
**£40–60**  *AL*

A pine Continental crofter's spinning box, 17in (43cm) wide.
**£25–35** *ASP*

A treen pot, inscribed 'A.O. The Priory St. Ives, 1854' 'Pear Tree'.
**£50–75** *WaH*

A Welsh pine miniature chest of drawers, c1870, 14in (36cm) wide.
**£100–125** *ASP*

A station master's pine luggage truck, c1880, 48in (122cm) high.
**£45–55** *ASP*

A pine coal scuttle, with metal mounts, 17in (43cm) wide.
**£45–65** *OCP*

A pine tool box, with drawers, 18in (46cm) wide.
**£40–50** *ASP*

A pine hat and coat stand, c1900, 74in (188cm) high.
**£75–85** *ASP*

*r.* A pine tool box, 1900, 18in (46cm) long.
**£20–30** *ASP*

A carved pine eagle, c1900, 37½in (95cm) high.
**£325–375** *ASP*

*r.* A varnished pine wheelbarrow, c1900, 28in (71cm) long.
**£35–45** *ASP*

# OAK & COUNTRY FURNITURE

Furniture historians recognise 'The Age of Oak' as being the years from 1500 to 1660, coming before the ages of 'Walnut', 'Mahogany' and 'Satinwood'. One could easily be misled into thinking no furniture was made in oak after 1660 or, indeed, that any other timber could possibly have been used before that date. 'Oak Furniture' seems to be a generic term applied to country-made pieces, as opposed to their sophisticated, city counterparts. Although much country furniture was made from oak, the generalisation encompasses a host of native timbers and country pieces are often found in chestnut, elm, ash, yew, walnut, pine, sycamore and the fruitwoods.

In the 18th century, these indigenous timbers were often stained with a dark dye, oiled and polished to simulate oak and thereby conform with popular fashion, and it is only in subsequent years that this finish has worn away, and allowed us glimpses of the enchanting timbers hidden below. One could easily be forgiven for dismissing an early 18th-century side table as oak, when upon closer examination, it was found to be walnut, fruitwood or even yew.

The type of timber, the condition of the piece, the proportion and patina, are important factors to collectors of this furniture, and as such can result in huge price differences. In general, all the country timbers are prized and have good colour and grain configuration, but rarer timbers such as yew, plum and cherry are infinitely more desirable. English cherry is rare, and as a rule was only used for smaller pieces (often constructed from narrow planks) or for turning or decorative work. It cannot be compared with French Provincial fruitwood furniture, which is of a softer, sunnier, more golden hue and fairly widely available.

Restoration work is tolerated in oak furniture, and often no attempt is made to conceal it. It is quite natural to find a 17th century chair with an 18th century replaced rail, or indeed a 19th century seat – in 300 years of use, it is only to be expected, but the restoration will be reflected in the price, especially when compared to a perfect example in museum condition. Restoration work that is unsympathetic or has attempted to enhance the object is not looked upon favourably. Late 17th century panelled oak coffers were often 'carved-up' in the 19th century, and the panels emblazoned with flowers, dates and intricate patterns. This type of carving is totally different to the simple style of an early craftsman, and may explain why two carved oak coffers could have such different values.

The late 19th/early 20th century saw a revival in fashion of early, dark, carved oak, and many 1930s beamed properties are furnished with these early reproductions. Machine made and heavily varnished, they are worlds apart from their forefathers, but they nevertheless have their own following.

Style and proportion are important factors to consider, but rather hard to quantify. In general, 'small is beautiful'. A tiny oak bureau, probably made for a lady or for the smallest cottage, is more pleasing than an example almost twice its size. A diminutive North Wales dresser with perfectly proportioned panels, a full canopy rack and a host of tiny spice drawers with original patina is a superior piece to an large housekeeper's dresser, recently removed from a farmhouse kitchen, stripped of layers of gloss paint and refinished!

Outstanding craftsmanship is often apparent, but in general country pieces were not signed or stamped. Some early oak court cupboards, chests or chairs have been carved with the owner's initials, and possibly a date if the piece was a marriage or dowry item.

Extensive research has been undertaken into the history of English chairs and many Windsor chair varieties and certain ladderbacks bear the maker's stamp or date. However, early stick chairs, rustic tables and occasional pieces which seem to have been carved from a solid tree trunk are often difficult to date or define. A dug-out, highbacked chair, carved from a massive section of elm begs the questions – when was the chair made? Moreover, how old is the elm tree from which it is carved? Rustic, simple items do have a unique charm, particularly if they have achieved a glorious colour and deep patina from daily use and polishing. Colour and patina are the foremost criteria for country furniture. Both go hand in hand, are impossible to fake and will be reflected in the asking price.

Ideally, one looks for a good colour, not just an overall blanket but a variety of tones, the palest areas where wear would have been greatest and darker sections where neither hands nor sunlight reached. The wood will be soft and silky to the touch and the piece should glow with a 3D depth.

Oak furniture was never produced in great quantities in the 17th and 18th centuries, and was not fashionable for mass production after the Industrial Revolution. It is very good value and in general far less expensive than the later, mahogany equivalent. Oak furniture seems to be particularly fashionable in Britain at the moment, and also with Continental customers since changes in customs regulations have broken down trading barriers.

Prices have remained fairly static while inflation has been kept low, with only outstanding items fetching soaring prices. Times are undoubtedly changing: interest in the field is increasing, especially amongst the younger, first-time furniture purchasers and, as there is a finite supply, prices can only go one way and that is up!

Derek Green

An oak dresser, with 3 frieze drawers above 2 panelled cupboards, c1780, 58in (147cm) wide.
**£2,500–3,000** *SKC*

An oak Welsh dresser, 18thC, 60in (152cm) wide.
**£2,800–3,500** *DDM*

A Georgian oak Welsh dresser, 64in (162.5cm) wide.
**£2,750–3,500** *BMM*

A joined oak high dresser, 65in (165cm) wide.
**£2,500–3,000** *L*

An oak Welsh dresser, in original condition, early 18thC, 51in (129.5cm) wide.
**£2,700–3,200** *WIL*

An oak dresser, the lower part with 3 frieze drawers, mid-18thC, 63in (160cm) wide.
**£2,500–3,000** *SC*

An oak dresser, from North Wales, early 18thC, 54in (137cm) wide.
**£2,500–3,000** *H*

An oak dresser, from North Wales, with good colour and patination, c1740, 63in (160cm) wide.
**£3,700–4,200** *H*

A George II oak and elm dresser, c1740, 80in (203cm) wide.
**£4,000–5,000** *SS*

*r*. A Georgian oak cottage dresser, with good patina, 57in (144.5cm) wide.
**£2,750–3,200** *L*

An oak dresser base, the inverted breakfront top above a central drawer and cupboard between reeded half columns, flanked by 3 drawers to either side, with outer channelled columns, on multiple bracket feet, one corner block missing, early 18thC, 72in (182.5cm) wide.
**£4,500–5,500** *C*

An oak dresser, with moulded top above drawers, on barley-twist legs.
**£2,000–2,500** *DN*

A George III elm dresser, with moulded top, three frieze drawers and shaped apron, on shell carved cabriole legs with pad feet, 66in (168cm) wide.
**£1,700–2,200** *DN*

An oak low dresser, with 7 moulded panelled drawers around a fielded panelled door, 18thC, 68in (172.5cm) wide.
**£1,600** *DN*

An oak dresser, the moulded fruitwood top above 3 frieze drawers and a pair of cupboard doors with geometric mitred mouldings, on turned stile feet, restored, c1700, 58½in (148cm) wide.
**£4,500–5,000** *S(S)*

A George III fruitwood dresser, the back with a plain gallery above 3 drawers, on plain turned tapered legs, restored, c1800, 64in (163cm) wide.
**£1,700–2,200** *Bon*

*l.* A George III oak enclosed dresser base, with moulded edged top, central drawer with ogee panelled door below, flanked on either side by 3 drawers with brass drop handles, panelled sides, moulded base and bracket feet, 73in (185cm) wide.
**£3,500–4,500** *AH*

A George III oak dresser, the moulded cornice above an open shelf back, on bracket feet, possibly reduced in width, c1790, 46in (117cm) wide.
**£2,000–3,000** *S(S)*

An oak dresser, with shaped apron carved with fan motifs and on square legs, early 19thC, 51in (129.5cm) wide.
**£3,200–3,800** *S*

An oak dresser, inlaid with satinwood and boxwood, on turned tapering legs, parts 18thC, 74½in (189cm) wide.
**£2,500–3,000** *CSK*

An oak Welsh dresser, on block feet, 18thC, 61in (154.5cm) wide.
**£3,200–3,800** *CSK*

An oak dresser, with baluster turned uprights and bun feet, joined by an undertier, 94in (239cm) wide.
**£1,500–2,000** *CSK*

An oak Welsh dresser carved with the letters 'A.M.O.W.B.', early 18thC, 64½in (163cm) wide.
**£2,500–3,000** *Bon*

A oak dresser, mid-18thC, 58in (147cm) wide.
**£1,600–2,000** *SBe*

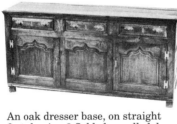

An oak dresser base, on straight feet, having 3 fielded panelled doors and 3 drawers over, 18thC, 71in (180cm) wide.
**£2,500–3,000** *JD*

A pair of oak dresser bases, probably adapted from a single dresser base, each with rectangular top above 2 frieze drawers and waved apron, on baluster turned uprights and block feet, part 18thC, 46in (117cm) wide.
**£3,000–3,500** *CSK*

An oak dresser and rack, with moulded dentil cornice and waved frieze, 18thC and later, 70in (178cm) wide. **£2,500–3,000** *CSK*

l. An oak and pine dresser, with chamfered square legs joined by a platform stretcher, restored, late 18thC, 55in (139cm) wide.
**£4,000–5,000** *S(S)*

An oak dresser, the upper section with a moulded cornice and 3 shelves flanked by inlaid uprights, the base with ebony stringing to the 3 frieze drawers and central simulated drawers, the 2 doors with crossbanded panels, on shaped stile feet, early 19thC, 63in (160cm) wide.
**£3,500–4,000** *Bea*

An oak dresser, with 3 shelves to the top, and 3 drawers to base, on 4 baluster supports and pot-board, 18thC, 68in (172.5cm) wide.
**£4,000–4,500** *RBB*

A stained dresser, with 3 shelves, 7 drawers and 2 cupboards, mid-Wales, c1780.
**£1,800–2,300** *COM*

A Welsh oak dresser, the boarded backed top with 3 shelves and hooks, the base with 3 frieze drawers, on 4 turned front supports to a potboard, and bracket feet, 18thC, 67in (170cm) wide.
**£3,500–4,000** *B*

An Irish dresser, with carved three-shelf top, 3 drawers and 2 cupboards to base, c1800.
**£4,000–4,500** *B*

An ash canopy cupboard dresser, with fielded panels to the doors and drawers, c1690.
**£12,000–15,000** *Ced*

An oak dresser, the upper section with planked plate rack, 3 small frieze drawers, block legs and potboard to base, 18thC, 57½in (146cm) wide.
**£2,500–3,000** *WL*

A George III oak dresser, the top with moulded cornice above 3 shelves, 3 frieze drawers above a shaped apron with two further small drawers to base, on turned legs with a platform base, 54in (137cm) wide.
**£2,800–3,300** *DN*

A Georgian fruitwood dresser, with open plate rack, above a base with 3 long drawers, on cabriole legs, alterations, 18thC, 62in (157cm) wide.
**£1,500–2,000** *MMG*

An oak dresser base, the 3 drawers cockbeaded and oak lined, shaped apron, cabriole front legs, brackets missing, square section back legs, old restoration, early 18thC, 73in (185cm) long.
**£1,500–2,000** *WIL*

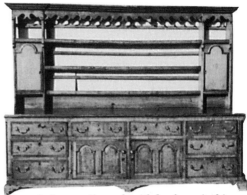

An oak dresser, the rack with lambrequin frieze above 3 central shelves flanked by arcaded doors to cupboards on either side, on a base with 4 frieze drawers, above two central cupboards, each with 2 arcaded fielded panels flanked on either side by 2 further drawers, and canted reeded corners, 18thC, 96in (243.5cm) wide.
**£7,200–8,000** *B*

A George III Montgomeryshire oak dresser base, with 3 cockbeaded frieze drawers above cockbeaded and shaped aprons, baluster turned legs, framed pot board, 75in (190.5cm) wide.
**£6,000–7,000** *P(S)*

A George II oak dresser, with open shelf back above a pair of frieze drawers and an ogee arched apron, the turned and square supports joined by a platform stretcher, reduced in size from a larger dresser, back probably associated, altered, 51½in (130cm) wide.
**£2,800–3,500** *S(S)*

An oak Anglesey dresser, with pine back, three-shelf rack, breakfront base, with 4 central drawers and quarter columns, one drawer and cupboard to each side, 19thC, 67in (170cm) wide.
**£2,200–2,700** *WIL*

A Charles II style oak dresser, with moulded cornice above open shelves and a pair of geometrically panelled frieze drawers, on turned and square legs, 54½in (138cm) wide.
**£950–1,200** *S(S)*

An oak dresser base, the moulded top above 3 frieze drawers, with columnar turned and square supports, mid-18thC, 75½in (192cm) wide.
**£3,000–3,500** *S(S)*

An oak dresser, the shallow raised back with small drawers, the base with drawers surrounding a cupboard, now on casters, damaged, late 18thC, 71in (180cm) wide.
**£4,000–4,500** *S(S)*

# Welsh Furniture

It may be a surprise to some that a small country such as Wales could have such an impact on the furniture market. But it is a strong indication of the quality and variety of furniture produced there, that such an astonishingly large proportion of collectable country furniture originated in Wales.

Produced from the early 16th century, evolving styles showed considerable innovation in response to local needs and owed little to urban fashion. Certain cupboards and chests, such as the 'coffor bach' the 'cwpwrdd tridarn' and 'cwpwrdd deuddarn',

*An oak 'coffor bach', with inlaid decoration in holly and bog oak in a design typical of West Wales, 1750–80.*

the are so distinctive that they are known universally by their Welsh names. But it is the dresser that has is achieved the greatest fame. So diverse that no two are identical, the Welsh dresser admirably combines both practical and decorative features, and the overall market for the more unusual examples has never been healthier.

With a reputation for being solidly constructed, with a fine polished finish, Welsh furniture was made to be functional, designed for a specific purpose, and often for a specific location. Local carpenters preferred to use native timbers – the most sought-after type of Welsh furniture today is made from figured red-black oak, which grew on exposed mountainsides. Although other woods such as ash, elm and fruitwood were used, a mixture of woods is often found in the same piece. This is an indication of the suitability of certain timbers for the particular parts, the availability of usable boards, or cost considerations.

During the 19th century, 'oak' dressers, for example, may commonly have comprised shelves and even potboards made from pine. The craftsmen, who were not full-time furniture makers, would also have produced everyday items, from spinning wheels to gates, using a range of techniques. This resulted in unexpected and interesting methods of construction, reflected in the frequent absence of dovetails from drawers, especially in the finely panelled cupboards from North Wales.

The demand for useful pieces had always been strong, but of course, the requirements of the modern home do not match those of the 18th century farmhouse. Certain items such as long tables and sets of chairs, were always scarce – cupboards deep enough to hold a hi-fi are decidedly rare! Furniture was traditionally an important acquisition, intended to be handed down the generations. The sheer quantity of large presses, dressers and chests found in Wales has led to much 'recycling', so be wary when buying – you may well be offered pieces that have been substantially altered to make them more suited to 20th century life.

Although basically utilitarian, Welsh dressers typically contain decorative embellishments including shaped panels, fretted friezes and carved or inlaid dates and initials. The presence of such elements adds considerably to the desirability of an item, and is reflected in the higher price. Remember, too, the fact that pieces were made to be used, and this will have resulted in everyday wear and tear, minor damage and variation in colour – all factors forming an important part of the furniture's appeal.

Recently, there has been emphasis on the identification of the precise regional origins of pieces, and the singularity of certain features suggests that local styles should be discernible. For instance, flowing designs of floral inlay were confined to a few areas in South Wales, and the famed 'cwpwrdd tridarn' was only found in Snowdonia. But plainer forms, such as stick chairs and stools, were produced over a wide area, thus making specific identification difficult.

*An oak 'cwpwrdd tridarn', with carved and inlaid embellishments, including marriage initials and '1731', Conwy Valley, Caernarfonshire.*

The last few years have witnessed a significant increase in interest from the home market for more unusual items, or those with a reliable provenance. Trade from North America and the Continent, who have both in the past imported vast numbers of Welsh dressers, cupboards and chests, still remains active.

Richard Bebb

*r.* A George III Welsh oak dresser, with associated back, on stile feet, base c1780, top early 19thC.
**£3,000–4,000** *S(S)*

An oak and inlaid dresser, the open shelf back with pilasters, the base with frieze drawers, a pair of panel doors with fan medallions flanking a central drawer and 2 dummy drawers, stile feet with shaped brackets, North Wales, early 19thC, 63in (160cm) wide.
**£4,500–5,500** *S(S)*

A George III elmwood Welsh dresser, late 18thC, 52½in (133cm) wide.
**£2,000–2,500** *SK(B)*

*r.* An oak dresser, the associated open shelf back above 4 shallow drawers, 5 frieze drawers above turned supports with fan-shaped angle brackets, on a platform base and square feet, South Wales early 19thC, 60½in (153cm) wide.
**£4,000–5,000** *S(S)*

An oak dresser, the associated open shelf back with a pair of cupboards, the base with 4 frieze drawers, an open recess and a pair of panel doors, on shaped bracket feet, restored, North Wales, early 19thC, 92½in (234cm) wide.
**£2,000–3,000** *S(S)*

A Georgian elmwood and fruitwood Welsh dresser, with open rack, above a base with 3 drawers, on cabriole legs, restored, 62in (157cm) wide.
**£1,000–1,500** *MMG*

An oak Welsh dresser, the 2 cupboards and 2 drawers, below a panelled plate rack, c1720, 50in (127cm) wide.
**£3,000–4,000** *KHD*

An oak dresser, in original condition, replaced brasses, North Wales, 50in (127cm) wide.
**£5,000–7,000** *H*

An oak Welsh dresser, the base with 3 frieze drawers, above 3 short drawers flanked by a pair of cupboards, c1750, 62½in (159cm) wide.
**£2,000–3,000** *S(S)*

A George III oak dresser, c1770, 64in (162.5cm) wide.
**£3,000–4,000** *S*

An oak Welsh dresser, with raised ogee arched panels, on ogee bracket feet, mid-18thC, 72in (182.5cm) wide.
**£7,000–8,000** *Bea*

A late Georgian oak Welsh dresser, with 6 drawers and 2 cupboard doors, later turned ebony handles, 69in (174.5cm) wide.
**£2,000–3,000** *C*

An oak Welsh dresser, with 3 frieze drawers, and 2 cupboard doors below, mid-18thC.
**£7,000–9,000** *PHA*

An oak Welsh dresser, with spice drawers, all crossbanded in burr oak, mid-18thC, 74in (188cm) wide.
**£6,000–7,000** *PJ*

An oak Welsh dresser, with fielded panelled cupboard doors, in original condition, 69in (175cm) wide.
**£3,000–4,000** *H*

*l.* An oak Welsh dresser, 18thC, 64in (162.5cm) wide.
**£3,000–4,000** *LRG*

A matched set of 6 Charles II carved oak Yorkshire chairs, now with figured seat cushions and loose covers, c1680.
£6,000–7,000  S(S)

A Charles I oak coffer, with moulded top above a fluted frieze, the panelled front carved with stylised flowerheads and initials 'AW' flanked by foliate strapwork and stile supports, Somerset, c1640, 42in (106cm) wide.
£1,500–2,500  S(S)

A Windsor chair, one arm repaired, mid-19thC.
£2,500–3,500  C

An oak bench, with a padded seat covered in close-nailed brown leather, on turned legs and square channelled stretchers, mainly 17thC, 60in (152.5cm) wide.
£2,700–4,000  C

An ebonised oak and fruitwood chest in 2 sections, inlaid with ivory and mother-of-pearl, dated '1652'.
£3,000–5,000  C

A Charles II oak bench, with a solid seat, the plain frieze with channels, on 4 baluster legs joined by stretchers, one stretcher replaced, 67in (170cm) wide.
£2,500–3,500  C

A William and Mary line inlaid burr yew chest, with later veneer and bun feet.
£6,000–7,000  C

A Welsh primitive chair, dry scraped down to its original paint finish.
£1,000–1,500  SWN

A Queen Anne oak bureau bookcase, with associated top, the featherbeanded fall revealing a stepped interior, on later bun feet, c1710, 79in (199cm) high.
£2,500–3,500  S(S)

r. An oak bureau, with fitted interior, 2 short and 3 long drawers, on bracket feet, early 19thC, 36in (91.5cm) wide.
£1,500–2,500  GAK

A beech and elm slat back
chair, c1880.
**£50–70**  *AL*

A Continental oak strong box, with 3 locks
and keys, c1730, 22in (55.5cm) wide.
**£600–800**  *KEY*

A miniature oak chest
of drawers, 19thC,
8in (20cm) wide.
**£150–160**  *Ber*

*r.* An oak spice
cabinet, with
11 interior
drawers, 16in
(40.5cm) wide.
**£300–350**  *JH*

A Welsh oak cobbler's bench, in
original condition, early 19thC,
38in (96.5cm) wide.
**£750–850**  *RYA*

A child's school desk,
26in (66cm) high.
**£25–35**  *Ber*

An ash dug-out shepherd's
chair, with a cupboard
beneath the seat, early
18thC, 24½in (65cm) wide.
**£1,000–1,200**  *RYA*

An early Victorian child's nursery
table, with original paint.
**£475–500**  *SWN*

An oak side table, c1690,
26in (66cm) high.
**£1,400–1,800**  *KEY*

An American bentwood chair,
with carving on the seat and
back, c1910.
**£120–135**  *Ber*

A scroll back Windsor
chair, c1880.
**£45–55**  *AL*

A table, the sycamore top with cleats, over a painted elm base, with 3 drawers, c1800.
**£1,000–1,400** *SWN*

An oak refectory table, 17thC,
57in (144.5cm) long.
**£2,200–2,400** *SPa*

A farmhouse Windsor carver,
with original green paint, 18thC.
**£500–600** *SWN*

A Windsor chair, with hickory
arms, original paint, possibly
American, 18thC.
**£750–950** *SPa*

A pair of yew wood highback
Windsor chairs, 19thC.
**£2,200–2,400** *SPa*

A beech and elm child's
chair, c1920.
**£30–35** *AL*

An elm night commode,
with carving, late 17thC.
**£500–700** *SWN*

A Welsh Windsor chair.
**£225–245** *PC*

A pine tavern table, heavily carved through
use, late 18thC, 60in (152cm) wide.
**£1,800–2,000** *SWN*

A chestnut washboard, with oak legs, 19thC,
69in (175cm) long.
**£400–450** *SPa*

A primitive Windsor comb-backed armchair, with traces of original paint, c1780.
**£1,000–1,500** *RYA*

A child's fruitwood chair, 19thC.
**£200–300** *SWN*

A stick back chair, c1880.
**£50–55** *AL*

A country stool, c1900, 10½in (26.5cm) high.
**£35–45** *Ber*

A set of wedge/wheel-back Windsor chairs, comprising: 3 side chairs and one carver, c1890.
**£300–335** *AL*

An oak panelled back carver chair, with a primitive crest, early 17thC.
**£1,500–1,800** *SWN*

A comb-back Windsor chair, with original paint, c1870.
**£650–850** *PC*

Eight ash and elm Windsor chairs, with draught patterned splats, 18thC.
**£2,000–2,200** *SPa*

*l.* A child's stick chair, with panelled seat, late 18C.
**£1,000–1,500**
*c.* A comb back beech and ash stick chair, c1800.
**£1,000–1,200**
*r.* A Welsh oak child's backstool/stick chair, c1700.
**£2,000–2,500** *CAL*

A Celtic elm box chair,
early 19thC.
**£750–800** *FHA*

A set of 4 Dutch ladder
back chairs, with rush
seats, c1880, 43in
(109cm) high.
**£750–800** *AnD*

A pair of ladder back chairs,
with rush seats, early 20thC.
**£100–115** *AnD*

A Continental lignum vitae
turned ladderback chair,
early 19thC.
**£1,200–1,800** *CAL*

An ash reclining ladderback chair,
with wrought iron ratchet
mechanism, c1800.
**£1,200–1,500** *CAL*

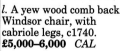

A rustic stick chair of
angular design and
construction, showing traces
of original paint.
**£2,000–2,500** *CAL*

*l.* A yew wood comb back
Windsor chair, with
cabriole legs, c1740.
**£5,000–6,000** *CAL*

A yew wood turner's chair, with an
oak panelled seat, early 17thC.
**£7,500–10,000** *CAL*

A pair of stick back chairs, with 2 iron rods, c1880.
**£100–120** *AL*

A child's school chair, c1920.
**£25–35** *Ber*

A bar back Windsor chair, c1880.
**£50–55** *AL*

A spindle back Windsor chair, c1880.
**£50–55** *AL*

A beech and elm chair, c1920.
**£30–40** *FAG*

A smoker's bow chair, c1900.
**£120–160** *FAG*

A penny seat chair, c1900.
**£40–50** *AL*

A folding chapel chair, c1900.
**£40–50** *AL*

A set of 4 French rush seat chairs, c1930.
**£230–250** *Ber*

A French rush seat chair, with original paintwork, early 19thC.
**£30–50** *FOX*

A pine step ladder, early 20thC, 58in (147cm) high.
**£20–45** *FOX*

A painted stool, with rush seat,
13in (33cm) high.
**£35–45** *Ber*

A chopping bench, c1850,
54in (137cm) wide.
**£130–150** *MIL*

An oak joined stool, the plain
top above a shaped frieze on
ring turned tapering legs tied
by block stretchers, mid-
17thC, 19½in (49.5cm) wide.
**£4,800–5,000** *Bon*

A kitchen stool, c1900,
22in (55.5cm) high.
**£50–60** *MIL*

An oak country stool, early
19thC, 17in (43cm) high.
**£50–65** *SHA*

An oak joined stool, the associated
top above a moulded frieze on
turned column supports tied by
block stretchers, mid-17thC and
later, 18in (46cm) wide.
**£200–250** *Bon*

A pair of oak joined stools, the bevelled
plank seats above moulded friezes on ring
turned column supports and peg feet,
18in (46cm) wide.
**£3,300–3,500** *Bon*

An oak stool, c1850, 22in (55.5cm) wide.
**£90–100** *MIL*

A George III Provincial oak and pollard oak linen press, with a moulded cornice above 2 panelled doors, plain interior with a well, 40in (101.5cm) wide. **£2,250–2,750** *C*

A North Wales oak clothes press, with arched panel doors above fielded drawers, on a later plinth base, late 18thC, 79in (201cm) wide. **£2,000–3,000** *S(S)*

A yew wood cupboard or press, early 18thC, 72in (182.5cm) wide. **£4,000–6,000** *CAL*

An oak press cupboard, with moulded cornice above 2 panelled doors, the base with panelled front and 2 drawers below, on stile feet, 51in (129.5cm) wide. **£800–1,000** *C*

A French oak buffet 'deux corps', with 4 doors, c1840, 57in (144.5cm) wide. **£1,800–2,000** *UC*

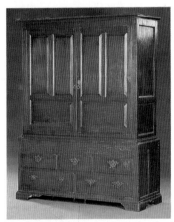

An oak clothes press, with a pair of fielded panel doors above drawers and bracket feet, cornice damaged, late 18thC, 61in (155cm) wide. **£1,800–2,200** *S(S)*

A Welsh sycamore two-part cupboard, 54in (137cm) high. **£3,000–4,500** *CAL*

A Shaker bone inlaid butternut cabinet, over 4 drawers, from Harvard Community, Mass., 36in (91.5cm) wide. **£18,000–19,000** *S(NY)*

An oak press cupboard, the moulded cornice above 2 fielded panelled doors, above 4 panels and 5 drawers, 61in (155cm) wide. **£3,000–4,000** *S(S)*

A Spanish walnut bread table, c1600,
37in (94cm) wide.
**£1,000–1,400** *FHA*

An oak gateleg occasional table, the top
with elliptical leaves, on bobbin turned
column, with square section stretcher
support, c1670, 26in (66cm) wide.
**£3,800–4,200** *Bon*

A burr oak joined folding table, the tilt-top
on slender baluster supports with a single
gateleg action, c1680, 31in (78.5cm) diam.
**£3,800–4,200** *Bon*

An oak refectory table, the later three-plank top with
end cleats, the frieze carved with a leaf scroll border,
with 6 baluster turned square legs joined by
stretchers, mid-17thC, 89in (226cm) wide.
**£2,500–3,500** *S(S)*

A sycamore and ash cricket table, the
top on turned legs joined by a platform
stretcher, eary 18thC.
**£3,000–4,000** *S*

An oak refectory table, with a cleated three-plank
top, the frieze carved with a foliate border, on
baluster turned and square legs, mid-17thC,
80in (203cm) wide.
**£2,250–2,750** *S(S)*

An oak gateleg table, the oval top with a later
pine frieze drawer, the baluster turned legs
joined by conforming stretchers, mid-18thC,
76in (193cm) wide. **£4,700–5,500** *S(S)*

An oak refectory table, the reduced top above a
channel moulded freize carved with lunettes, on
block feet, mid-17thC, 87in (220cm) wide.
**£1,800–2,500** *S(S)*

A Welsh oak bureau cabinet, with stepped interior, mid-18thC, 37in (34cm) wide.
**£7,500–8,500**  *CoA*

A Welsh oak and deal food cupboard, with fruitwood spindles, 18thC, 31½in (80cm) wide. **£4,500–5,500**  *CoA*

A Welsh oak 'cwpwrdd tridarn', 17thC, 54in (37cm) wide.
**£8,000–10,000**  *CoA*

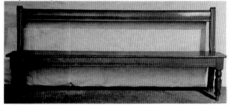

A pair of Victorian benches, 72in (182.5cm) wide.
**£200–250**  *AnD*

An oak dining and shove ha'penny table, with incised diagonal lines and arcaded frieze, on ring turned legs joined by stretchers on block feet, early 18thC, 81½in (207cm) long.
**£4,500–6,000**  *C*

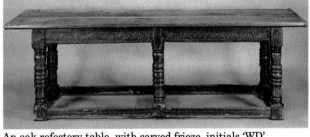

An oak refectory table, with carved frieze, initials 'WD', early 17thC, 103½in (263cm) wide. **£6,500–7,000**  *Bon*

A Welsh oak chest of 3 long drawers, c1790, 18in (46cm) wide.
**£900–1,100**  *KEY*

An oak chest of drawers, with 2 short and 3 long drawers, on bracket feet, c1820, 47in (119cm) wide.
**£800–900**  *UC*

An oak tilt-top table, c1760, 34in (86cm) diam.
**£450–500**  *MIL*

An oak chest of 2 short and 4 long drawers, 42in (106.5cm) wide.
**£1,700–2,000**  *S(S)*

A Welsh cottage dresser, with
potboard, original hooks, late
18thC, 56in (142cm) wide.
**£3,000–4,000** *SWN*

An oak dresser, the rack with
a moulded cornice above
2 shelves, the base with 3 frieze
drawers and and 4 false central
drawers, on bracket feet, mid-
18thC, 56½in (143cm) wide.
**£3,250–3,750** *Bon*

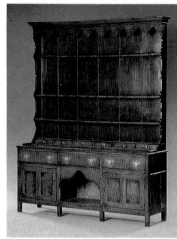

A oak Welsh dresser, on stile feet,
late 18thC, 69in (175cm) wide.
**£5,800–6,200** *S(S)*

An oak Welsh dresser, the raised
back with projecting cornice above
notched beading, the base with
3 frieze drawers, on stile feet,
mid-18thC, 58in (147cm) wide.
**£6,500–7,000** *S(S)*

An oak Welsh dresser, with potboard
and 3 shelves above 3 drawers, c1770,
56in (142cm) wide.
**£3,000–4,000** *KEY*

An oak dresser, the rack with
ogee moulded cornice, the
base with 2 frieze drawers,
2 false central drawers, and
2 cupboard doors, on bracket
feet, mid-18thC, 55in
(139.5cm) wide.
**£3,800–4,200** *Bon*

A George II oak dresser, with
3 plate rails, on chamfered
legs with a platform base,
58in (147cm) wide.
**£3,800–4,200** *DN*

A George III oak Welsh dresser,
with a shaped apron, on baluster
legs, with a platform base and
stump feet, 67½in (171cm) wide.
**£6,250–6,750** *DN*

An oak Welsh dresser, the associated
shelf back above 5 mahogany crossbanded drawers and 2 cupboard doors,
on later backet feet, 79½in (202cm) wide.
**£3,000–3,500** *S(S)*

A George III oak Welsh dresser, the shelf back above 5 frieze drawers and a pierced apron, on turned column supports, with a platform undertier on block feet, restored, late 18thC, 65in (165cm) wide.
**£3,500–4,000** *Bon*

An oak Welsh 'cwpwrdd tridarn', the canopy with columns, the central section with turned pendants and recessed cupboards, 2 frieze drawer and 2 panelled doors below, Harrods label, restored, early 18thC, 52in (132cm) wide. **£3,800–4,200** *S(S)*

A West Country oak dresser, the associated open shelf back above 3 frieze drawers, on reduced turned legs, early 19thC, 69in (175cm) wide. **£2,000–2,500** *S(S)*

A North West region oak dresser, the moulded cornice above an open shelf back, the base with 3 crossbanded frieze drawers and a valanced apron, on cabriole legs with pad feet, late 18thC, 78in (198cm) wide.
**£5,000–5,500** *S(S)*

An oak and pitch pine dresser/bookcase, with glazed doors above 6 drawers and 2 cupboard doors, 19thC, 72in (182.5cm) wide.
**£3,000–4,000** *CCP*

A North Country oak dresser, the open back rack with 3 open shelves, the base with 2 tiers of 3 graduated drawers and a central drawer over 2 panelled doors, on 3 front bracket supports, 18thC, 82in (208cm) wide.
**£2,750–3,250** *LAY*

An oak Welsh dresser, with a raised open shelf back, the base with 3 drawers, on profile baluster and square supports joined by a platform base, late 18thC, 67in (170cm) wide.
**£3,500–4,000** *S(S)*

An oak Welsh dresser, the shelf back above a pair of frieze drawers, on square supports, late 18thC, 57in (145cm) wide.
**£4,250–5,000** *S(S)*

An oak dresser, the reduced raised back with dentilled cornice and shaped frieze above 3 open shelves, the base with 3 drawers on cabriole legs, c1770, 72in (183cm) wide.
**£3,250–4,000** *S(S)*

An oak dresser/mule chest, with hinged top above 6 false and 3 real drawers, late 18thC, 61in (155cm) wide. **£2,500–3,000** *S(S)*

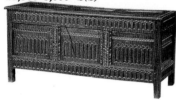

An oak coffer, the hinged top above a stop-fluted panelled front and sides, mid-17thC, 57in (144cm) wide. **£1,500–2,000** *S(S)*

An Essex County, Massachusetts, Pilgrim Century oak blanket chest, with geometric carving, c1660, 45in (114cm) wide. **£45,000–55,000** *S(NY)*

An oak plank coffer, c1870, 37in (94cm) wide. **£650–700** *MIL*

An oak mule chest, with 2 small drawers, 18thC, 25in (63.5cm) wide. **£250–300** *WaH*

An oak mule chest, with 4 arched panels, 2 drawers, the interior fitted with a candle box, 2 drawers, 18thC, 57in (144.5cm) wide. **£1,200–1,500** *CCP*

An oak dresser/mule chest, crossbanded with mahogany, the front with 4 panels and 3 drawers, late 18thC, 59in (150cm) wide. **£750–900** *S(S)*

An oak coffer, of 6 planks, original hinges and lock, mid-17thC, 56in (142cm) wide. **£1,000–1,250** *SWN*

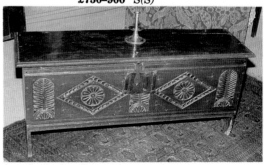

An oak plank coffer, with original carving and ironwork, c1650, 44in (111.5cm) wide. **£700–800** *KEY*

A primitive elm settle, of bowed plank construction, carved with various initials, late 17thC, 98in (249cm) wide. **£2,000–2,500** *Bon*

An elm bacon settle, with original interior wrought iron meat hooks, 30in (76cm) wide. **£3,500–5,500** *CAL*

An oak high backed winged armchair or settle, with a drawer to the base, c1780. **£2,500–3,500** *CAL*

A miniature arched back elm settle, with lift-up seat, constructed in the manner of a six-plank coffer, c1740, 36in (91.5cm) wide. **£2,000–2,500** *CAL*

A walnut dresser base,
48in (122cm) wide.
**£10,000–12,000** *CAL*

An oak dresser base, with 3 frieze drawers and 2 central
drawers, flanked by panelled cupboard doors, on block feet,
restored, mid-18thC, 72in (182cm) wide. **£2,500–3,000** *Bon*

A Canadian Waterloo County Mennonite
cherrywood sideboard, c1880, 50in (127cm) wide.
**£700–800** *RIT*

An oak serving table, with 3 drawers, late 17thC,
72in (182.5cm) wide.
**£8,000–10,000** *CAL*

A French carved and decorated
cherrywood low buffet, with original
ironwork, c1790, 50in (127cm) wide.
**£3,500–4,000** *CAL*

A cherrywood dresser base, with 2 panelled doors
beneath 3 drawers, c1690, 72in (182.5cm) wide.
**£8,000–10,000** *CAL*

A Georgian oak Welsh dresser base, with 3 frieze drawers
interspersed with fluted panels above an apron fitted with 3 ogee
arches, on ring turned baluster supports joined by a platform
stretcher, on bracket feet, restored, mid-18thC, 76in (193cm) wide.
**£13,000–15,000** *S(NY)*

A French Provincial cherrywood
low buffet, with scratch-carving to
the drawers, and original wrought
iron, c1780, 50in (127cm) wide.
**£3,000–3,500** *CAL*

A Welsh oak cricket table, 18thC.
**£400–500** *OSc*

An oak tavern table, c1830.
**£600–800** *CCA*

A George III oak and
elm cricket table, with
a shelf, c1800.
**£600–700** *PHA*

An oak gateleg table, fitted with
a drawer, 17thC.
**£1,600–1,900** *NCr*

An oak gateleg dining table,
c1900, 53in (135cm) wide.
**£1,500–2,000** *SC*

An oak gateleg table, late
17thC, 64in (163cm) extended.
**£3,000–3,600** *SC*

A Welsh oak and elm farmhouse table,
with 2 drawers, c1820.
**£600–800** *OSc*

A George III country oak
farmhouse table, one leaf
missing, 94in (239cm) long.
**£1,800–2,200** *L*

A Tudor refectory table, mid-16thC,
125½in (317.5cm) long.
**£2,500–3,500** *SBA*

A William and Mary oak double action gateleg table, with frieze drawer and twelve square and baluster turned supports with conforming stretchers, 74in (188cm) extended.
**£6,000–8,000**  *S(S)*

A French walnut folding wine tasting table, c1850, 42in (106.5cm) diam.
**£800–950**  *UC*

*l.* A cherrywood oval table, c1880, 45in (114cm) wide.
**£700–800**  *MofC*

An oak gateleg table, the oval moulded top above two frieze drawers, on block and turned legs with shaped aprons, joined by stretchers, the flaps re-tipped, 18thC, 59in (149cm) wide.
**£1,500–2,000**  *P*

A Charles II oak gateleg table, the top with elliptical leaves above a drawer, on baluster turned columns, joined by ball turned stretchers, c1670, 59in (149.5cm).
**£800–1,000**  *Bon*

An oak gateleg table, with hinged top, on turned baluster supports joined by stretchers, on block feet, 96in (244cm) extended.
**£800–1,000**  *CSK*

A Charles II oak gateleg table, the drop-leaf top raised above a shallow frieze drawer with moulded front and raised upon spiral-twist legs, stretchers and gates on either side, late 17thC, 48in (122cm).
**£1,200–1,700**  *B*

A New England maplewood butterfly table, the base with old colour, restored top and drawers, 38in (96.5cm) wide.
**£500–600**  *SK(B)*

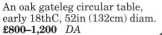

An oak gateleg circular table, early 18thC, 52in (132cm) diam.
**£800–1,200** *DA*

An oak gateleg dining table, late 17thC, 73in (185cm) extended.
**£4,000–5,000** *B*

A gateleg table, with a pearwood top, mid-17thC, 29in (74cm) wide.
**£1,500–1,800** *SKC*

An oak gateleg table, late 17thC, 45in (114cm) extended.
**£800–1,200** *SKC*

An oak gateleg table, with twin-flap top and one panelled drawer, on later bun feet, restorations to top, some replacements to legs, top extended, part late 17thC, 60in (153cm) wide.
**£1,500–2,000** *C*

An 18thC style oak oval gateleg dining table, with single frieze drawer, supported on ring turned legs with plain stretchers, 40in (101.5cm) wide.
**£700–900** *DDM*

An oak oval gateleg dining table, with plain top, frieze drawer, turned supports and plain stretchers, 60in (152cm) extended.
**£1,200–1,700** *DDM*

A William and Mary oak gateleg table, with a drawer, on square and bobbin turned legs, late 17thC, 56in (142cm) extended.
**£2,200–2,500**  *S(S)*

A Charles II oak gateleg table, with spiral twist end supports, restored, late 17thC, 30½in (78cm) extended.
**£1,600–2,000**  *S(S)*

A George III oak side table, the moulded top above one long and 2 short drawers, with a shaped apron, on chamfered square legs, damaged, late 18thC, 33½in (85cm) wide.
**£800–1,000**  *S(S)*

*r.* An oak credence table, the circular top falling over a single gate to a base of 4 cannon barrel turned legs beneath an incised frieze with a potboard beneath, early 17thC, 37in (94cm) wide.
**£2,500–3,000**  *B*

A Shaker cherrywood, two- drawer trestle-base work table, the top with rounded corners above a two-drawer frieze, the supports jointed by a turned medial stretcher, on slightly arched shoe feet, Kentucky, 1850–70, 24½in (62cm) wide.
**£1,500–2,000**  *S(NY)*

*l.* An oak side table, with a moulded top above one long and 3 short drawers, with a shaped apron, on tapered square legs, South Wales, late 18thC, 31in (79cm) wide.
**£1,000–1,200**  *S(S)*

An oak side table, the moulded top above a frieze drawer, on block and turned legs, joined by stretchers, turned feet, early 18thC, 29in (74cm) wide.
**£400–600**  *P*

*l.* A Continental oak refectory table, the top above two frieze drawers, on rounded square tapering legs joined by box stretchers, associated, 18th/19thC, with two later stretchers, 87½in (222cm) wide.
**£4,000–5,000**  *C*

A dairy table, in original finish, c1870, 20in (51cm) wide.
**£220–250** *MIL*

A Spanish walnut rustic table, 18thC.
**£1,000–1,500** *Ced*

A late Victorian oak press table with 2 drawers, turned ebony handles, with splayed front legs, 35in (89cm) extended.
**£150–250** *AP*

An oak and ash tavern table, the three-plank top above X-shaped end supports, early 19thC, 61½in (156cm) wide.
**£1,850–2,000** *S(S)*

A Charles II oak refectory table, with three-planked top, on a separate base of 4 baluster-turned legs united by one carved and one plain frieze, inscribed '1667', with a heavy all-round stretcher at the base, good colour and original patination, 99in (251.5cm) wide.
**£6,000–7,000** *B*

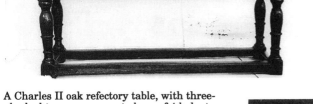

A Jacobean oak refectory table, the plank top on bulbous gadrooned pedestals and X-form plinths, 147in (374cm) wide.
**£21,500–25,000** *C(NY)*

A pine and ash long tavern table, with shove halfpenny markings, c1800.
**£1,000–1,200** *COM*

*r.* An oak tavern table, the top supported by X-form base, with faceted supports, 19thC, 56in (142cm) wide.
**£8,000–9,000** *S(NY)*

An oak side table, the projecting top above columnar-turned and square legs joined by peripheral stretchers, c1700, possibly associated, 48½in (123cm) wide. **£1,200–1,700** *S(S)*

An oak side table, the top above a plain frieze, on baluster turned legs joined by stretchers, late 17thC, 35in (89cm) wide. **£500–600** *P*

A New England William and Mary turned tavern table, on turned legs joined by a stretcher, painted black, restored, 22in (56cm) wide. **£500–600** *SK(B)*

A pine and elm tavern table, with X-frame, c1830. **£1,000–1,200** *COM*

## Colour and Patina

Rustic, simple items have a unique charm, particularly if they have achieved a glorious colour and deep patina from daily use and polishing. Colour and patina are the foremost criteria for country furniture. Both go hand-in-hand, are impossible to fake, and will be reflected in the asking price. Ideally, one looks for a good colour – not just an overall blanket of colour, but a variety of tones from almost blond to black. The palest areas where wear would have been greatest, and darker sections that were out of reach of hands or sunlight. The wood will be soft and silky to the touch, and the piece should glow with a three-dimensional depth.

*r*. A New England pine and poplar harvest table, the top supported on four angled legs with stretchers, 78in (198cm) wide. **£2,000–2,500** *MMG*

An oak gateleg table, the top above an end frieze pine-lined drawer, baluster ogee turned block legs and stretchers, on turned feet, late 17thC, 42in (106.5cm) wide. **£800–1,000** *WW*

A French cherry wood table, on brass casters, 1830, 42in (106.5cm) diam. **£520–600** *GD*

An oak refectory table, on 6 inverted baluster legs united by stretchers at floor level, early 17thC with new solid oak top, 157½in (427cm) long. **£1,650–2,000** *WL*

A Charles II oak credence table, with folding demi-lune top above a central panelled frieze drawer, on turned baluster column supports tied by block stretchers, c1640, 49in (125cm) wide.
**£4,500–5,000** *Bon*

A Charles I style oak monk's table, with boarded hinged top, a boarded seat and a drawer, the square and turned legs joined by peripheral stretchers, made-up, 42½in (107cm) wide.
**£900–1,000** *S(S)*

A pine and walnut wine table, with carved dolphin base, c1870, 23in (59cm) diam.
**£250–300** *AF*

A Charles II oak side table, with moulded rectangular top, on bobbin-turned and square legs joined by peripheral stretchers, late 17thC, 33in (84cm) wide.
**£900–1,200** *S(S)*

A Queen Anne oak side table, with moulded top above a frieze drawer, the slender turned and square legs joined by peripheral stretchers, early 18thC, 30in (76cm) wide.
**£2,000–2,500** *S(S)*

An oak and fruitwood draw-leaf dining table, French or Flemish, the cleated top above turned and square legs joined by shaped stretchers, on later turned feet, mid-18thC, 106in (269cm) long.
**£3,000–3,500** *S(S)*

*l.* A small oak table, c1920s, 16½in (42cm) diam.
**£80–110** *JHW*

A chestnut table, late 19thC, 60in (152cm) diam.
**£500–600** *CUL*

An Irish yew wood wake table, with oval drop leaf, 18thC, 29in (74cm) high.
**£2,500–3,000** *AF*

A French Provincial Normandy pear wood table, with oak frame, single centre drawer, tapered legs, 80in (203cm) long.
**£200–300** *AF*

# French Provincial Furniture

The past five or six years have seen a huge increase in the importation of French provincial antique country furniture to England. As 'French country' becomes a recognised look, it is important to consider certain factors before buying French furniture.

Invariably, the French 'restore' their tables, a process that involves noticeable and unacceptable practices, including removing the top to close up shrinkage gaps by trimming down one side of the cleats (the smaller plank at each end binding the main plank at right angles), leaving one side with a new worked surface. Many work tables were altered to make them more valuable as dining tables, by removing drawers and shaping rails to leave low corner brackets, and cut up to a shallow rail leaving knee space.

Age and style are important: one type of table from northern France, dated 1680–1780, is very similar in style to a late 17th century/early 18th-century English table – with large square section chamfered legs and a generous thick top – usually in chestnut. Many have been sold as English, and go well with English furniture. Very plain tables with square section legs joined by H-stretchers from about 1760 to 1880, follow a popular style in England and France, teaming well with English vernacular chair types. By the mid-19th century, French tables had heavily turned legs, often in well-figured walnut, and are used in England as kitchen dining tables. These are commanding between £600 and £1,200.

A late 18th century English ten-seater farmhouse dining table, that has a thick two-plank cleated top with a good overhang at each end, in well patinated oak, elm, ash or sycamore, would command in excess of £5,000. The French equivalent in oak, elm, ash, chestnut or cherrywood, mostly from northern France and much prized in England, would cost about £2,500.

Quality French (and English) dining tables have doubled in value over the past few years and the price differential is narrowing. As fine French tables are becoming rarer in Britain, the French are becoming more reluctant to part with them.

French country chairs are not popular in Britain, although recently there has been a vogue for painted rush-seated ladder backs from Provence. Original sets are very desirable reaching prices of £3,000–4,000 for a three-seater banquette. But be warned – reproductions exist complete with distressed paint surface.

We tend to match French farmhouse tables with our traditional English country ladder back, spindle back or Windsor type chair.

The desirability and value of an exceptional dresser, court cupboard or chest of drawers means they exact a high price, but it is still possible to buy fine French provincial pieces for competitive prices. Commodes or chests of drawers are the highlight of French provincial furniture. Offered frequently at £10,000 or more they are often considered too flamboyant for English taste, usually outshining heavily geometrically moulded English chests and plain, flat fronted ones.

Armoires (wardrobes) with 'Napoleon hat' type cornices are very popular – usually inlaid, decorative and elegant, as opposed to the rare, rather ungainly, early English country form. A plain armoire would fetch between £2,500–3,500. A huge advantage of the French armoire, is that the doors are removable and the carcass may be knocked apart for easy transportation.

Whatever one chooses to buy, it is above all, important to look for a genuine patina over the scars of generations. It is this which gives any piece of country furniture its vital magic.

When looking at 'restored' tables, look for a new worked surface on the cleats, showing shrinkage gaps have been closed up. Shadow marks on the underside of the table top planks indicate recentering on the frame has taken place, and look for 'length shrinkage' – a sure sign of trouble as the one has been reduced to create a bigger overhang. Note any signs of a mechanical circular saw as these do not predate 1840. On altered work tables, fresh underside rail edges or even staining to conceal them are of note.

Wear to both English and French tables can be easily identified: wear to stretchers, finger marks, grimy patina around underside edges of tops, shrinkage of timber, wear to feet. Colour, surface and patina are most important – washed off and repolished tables lose value and evidence of age.

Robert Young

A 17thC style oak cupboard, with split bobbin and turned mouldings, the triple panel front including a pair of arched panel doors, the square and turned legs joined by peripheral stretchers, 45½in (112cm) wide.
**£950–1,200** *S(S)*

An oak cupboard in two parts, possibly East Anglian, with a frieze drawer and 3 panel doors above a shaped apron, alterations, late 17thC, 41½in (106cm) wide.
**£1,800–2,500** *S(S)*

A George III oak wall cupboard, with shelves enclosed by a panelled door, 26½in (67cm) wide.
**£450–500** *DN*

An oak cupboard, with shelves enclosed by one panelled door, with iron hinges, 17thC, 21½in (54cm) wide.
**£200–250** *DN*

An oak cupboard, with punch heightened decoration of lunettes, stylised paterae and dentil geometric motifs, enclosed by a panelled door, traces of green paint, 17thC, 20½in (52cm) wide.
**£2,200–2,800** *C*

A rare medieval dug-out cupboard, with single door and iron strap hinges.
**£3,800–4,200** *B*

A small oak food cupboard, with potboard base, c1870, the handles and hinges later replacements.
**£3,500–4,500** *Ced*

A George III oak food cupboard, inlaid with mahogany geometric motifs, the moulded cornice above a pair of doors with perforated panels enclosing shelves, the base with 2 short and 2 long-drawers lacking feet, late 18th/early 19thC, 43½in (110cm) wide.
**£2,000–2,500** *S(S)*

An oak press cupboard, with a pair of panelled doors above a panelled frieze on stile feet, restored, c1670, 49½in (126cm) wide.
**£1,700–2,000** *Bon*

A Queen Anne oak press cupboard-on-chest, the panelled doors enclosing hanging space, 4 panels below, on stile feet, restored, early 18thC, 46½in (117cm) wide.
**£1,000–1,500** *S(S)*

An oak court cupboard, with fielded panel doors, 17thC, 53in (134.5cm) wide.
**£1,800–2,000** *RBB*

A Welsh oak cupboard, in two parts, fitted with cupboard doors and drawers, with engaged columns, on bracket feet, inscribed 'A.I. 1798', late 18thC, 60in (152cm) wide.
**£5,000–6,000** *S(NY)*

A Federal cherrywood cupboard, with projecting cornice over glass doors enclosing shelves, above 3 panelled drawers and a pair of cupboard doors, on bracket feet, 19thC, 63in (160cm) wide.
**£1,500–2,000** *LHA*

An oak hanging corner cupboard, enclosing 3 shelves, the shaped moulded panel door with central inlaid rosette, 27in (69cm) wide
**£450–550** *DA*

A Pennsylvanian walnut cupboard, with glazed doors to top, 3 drawers and cupboards to base, restoration, 70in (177.5cm) wide.
**£3,500–4,000** *SK(B)*

A George III oak hanging corner cupboard, the moulded cornice above a fielded panelled door enclosing shaped shelves, the canted sides with stop-fluted pilasters, late 18thC, 36in, (91.5cm) wide.
**£700–800** *S(S)*

A George III oak hanging corner cupboard, the moulded cornice above a pair of mahogany crossbanded and floral inlaid panelled doors with one true and two false drawers beneath, late 18thC, 35in (89cm) wide.
**£650–800** *Bon*

An oak corner cupboard, the moulded cornice above a crossbanded door with central inlaid paterae, on a moulded plinth base, 18thC, 32in (81cm) wide.
**£600–700** *P*

A walnut carved glazed buffet, probably mid-Atlantic States, with three painted shaped shelves, glazed door and a single shelf behind the recessed door flanked by fluted columns, old darkened surface, restored, 1790–1820, 48in (122cm) wide.
**£1,700–2,200** *SK(B)*

*r.* A poplar wood glazed corner cupboard, probably Pennsylvania, refinished (minor repairs), c1810, 43in (109cm) wide.
**£2,000–2,500** *SK(B)*

A Federal cherrywood four-door corner cabinet, late 18thC, 55in (139.5cm) wide.
**£1,000–1,500** *LHA*

A New England cherrywood corner cupboard, old refinish, (minor imperfections), c1810, 42in (106.5cm) wide.
**£1,350–2,000** *SK(B)*

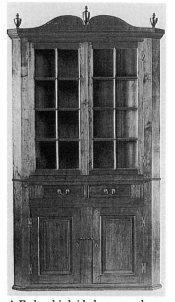

A Federal inlaid cherrywood corner cupboard, the shaped pediment with three carved urn finials above two glazed doors enclosing 3 shelves, 2 drawers and two raised panelled doors enclosing a shelf, on plinth base, 49in (125cm) wide.
**£2,700–3,200** *CCS*

A George III oak standing corner cupboard, the moulded cornice above two fielded panelled doors, flanked by canted corners, mid-18thC, 40in (101.5cm) wide.
**£1,200–1,700** *Bon*

## Locate the source

*The source of each illustration in* **Miller's Pine & Country Buyer's Guide** *can easily be found by checking the code letters at the end of each caption with the Key to Illustrations located at the front of the book.*

*l.* An elm standing corner cupboard, with dentil cornice and a pair of arched parallel doors, 19thC.
**£1,850–2,000** *DN*

An oak chest, with 2 short and
2 long drawers, on bracket feet,
some original brass handles and
escutcheons, early 18thC, 36in
(92cm) wide.
**£340–400** *WIL*

## Followers of Fashion

The fashion in furniture hardware – handles,
locks, hinges and escutcheons changed
regularly, and owners can be seen to have
updated their furniture, leaving behind the
evidence of time. Look closely at a chest of
drawers. You may well see evidence of the
original drop handles, replaced by later plates,
sometimes by two or even three progressively
larger sets and lastly, perhaps, a Victorian
glass or china knob. Dealers will often rehandle
a piece, putting back whatever is most
appropriate, but the scars are hard to disguise
and original hardware is obviously a premium.

A simulated maple chest
of drawers, c1860, 36in
(91.5cm) wide.
**£400–450** *PEN*

An unusual oak chest of
drawers, with linen
press, c1800.
**£1,200–2,000** *Ced*

An oak chest of drawers, late
18thC, 44in (111.5cm) wide.
**£650–850** *WV*

An oak chest of drawers, with
mitred mouldings and later
pierced bracket feet, late 17thC,
42½in (107cm) wide.
**£950–1,000** *S(S)*

A William and Mary oak chest
of drawers, restored, late 17thC
35½in (90cm) wide
**£1,800–2,200** *SK(B)*

A George III oak chest of
drawers, with 4 long graduated
drawers, on bracket feet, c1770,
34in (87cm) wide.
**£700–750** *Bon*

*l.* A James II oak chest, the
rectangular moulded top
above 2 short and 3 long
geometrically moulded
drawers, on later shaped
bracket feet, 36in (92cm).
**£1,200–1,500** *P*

*r.* A maple chest of 4 drawers,
New England, old bale
brasses, refinished, restored,
c1790, 33in (84cm) wide.
**£1,200–1,500** *SK(B)*

A Jacobean oak tester bed, with cup-and-cover turned end posts below a nine panel tester with moulded cornice, legs rebuilt, tester possibly of a later date, 54in (137cm) wide.
**£4,000–4,500**   *P(M)*

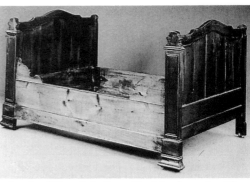

A pair of French fruitwood bedsteads, each with arched panelled headboard and footboard, panelled uprights and joined by siderails with shaped spandrels, mid-19thC, 80in (204cm) wide.
**£800–1,000**   *CSK*

*r.* An oak cradle, with a domed canopy, tapering sides and lunette shaped rockers, 18thC, 35½in (50cm) wide.
**£260–300**   *P*

An oak tester bed, with a panelled canopy with cavetto moulded cornice and headboard, the foot board with turned posts and moulded panels, on solid end supports, parts 17thC, 58in (147cm) wide.
**£2,500–3,000**   *Bon*

An oak tester bed, the headboard with a pair of floral marquetry panels, above carved arcades with recessed foliate fruiting tendrils, and the box spring, Yorkshire, parts 17thC, 69in (176cm) wide.
**£7,000–9,000**   *CSK*

A French chestnut enclosed double bed, early 19th.
**£1,500–1,800**   *Ced*

An oak tester bed, the panelled headboard with a carved figure, on square block feet, 17thC and later, made up, 58in (147cm) wide.
**£3,500–4,500**   *S(S)*

*r.* An oak tester bedstead known as 'The Lovely Hall Bed', with 24 pierced carved panels, the end posts carved with 'R' and 'I', early 16thC, 158in (400cm) wide.
**£25,000–30,000**   *S(S)*

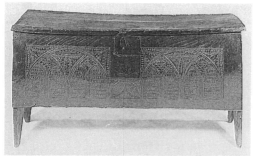

An oak chest, the moulded plank top enclosing a lidded candle box above a lunette and chip-carved painted front, with arcaded end supports, restored, mid-17thC, 48½in (123cm) wide.
**£1,500–2,000** *Bon*

A Charles II joined oak chest, the panelled top above a frieze applied with ovoid bosses and 3 leaf and sunburst carved panels flanked by split balusters, Yorkshire, c1660, 49in (125cm) wide.
**£700–800** *Bon*

A Jacobean oak chest, the moulded hinged top above a panelled and carved case, plank legs, late 17thC, 55½in (140cm) wide.
**£800–1,000** *SK(B)*

An oak coffer, the rising plank top above a front with a gouge-decorated frieze and 2 arcaded panels with carved decorations and stylised pilasters, early 17thC, 40in (101.5cm) wide.
**£1,200–1,700** *B*

An oak coffer, the panelled hinged top enclosing a plain interior with a till, the linen-fold panelled front above block feet, restorations, part 16thC, 49¼in (125cm) wide.
**£1,500–2,000** *C*

An oak joined chest, with panelled hinged top and a frieze of stop-flutes, 17thC, 40½in (102cm) wide.
**£650–750** *DN*

An oak mule chest, the moulded top, previously hinged at the back, above a fall-front of 4 fielded arched panels, 3 drawers and ogee arched aprons, on scrolling plank feet, alterations, mid-18thC, 55½in (141cm) wide.
**£600–800** *P*

An oak coffer, the hinged lid with 4 moulded panels above an arcaded frieze and conforming panelled front, on plank feet, 17thC, 51¼in (130cm) wide.
**£500–600** *P*

An oak six-plank chest, with
scratch carved decoration, c1700,
24in (61.5cm) wide.
**£750–950** *OSc*

A Commonwealth oak coffer, the moulded
hinged top above a twin panel front, on
stile feet, c1650, 37½in (95cm) wide.
**£900–1,200** *S(S)*

An oak coffer, 17thC, 41in
(104cm) wide.
**£1,000–1,200** *OB*

An oak coffer, 18thC,
60in (125.5cm) wide.
**£800–1,000** *C*

A small oak six-plank chest,
mid-17thC, 31½in (80cm) wide.
**£800–1,200** *S*

An oak coffer, with plain
hinged top and front, 18thC,
35in (89cm) wide.
**£200–250** *DDM*

An oak 3 panelled coffer,
with carved top rail and
ebony and holly chevron
inlay, raised on high stiles,
17thC, 42in (106.5cm) wide.
**£700–800** *TM*

An elm blanket chest, 18thC,
42in (106.5cm) wide.
**£120–150** *JMW*

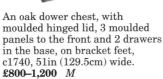

An oak dower chest, with
moulded hinged lid, 3 moulded
panels to the front and 2 drawers
in the base, on bracket feet,
c1740, 51in (129.5cm) wide.
**£800–1,200** *M*

A carved elm coffer, 18thC,
38in (96cm) wide.
**£600–800** *PCA*

An oak and fruitwood chest, lead scratch carved
with compass decoration, c1690, 42in (106.5cm).
**£800–1,200** *OSc*

An oak chest, with scratch carved
decoration, c1670, 36in (91.5cm).
**£750–1,000** *OSc*

An oak coffer, with panelled top and
sides, 18thC.
**£400–600** *DaD*

An oak triple panel coffer, with iron latch, late 17thC,
50in (127cm) wide.
**£300–400** *AP*

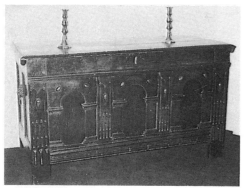

An oak coffer, with moulded top and 3 panel
front with arcaded fluted decoration, 17thC,
39in (99cm) wide.
**£500–600** *AP*

An oak coffer, with carved front, 57in (144.5cm) wide.
**£500–550** *GD*

An oak chest, with two-plank top, 4 shaped, raised
and fielded panels to front and 2 drawers to base,
on ogee bracket feet, restored, late 18thC, 55in
(140cm) wide.
**£500–600** *WIL*

An oak coffer, with 3 panels, late 17thC,
47in (119cm) wide.
**£350–450** *AP*

A mule chest, 18thC, 48in (122cm) wide.
**£650–750** *WV*

An oak chest, the top with 3 panels, and original hinges,
the 3 front panels carved with roundels and arcading to
top rail, slight restoration to lid, 17thC, 42in (107cm) wide.
**£660–900** *WIL*

An oak and mahogany crossbanded blanket chest, Cheshire, the panelled top above 4 dummy and 3 real drawers flanked by reeded pilasters, on ogee bracket feet, late 18thC, 55½in (141cm) wide.
**£1,300–1,700** *S(S)*

A Charles II oak chest, the moulded hinged top above a triple panel front carved with stylised arches within S-scroll borders, on stile feet, late 17thC, 55½in (140cm) wide.
**£650–700** *S(S)*

A North Country carved oak chest, the moulded hinged top above a lunette frieze and a triple panel front with stylised foliate motifs within inlaid geometric borders, on stile feet, mid-17thC, 58in (147cm) wide.
**£680–720** *S(S)*

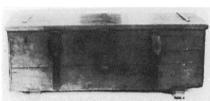

An oak ecclesiastical plank chest with iron strap hinges and hasps the rising lid enclosing a fitted interior with an ecclesiastical safe compartment with further rising lid, on sledge feet, formerly with three internal locks, 16thC, 53in (134.5cm) wide.
**£1,500–2,000** *B*

*r.* A William and Mary carved oak boarded chest, with hinged cover, the carved front bearing the initials 'WS' and dated '1696', 40½in (103cm) wide.
**£1,300–1,600** *S(S)*

A small oak coffer, with three-panel rising lid above a front of three panels with stylised foliate decoration and spandrels beneath, 17thC, 44in (111.5cm) wide.
**£420–450** *B*

An oak five-panelled coffer, 17thC, 37in (94cm) wide.
**£800–1,000** *MIT*

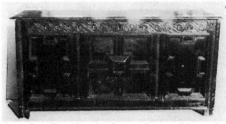

An oak coffer, the plank top above a frieze of scrolls and a three-panel front with moulded decoration, late 17thC, 62in (157cm) wide.
**£780–850** *B*

An oak coffer, 18thC, 30in (77cm) wide.
**£450–500** *DaD*

An oak coffer, the rising plank top above a carved front and lunette carved frieze, 3 panels with applied lozenge decoration within carved arcades, 17thC, 53in (134.5cm) wide.
**£450–500** *B*

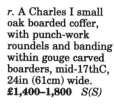

*r.* A Charles I small oak boarded coffer, with punch-work roundels and banding within gouge carved boarders, mid-17thC, 24in (61cm) wide.
**£1,400–1,800** *S(S)*

A Westmorland oak coffer, the rising top above a three-panelled front with gouged decoration, above applied arcades and pilasters, 17thC, 51in (129.5cm) wide.
**£600–700** *B*

A Queen Anne oak boarded coffer, the hinged top above an incised front panel with an iron lockplate, flanked by the date '1709', on trestle shaped supports, early 18thC, 35½in (91cm) wide.
**£560–600** *S(S)*

A Yorkshire oak double coffer, the panelled top above a frieze with incised decoration surrounding the initials 'P.S. 1702', early 18thC, 72in (182.5cm) wide.
**£600–650** *B*

*l.* An oak coffer, with panelled top, the front carved with leafage and scroll designs, dated '1693', 52in (132cm) high.
**£620–650** *RBB*

A late Victorian oak blanket box, with original hinges, c1820, 44in (111.5cm) wide.
**£200–240** *POT*

A Military camphor wood box, brass hinges, 38in (96.5cm) wide.
**£350–400** *AF*

An elm plank coffer, with arcadian carving, original lock plate, 17thC, 54in (137cm) wide.
**£450–550** *AF*

A George III oak bureau, with fall front and fitted interior, the base with 4 graduated drawers, brass bail handles, on bracket feet, 37in (94cm) wide.
**£1,750–2,000** *WIL*

*r.* An ash country bureau, with fitted interior, 18thC, 36in (91.5cm) wide.
**£1,450–1,650** *GD*

*r.* A George III oak bureau, the cleated fall enclosing fitted interior above 4 graduated drawers, on later ogee bracket feet, late 18thC, 36in (92cm) wide.
**£1,500–2,000** *S(S)*

An oak bureau, the interior with pigeonholes, 5 drawers, 3 secret drawers and a sliding well, the lower section with 2 short drawers and 2 long drawers, on bracket feet, early 18thC, 37in (94cm) wide.
**£1,300–1,500** *P*

A George III oak and mahogany crossbanded bureau, late 18thC, 39in (99cm) wide.
**£1,800–2,200** *S(S)*

## Locate the source

*The source of each illustration in* Miller's Pine & Country Buyer's Guide *can easily be found by checking the code letters at the end of each caption with the Key to Illustrations located at the front of the book.*

A George II oak bureau, the fall front enclosing a fitted interior above 2 short and 2 long drawers, on bracket feet, 33½in (85cm) wide.
**£3,200–3,500** *DN*

A George III oak bureau, with fall front enclosing a fitted interior, above four long drawers, on bracket feet, 38in (96.5cm) wide.
**£1,200–1,500** *DN*

A George III oak bureau, with fitted interior, above 4 long drawers with brass handles, on bracket feet, 40in (101.5cm).
**£1,200–1,500** *DN*

An oak high-back settle, the five-panel back above a box base with lift-up seat and panels beneath, turned supports to side arms, original colour and patination, 18thC, 67in (170cm) wide.
**£1,000–1,500** *B*

A George II style oak settle, with moulded crested rail above five arched fielding panels to the back, shaped arm supports, square fluted legs with a gold dralon squab cushion, basically 18thC, 80in (203cm) long.
**£500–700** *HCC*

An oak settle, the back with 3 panels, the base with open arms and single central drawer, 45in (115cm) long.
**£550–600** *LAY*

An oak settle, the back with 5 stylised foliate carved panels, solid seat and chamfered legs, restored, Lancashire/Cheshire, late 17thC, 71in (180cm) long.
**£1,500–2,000** *S(S)*

A George III oak settle, the back with 4 shaped panels.
**£400–500** *DaD*

An oak box settle, the back with 4 raised and fielded panels, hinged seat, front of replaced base with 5 square fielded panels, open arms, 17thC, 51in (130cm) long.
**£3,100–3,500** *WIL*

An oak settle, with four-panelled back and cushioned seat, Lancashire, 18thC.
**£650–800** *W*

A pair of French cherrywood benches, late 19thC, 85in (216cm) long.
**£250–400** *HGN*

An elm and oak hall bench, the back inscribed '1736', on reduced stump supports, mid-18thC, (105 by 152cm) long.
**£2,000–2,600** *SBA*

An oak high wing-back concave settle, the seat with 2 drawers, 18thC, 50in (127cm) wide.
**£1,200–1,600** *DDM*

An elm bacon settle, c1800, 77in (195.5cm) high.
**£2,000–2,500** *W*

A Welsh oak settle, the top rail carved and dated '1687', the base fully enclosed with a small removable lid inserted in the seat, the top 17thC, the base made up later, 46in (117cm) wide.
**£800–900** *SC*

An elm bacon settle, the back with single cupboard below 4 short drawers, solid seat, with a cupboard below, c1720, 56in (142cm) wide.
**£2,000–2,250** *SKC*

An oak four-panel settle, 17thC, 72in (182.5cm) wide.
**£1,800–2,400** *AGr*

An oak settle, dated '1740', 44in (111.5cm) wide.
**£2,800–3,000** *JAC*

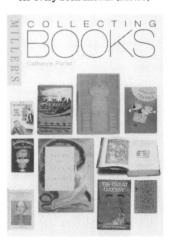

*l.* An oak and chestnut settle, 18thC, 58in (1147cm) wide.
**£1,000–1,200** *PCA*

A Charles II oak joined stool, with
moulded top above a fretwork
apron, on baluster turned and
square legs joined by stretchers,
late 17thC, 17½in (44cm) wide.
**£1,500–1,800**   *S(S)*

A Queen Anne oak close stool,
3 three dummy drawers, on
later turned feet, early 18thC,
19in (48cm) wide.
**£1,200–1,500**   *S(S)*

An oak joined stool, c1850,
14in (36cm) wide.
**£150–200**   *MofC*

A Charles II oak joined stool, c1650,
17in (43cm) wide.
**£500–600**   *WaH*

*r.* An oak joined
stool, with moulded
top above a frieze
carved with the
initials 'HB', on
bobbin turned
legs tied by
block stretchers,
restorations, top
possibly associated,
mid-17thC, 18½in
(47cm) wide.
**£800–900**   *Bon*

An elm rustic stool, early 19thC,
18in (45.5cm) high.
**£25–35**   *WCA*

An oak fireside or dairy
stool, c1800.
**£70–150**   *Ced*

A child's oak joined stool on
baluster turned legs, c1680,
late 17th/early 18thC, 12in
(30.5cm) square.
**£650–750**   *RYA*

*l.* A pine milking
stool, c1870,
12in (31cm) wide.
**£25–35**   *ASP*

*r.* An oak joined stool, the
moulded top above turned
and square legs joined by
stretchers, early 18thC,
15in (39cm) wide.
**£1,800–2,000**   *S(S)*

A saddle seat stool, c1860,
32in (81cm) high.
**£50–60**  *AL*

A late Georgian elm and ash
stool, 18in (46cm) wide.
**£75–100**  *OA*

A country stool, 19thC,
25in (64cm) high.
**£80–100**  *JAC*

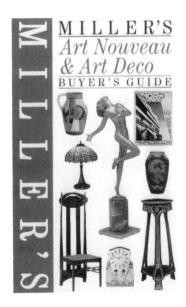

A milking stool, 1880,
12in (31cm) high.
**£35–50**  *AL*

An elm stool, c1880,
21in (53cm) high.
**£45–60**  *W*

A Victorian sycamore stool.
**£40–60**  *W*

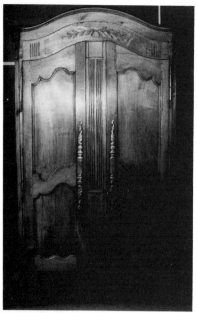

A Normandy cherrywood armoire, c1820, 52in (132cm) wide.
**£2,000–2,250**  *PEN*

A French provincial oak bonetière, with shell-carved crest over a double panelled door, on stile feet, 30in (76cm) wide.
**£1,000–1,500**  *MMG*

An oak armoire, 18thC.
**£1,600–1,800**  *CUL*

*r.* A French chestnut armoire, from Quimper in Brittany, c1790, 52in (132cm) wide.
**£1,750–1,900**  *GD*

*l.* A French oak armoire, 17thC.
**£3,000–5,000**  *AnD*

A carved oak armoire, Southern French or Spanish, the flared cornice above a pair of rounded carved panelled doors with foliate borders enclosing hanging space, below 4 carved apron panels, on stile feet, restored, early 18thC, 56½in (143cm) wide.
**£1,800–2,200**  *S(S)*

A chestnut armoire, 19thC, 48in (122cm) wide.
**£1,850–2,000**  *CUL*

An oak hanging press, with Gothic fielded panels, on bracket feet, c1760, 51in (129.5cm) wide.
**£1,500–2,500**  *POT*

A panel back lambing armchair, with shaped toprail, fielded panel back, outset wings with flat arms and enclosed sides, the sprung seat with panelled base, c1740.
**£2,000–3,000** *S*

A lambing chair, of primitive form, partly in elm, the panel seat with drawer beneath, 55in (140cm) high.
**£2,000–2,500** *L*

*r.* A George I oak lambing chair, with a rope seat, c1725.
**£1,600–2,200** *PHA*

A William IV oak and alder rocking lambing chair, c1830.
**£1,850–2,000** *PHA*

A rare elm dug-out chair, 18thC, 26in (66cm) wide.
**£6,000–6,500** *RYA*

An early Georgian elm lambing chair, with original paint.
**£7,000–7,500** *SWN*

A yew wood Windsor chair, 18thC.
**£900–1,200** *MMB*

A pair of yew wood Windsor elbow chairs, with bow backs and pierced splats, dished elm seats and crinoline stretchers joining the turned supports, early 19thC.
**£1,400–1,800** *L*

A set of 8 yew and elm Windsor high-back elbow chairs, with pierced splats, mid-19thC.
**£12,000–15,000** *N*

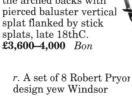

A walnut Windsor armchair, with an arched cresting rail and outscrolled arms with spindle supports, damaged arm, mid-18thC. **£1,000–1,500** *Bea*

A Georgian beech and elm Windsor chair, and a beech and elm Mendlesham chair, with curved arms above a solid seat on turned legs and stretchers, 19thC.
**£400–500 each** *CSK*

A yew and elm Windsor armchair, with pierced vase-shaped splat, early 19thC, 35in (87.5cm) high.
**£600–800** *TEN*

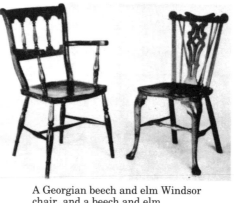

*l.* A set of 6 ash and elm Windsor chairs, including 2 armchairs, the arched backs with pierced baluster vertical splat flanked by stick splats, late 18thC.
**£3,600–4,000** *Bon*

*r.* A set of 8 Robert Pryor design yew Windsor armchairs, c1800.
**£6,000–8,000** *H*

A harlequin set of 8 yew wood Windsor armchairs, with decorative splats, early 19thC.
**£7,000–10,000** *H*

A set of 6 yew wood Windsor style chairs with crinoline stretchers pierced and stick backs.
**£6,000–7,000** *BA*

A yew-wood Windsor chair, c1800.
**£900–1,200** *MAT*

An elm Windsor armchair,
c1825. **£300–400** *LL*

A Windsor armchair, with
part yew-wood back, c1800,
35in (89cm) high.
**£400–600** *S*

A beech and elm Windsor
chair, c1840.
**£300–450** *LL*

An elm Windsor chair, c1850.
**£400–500** *LL*

An elm and ash Windsor chair,
with crinoline stretcher, c1850.
**£500–600** *DEB*

A yew-wood Windsor chair, c1800.
**£800–1,200** *MAT*

A set of 6 country elm and
ash Windsor chair, c1900.
**£400–600** *DEB*

An elm and and ash Windsor
chair, c1850.
**£400–600** *DEB*

A matched set of 8 low back yew Windsor armchairs, with standard splats, c1820. **£6,000–8,000** *H*

Two Victorian yew and elm Windsor armchairs, each with an arched pierced splat and spindled rail back, above outscrolled arms on bobbin-turned supports and solid saddle seat. **£1,000–1,500** *CSK*

An elm and ash Windsor elbow chair, with pierced wheel splat, turned supports with an H-stretcher. **£280–400** *CDC*

An ash and elm comb back Windsor chair, with a yoke-shaped crest rail, bowed arm rail with shaped front supports and turned legs, mid-18thC. **£300–500** *DWB*

Six yew, elm and beechwood Windsor armchairs, the bowed rail and pierced splat backs above saddle seats on ring-turned tapering legs, joined with crinoline cross stretchers. **£4,800–6,000** *CSK*

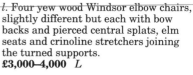

*l.* Four yew wood Windsor elbow chairs, slightly different but each with bow backs and pierced central splats, elm seats and crinoline stretchers joining the turned supports. **£3,000–4,000** *L*

A yew wood Windsor rocking chair, with an elm seat, c1790. **£1,200–1,500** *CDE*

A pair of yew wood Windsor armchairs, 18thC. **£1,200–1,400** *B*

A Windsor yew and elm armchair, the arched back with pierced splat and baluster supports, with moulded seat, on baluster legs, later rockers. **£1,200–1,500** *C*

A Windsor open armchair, with yew wood hoop back rails and arms, elm seat, on turned supports with crinoline hoop stretcher. **£900–1,200** *CDC*

*r.* A set of 6 Windsor armchairs, stamped 'F. Walker Rockley', early 19thC.
**£3,000–6,000** *CSK*

*Frederick Walker was born at Thornhill, near to Leeds, in 1798. In 1823 he was a member of the Gamston Methodist Society, and by 1828 he was a member of William Wheatland's class at Rockley. He became class leader himself in 1831, and remained so for at least 30 years. By 1851, he and his son, Henry, were the only remaining chair makers in the parish, where they were specifically called Windsor chair makers.*

*l.* A harlequin set of 7 George IV elm and yew wood Windsor armchairs, two stamped 'Wheatland Rockley'.
**£4,500–6,000** *CSK*

*William Wheatland is first recorded as a chair maker living and working at Beardsalls Row, East Retford, Notts, in 1822. In 1821 he was the Wesleyan leader in the small parish of Gamston which lies close to the hamlet of Rockley. By 1828 he is recorded as chair maker and Wesleyan Class leader in Rockley. By 1841 William Wheatland is no longer recorded as living in the parish.*

An elm Windsor armchair, mid-19thC.
**£200–300** *OMH*

A small elm rail back Windsor type armchair, c1850.
**£120–180** *OMH*

*Above left.* A low back yew wood Windsor armchair, with an elm seat, late 18thC.
**£400–500**
*Above right.* A low back Windsor armchair in elm and yew, early 19thC.
**£500–700** *MAX*

*r.* A set of 8 yew wood low back armchairs, late 18thC.
**£8,000–12,000** *H*

A set of 5 yew wood Windsor elbow chairs, with elm seats, early 19thC.
**£3,500–4,200** *GD*

A broad arm North Country elm Windsor chair, c1860.
**£800–1,000** *OMH*

*r.* A matched set of 8 ash and elm Windsor armchairs, with stick backs and solid seats.
**£2,500–3,200** *SS*

*l.* An ash and elm high back Windsor chair, c1830.
**£300–400** *KEY*

A harlequin set of 12 yew wood broad arm Windsor chairs.
**£8,500–9,500** *MGM*

A large yew and elm Windsor armchair, on ring-turned legs, c1830.
**£2,000–3,000** *C*

An ash and elm Windsor chair, early 19thC.
**£250–350** *OSc*

A set of 6 small Windsor chairs with saddle-shape elm seats and front cabriole legs with pad feet, late 18thC.
**£3,300–3,600** *L*

An ash and elm Windsor chair, with crinoline stretcher, 19thC, 19in (49.5cm) wide.
**£450–650** *PCA*

*r.* A broad arm yew wood Windsor chair, 19thC.
**£900–1,000** *TM*

*r.* A fruitwood and elm Windsor chair, 19thC, 15in (38cm) wide.
**£150–200** *PCA*

Two yew wood Windsor chairs, one with replaced crest rail, 19thC.
**£900–1,000** *DWB*

A set of 8 elm ladder back dining chairs, early 19thC.
**£3,000–4,000** *PWC*

*l.* A pair of elm Windsor wheel-back farmhouse elbow chairs, with H-stretchers.
**£600–700** *JD*

An ash, elm and fruitwood Windsor high-back chair, with 'Christmas tree' decorated splat, c1860.
£350–450 *OSc*

A scroll back Windsor chair.
£65–75 *AL*

A George III ash Windsor armchair, with a fruitwood cresting rail and sycamore seat, on turned legs.
£800–1,200 *S(S)*

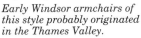

A mid-Georgian elm Windsor armchair, with waved toprail, railed back with pierced splat, cabriole legs and pad feet.
£1,500–2,000 *C*

*Early Windsor armchairs of this style probably originated in the Thames Valley.*

A pair of brace back Windsor side chairs, on baluster and ring turned legs joined by swelled stretchers, New England, late 18th/early 19thC.
£2,000–3,000 *CNY*

A simple rail back elm Windsor armchair, c1800.
£500–600 *OMH*

An elm, beech and yew framed Windsor armchair, 18thC, with later squab seat.
£600–900 *WHL*

Two comb-back Windsor elbow chairs, in ash and elm and some yew-wood, minor variations, 18thC.
£2,000–2,500 *L*

A Windsor sack-back armchair, on baluster and ring turned legs joined by turned stretchers, New England, 19thC.
£1,000–1,500 *CNY*

An ash Windsor armchair, early 19thC.
**£500–600**  *CSK*

A low back Windsor chair, with shaped seat and single bow back, c1780.
**£650–850**  *OSc*

A pair of yew and elm Windsor low back armchairs, the horseshoe arms with scroll terminals, the solid seats on turned legs joined by stretchers, late 18th/early 19thC.
**£2,500–3,000**  *Bea*

A set of 6 Windsor chairs, and 2 armchairs, c1840.
**£2,200–2,500**  *OSc*

Six ash and elm Windsor armchairs, with spindle filled hoop backs, horseshoe arms, solid seats and turned legs joined by stretchers.
**£2,500–3,000**  *Bea*

A yew wood Windsor chair, with crinoline stretcher and pierced splat, c1850.
**£750–850**  *OSc*

A set of 7 beech, fruitwood and elm Windsor scroll back chairs, one with arms, each with triple baluster spindles beneath an arcaded top rail, dished panel seat and turned underframe, repaired, stamped 'RW' on rear edge of seat, 19thC.
**£1,400–1,600**  *L*

*This style of chair was made by many of the High Wycombe chair manufacturers.*

A West Country Windsor armchair, c1800.
**£500–600**  *KEY*

A yew Windsor chair, early 19thC.
**£800–1,000**  *AS*

## Windsor Chairs

- unknown before 1720s
- basically Georgian tavern and coffee house chairs
- earliest examples have comb backs, plainly turned splayed legs, no stretchers
- cabriole legs suggest a date between 1740–70
- hooped back introduced c1740
- wheel splat introduced c1790
- Gothic Windsors, recognised by the carving of their spats and their pointed-arch backs, made between 1760–1800
- some better quality Windsors stained black or japanned black or green; these are more valuable in original condition - do not strip them
- most desirable wood is yew, followed by elm
- some mahogany Windsors were made for the gentry, and are always of good quality
- curved stretchers, carved and well proportioned backs add to value

A matched set of 6 Billinge Wigan ladder back chairs, plus 2 armchairs, c1800.
**£3,800–4,500** *H*

A fruitwood ladder back elbow rocking chair, with rush seat, on turned supports, 19thC.
**£300–400** *GD*

A set of George III elm ladder back chairs, on pad feet, c1790.
**£2,200–2,600** *SS*

A set of 7 oak framed ladder back dining chairs, late 19thC.
**£600–800** *PCh*

Eight ladder back dining chairs, with rush and string seats, 2 carvers and 6 singles, late 18thC.
**£3,800–4,800** *A*

*l.* A set of 6 George III oak and elm ladder back chairs, c1800.
**£1,000–1,500** *S(S)*

A set of four Macclesfield chairs.
**£2,000–2,500** *Bro*

A set of 6 Wigan ash and elm ladder back chairs, c1780. **£1,500–2,000** *P(EDH)*

A set of 6 plus two
Macclesfield ladder back
chairs, with distinctive
top rails.
**£3,500–4,000** *H*

An ash and elm ladder back
elbow chair, 18thC.
**£600–700** *CW*

A set of 6 elm and ash country
ladder back chairs, with
American influence, c1740.
**£1,800–2,200** *DEB*

An elm and ash country
ladder back chair, c1760.
**£150–175** *DEB*

A set of 8 George III ash, elm
and fruitwood ladder back
chairs, including a pair of
armchairs.
**£3,000–4,000** *Bon*

An 18thC ladder back chair.
**£150–200** *TJ*

A slat back maple armchair, with
ball and ring turned finials and flat
arms, above a rush seat, on cylinder-
and-ball turned legs joined by a
double turned stretcher, New York
or Connecticut, late 18thC.
**£2,200–2,700** *CNY*

An 18thC style ladder back
carver chair, with rush seat,
on turned legs and stretcher.
**£150–200** *DDM*

A George III oak ladder
back armchair, c1800.
**£300–400** *SS*

A harlequin set of 12 elm chairs, including 2 armchairs, with rush seats.
**£3,200–3,700** *CSK*

A set of 8 oak and ash spindle back chairs, including a pair of armchairs, with rush and woven seats, on turned legs joined by stretchers, on pad and ball feet, spindle splats partially lacking, seats differ, early 19thC.
**£1,500–2,000** *S(S)*

A set of 6 ash spindle back chairs, probably from Cheshire, each with a shell carved top rail and rush seat, on turned legs joined by stretchers, with pad feet, stamped 'C. Leicester', mid-19thC.
**£1,200–1,500** *S(S)*

*Charles Leicester is recorded as a chair maker with premises at 120–121 Chestergate, Macclesfield, Cheshire. He shared these premises with his son Charles, until they both moved to Derby Street c1855.*

An ash spindle back armchair, with a pierced splat back, and shaped seat, on turned supports with a hoop form stretcher.
**£400–600** *OL*

A matched set of 8 ash and birch spindle back chairs, including a pair of elbow chairs, with rush seats and turned tapering legs joined by stretchers, on pad and bun feet, seats re-rushed, Lancashire/Cheshire, c1900.
**£2,500–3,000** *S(S)*

A matched set of 8 ash spindle back dining chairs, on pad and ball feet, c1900.
**£2,800–3,800** *S*

A mixed set of 5 Lancashire spindle back dining chairs, including one elbow chair, 19thC.
**£800–1,200** *PC*

A matched set of 8 north country spindle back dining chairs, in fruitwood and ash, including one elbow chair, with rush seats, turned legs and stretchers, early 19thC.
**£2,300–2,800** *P(S)*

An elm armchair, reduced in height, with rockers added.
**£200–300** *CDE*

An elm smoker's bow chair, c1900.
**£300–400** *Ph*

A Victorian elm and yew-wood smoker's bow chair.
**£700–900** *JMW*

A desk chair, c1900. **£350–450** *Ph*

A set of 5 Irish beechwood penny seat and stick back chairs, c1890.
**£500–700** *UC*

A primitive oak and ash chair, 18thC.
**£1,000–1,200** *RYA*

A set of 4 country stick back chairs.
**£300–400** *MGM*

A set of 3 Hereford style kitchen chairs, late 19thC.
**£150–180** *TRU*

A set of 6 elm kitchen chairs, early 20thC.
**£200–250** *JMW*

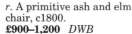

An Irish ash and elm famine chair, Co. Kerry, c1840, 21in (54cm) high.
**£350–450** *UC*

*r.* A primitive ash and elm chair, c1800.
**£900–1,200** *DWB*

An elm bobbin back
farmhouse armchair, c1840.
**£150–175** *OMH*

An elm slat back
cottage armchair,
c1880, 26in (65cm) wide.
**£70–85** *OMH*

A 'Busby's Stoop' rocking
chair, c1880.
**£200–250** *PIN*

A pair of Thonet beech
dining chairs, c1910.
**£50–65** *OMH*

A set of 6 wheelback chairs,
with cabriole legs and crinoline
stretchers, c1950.
**£250–300** *PIN*

A pair of Georgian yew-wood and
elm chairs.
**£2,500–3,000** *HWO*

A wheel back chair.
**£75–95** *AL*

A George III oak wing back armchair,
the panel back above a webbed seat and
an enclosed base with a lateral frieze
drawer, on stile feet, Lancashire/
Yorkshire Dales, late 18thC.
**£3,000–3,500** *S(S)*

An Irish fool's chair, 19in
(48cm) wide.
**£100–150** *PH*

A folding chair.
**£100–150** *AL*

A closely matched set of 8 Lancashire spindle back
chairs, with Chippendale ears, late 18thC.
**£4,000–5,000** *H*

A Welsh primitive oak and ash comb back armchair, with semi-circular seat and triple splayed legs.
**£700–900** *S(S)*

An ash and elm comb back corner chair, with a rush seat, 18thC.
**£800–900** *OS*

Two elm and fruitwood Mendlesham open armchairs, each with a spindle back inlaid with boxwood, one with vase-shaped splat, with solid seats on turned tapering legs joined by turned H-shaped stretchers, early 19thC.
**£1,200–1,700** *C*

A yew wood comb back elbow chair, on cabriole legs with crinoline stretcher, 18thC.
**£800–1,200** *JD*

A yew and elm low comb back armchair, on turned legs with a bowed stretcher, late 18thC.
**£1,000–1,200** *Bon*

A pair of Mendlesham chairs, the backs line-inlaid, with turned spindle and ball decoration, the solid elm seats on turned legs.
**£900–1,000** *NSF*

An ash and elm comb back chair, 41in (104cm) high.
**£800–1,000** *LA*

A Suffolk Mendlesham chair in cherrywood with an elm seat and boxwood stringing, c1820.
**£1,000–1,200** *OS*

*l.* An ash and elm comb back Windsor chair, 18thC.
**£400–600** *TM*

An elm Mendlesham chair.
**£300–400** *GT*

A kitchen chair.
£75–95  *AL*

A yew wood smoker's chair.
£600–850  *MAT*

A Victorian elm child's chair, from the village school at Preston, Kent, 24in (62cm) high.
£40–50  *PC*

A Tiverton chair, beech with elm seat, with contemporary tin repairs.
£200–250  *AL*

A pair of Victorian pine hall chairs, c1850.
£300–400  *AL*

An elm and beech kitchen chair.
£50–60  *WHA*

A lathe back chair.
£50–60  *AL*

A beechwood armchair, with a rush seat, 36in (92cm) high.
£200–250  *AL*

*l.* A set of 8 Victorian elm chairs, including 2 armchairs, on club legs joined with cross stretchers, and a set of 4 similar side chairs.
£3,800–4,200  *CSK*

*r.* A Scottish armchair, in ash and walnut, with burr wood veneered panel, one back support repaired, originally with a front stretcher, veneer later, c1680.
£700–900  *S*

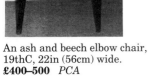

An ash and beech elbow chair, 19thC, 22in (56cm) wide.
£400–500  *PCA*

A set of 8 Wigan ladder back chairs, in original condition, late 18thC.
£3,800–4,800  *H*

A rocking chair, c1880, 24in (61cm) wide.
£300–400  *W*

An Irish famine chair, c1840.
**£250–300** *GPA*

A set of 4 smoker's chairs,
c1860, 26in (66cm) wide.
**£800–1,000** *W*

An armchair, with a new
rush seat, c1870.
**£200–280** *AL*

A pair of oak bobbin turned
elbow chairs, with vertical splats
and finials, the solid seats on a
similar turned underframe.
**£800–1,200** *P*

A beech corner chair, with a rush
seat, 27in (69cm) wide.
**£200–250** *AL*

An elm and beech
kitchen chair.
**£80–100** *WHA*

A pine and wicker Orkney
chair, 19thC.
**£175–200** *ARK*

An Arts & Crafts hall
chair, 24in (61cm) wide.
**£200–300** *W*

An elm country chair, c1760.
**£350–400** *PCL*

A Welsh primitive chair, with an oak
seat and sycamore spindles, c1800.
**£900–1,200** *OSc*

*r.* A set of 6 elm
farmhouse dining
chairs, c1820.
**£350–450** *OMH*

*r.* An elm,
ash and oak
Yorkshire
spindle-back
rocking
chair, 42in
(105cm) high.
**£250–300**
*SSD*

A set of 6 matched elm Windsor open arm elbow chairs, the saddle shaped seats on turned legs with stretchers.
**£3,400–3,800** *GC*

A pair of elm side chairs, with spindle backs and panel seats, on turned supports with stretchers.
**£600–800** *LRG*

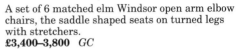

A pair of yew Windsor domino back chairs, 18thC.
**£1,000–1,200** *PCA*

A yew and elm Windsor armchair, with spindle filled hoop backs and horshoe arms, solid seats and on baluster turned legs joined by stretchers, stamped 'Hubbard', early 19thC.
**£1,000–1,500** *Bea*

An elm chair, with a new rush seat, c1820.
**£300–400** *AL*

A pair of yew and beechwood Windsor chairs, c1800. **£1,000–1,500** *S*

*r.* An Ash and elm Windsor rocking chair, c1830.
**£700—900** *KEY*

An open arm Windsor chair.
**£700–900** *AS*

A French fruitwood corner seat, with storage under seat, 1880s, 22in (56cm) wide.
**£340–380**  *GD*

An oak panel back armchair, the scroll cresting rail above lozenge carved splat, the solid seat with columnar turned legs joined by peripheral stretchers, Yorkshire, feet restored, mid-17thC.
**£2,000–2,500**  *S(S)*

A Victorian Gothic style chair.
**£500–600**  *WaH*

An English dug-out armchair, mid-18thC.
**£650–750**  *Ced*

An oak rocking chair, possibly Lancashire/Yorkshire, the foliate-carved cresting with the date '1748' flanked by later wings, the upholstered drop-in seat above a panelled base, on rocking supports, split to back, late 18thC.
**£1,200–1,500**  *S(S)*

An oak lambing chair, with upholstered winged back, scrolled arms, webbed seat, panelled base with side drawer and pierced brass handle, 18thC.
**£550–600**  *AH*

A Welsh primitive commode chair, c1780.
**£750–800**  *COM*

A French child's chair, with rush seat, c1900, 21in (53cm) high.
**£60–80**  *WaH*

A primitive comb backed Windsor armchair, with a lobster pot cresting above a thick ash seat, c1770.
**£1,200–1,500**  *RYA*

A Victorian smoker's bow chair, with beech back and elm seat, c1890.
**£130–150** *OPH*

An Irish súgán chair, replaced back rail, late 19thC.
**£50–70** *FOX*

*'Súgán' means twisted lengths of straw.*

A pair of matched Victorian smoker's bow chairs.
**£275–375** *POT*

An Irish ash and elm stick chair, original paint, early 19thC.
**£200–250** *AF*

A beech desk chair, c1890.
**£50–60** *AL*

An ash smokers bow chair, c1870.
**£150–200** *HON*

An Irish mixed wood famine chair, c1840.
**£175–275** *Byl*

A Bavarian oak chair, with exotic wood inlays of birds and deer, tapered legs.
**£150–200** *AF*

An Irish beech carver chair, with string seat, c1880.
**£75–125** *Byl*

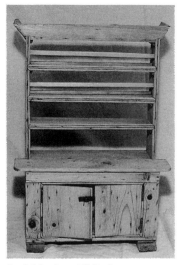

An Irish pine child's dresser,
c1870, 16½in (42cm) wide.
**£75–125** *Byl*

A mixed wood child's
chair, c1880.
**£60–75** *HON*

A pine single door children's
wardrobe, made from ceiling
boards, c1900, 36in
(91.5cm) wide.
**£285–325** *OCP*

A Continental pine rocking cradle,
c1890, 37in (94cm) long.
**£150–175** *ASP*

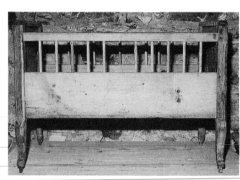

A European pine cradle, c1870,
38in (96.5cm) wide.
**£100–150** *AF*

*r.* A child's famine
chair, c1850, 21in
(53cm) high.
**£220–270** *OCP*

*l.* A child's pine cart,
early 20thC, 18in
(46cm) wide.
**£100–120** *WAC*

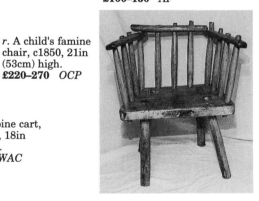

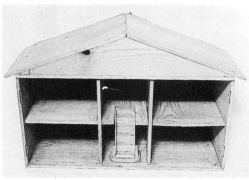

A Continental pine child's cot, c1860,
35½in (90cm) high.
**£150–250** *AF*

A pine doll's house, c1930, 26½in (67cm) wide.
**£60–70** *OPH*

A child's Windsor chair, with original green paint, c1800.
**£250–300** *KEY*

A Welsh elm child's chair, with a shaped top rail over a spindle back, raised on splay supports, mid-18thC, 14in (36cm) high.
**£700–800** *P(M)*

A child's oak chair, c1800, 29½in (75cm) high.
**£400–450** *PC*

A Welsh comb back child's Windsor armchair, 18thC.
**£1,200–1,400** *RYA*

A Victorian Orkney oak framed child's chair, the enclosed curved back in bound rush, with open flat scroll arms and woven sea-grass seat.
**£600–800** *GA(W)*

*This chair is reputed to be made of oak from St Magnus Cathedral.*

A George III mahogany child's chair, and a stand.
**£450–650** *PC*

A yew and elm Windsor elbow chair, with crinoline stretcher.
**£700–900** *BHW*

An elm and ash child's school chair, c1880.
**£250–350** *DEB*

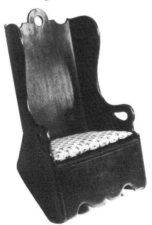

A mahogany child's rocking chair, c1770. 23½in (60cm) high.
**£1,200–1,800** *PC*

A primitive child's chair, with original red paint, 19thC, 18in (45.5cm) high.
**£250–300** *PCA*

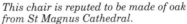

A child's Windsor chair, c1875.
**£100–150**  *PIN*

An oak cradle, Dutch or German,
17thC, 38½in (98cm) wide.
**£1,500–2,000**  *C*

A child's yew wood and elm
Windsor armchair, with an
arched stick back and
turned splayed legs joined
by crinoline stretchers,
early 19thC.
**£1,000–1,500**  *S(S)*

*l.* A child's walnut armchair
with humped cresting rail,
solid vase form splat,
shaped arms and elm seat
on outsplayed turned legs
with baluster turned
stretchers, damaged, 18thC.
**£350–450**  *NSF*

*r.* A child's school chair,
c1920, 24in (62cm) high.
**£30–50**  *AL*

A spice rack,
possibly a child's
dresser, with black
porcelain handles,
28in (71cm) high.
**£200–300**  *AL*

A Victorian baby walker, 18in
(46cm) high.
**£150–200**  *PH*

A Welsh turned stool, in
sycamore, 11in (29cm) high.
**£100–150**  *IW*

A child's trolley, late 17thC, 20in
(51cm) wide.  **£600–700**  *PH*

A child's chair,
30½in (78cm) high.
**£30–50**  *AL*

A primitive Welsh
chair, c1780.
**£1,000–1,500**  *CCA*

A pine cot, with porcelain handles, 41in (104cm) long.
**£145–175** *CHA*

A pitch pine child's washstand, c1880, 21½in (55cm) wide.
**£250–300** *MCA*

A child's elm chair, mid-18thC, 12in (30.5cm) wide.
**£500–650** *RYA*

An early pine rocking cradle, c1830, 39in (99cm) long.
**£250–300** *AL*

A pine doll's cradle, c1850, 18½in (47cm) long.
**£100–150** *AL*

A Welsh oak child's rocking armchair, 18thC, 22in (56cm) high.
**£200–300** *SC*

A pine high chair which converts to a play table, with porcelain beads, 38in (96.5cm) high.
**£95–100** *LAM*

A pine cot/cradle, c1850, 34in (86cm) long.
**£300–350** *AL*

## Children's Furniture

The children's furniture illustrated in this guide no longer complies with EC safety regulations, and must not be used for its original purpose.

*r.* A pine high chair, c1850, 40in (101.5cm) high.
**£120–175** *AL*

*l.* A child's beech high chair, with new cane seat.
**£45–55** *AL*

A beech high chair, which converts to a play pen, c1920.
**£150–200** *AL*

A simulated bamboo pine cot, 28in (71cm) wide.
**£250–300** *PH*

A pine child's chair, c1920, 19in (49cm) high.
**£30–50** *AL*

# EARLY PAINTED FURNITURE

A late 17th century oak chest of drawers with original bun feet made £24,200 at auction. Without one addition to it, the price would have been nearer £1,500. Why? Because it was decorated with paint! This may seem surprising, but the chest, not decorated until the early 19th century, is one of the many items of early painted furniture that is now attracting a great deal of interest. Although the species itself is not well documented, recent research is turning up many interesting facts about both materials and methods used for this particular type of decoration.

Domestic and ecclesiastical British furniture has been decorated with paint and coloured pigment since medieval times and following the flamboyant Gothic period, the painting style of furniture and domestic wooden objects changed. It fell into three categories: monochrome, polychrome (geometric or floral) and simulation.

Monochrome, the most common form of decoration, was simply a coat or two of single-coloured paint usually applied as protection against weather and general household wear and tear. Used on uncarved softwood, its decorative merits lie within the colour chosen, and the effect that years of wear and tear, patina and fading has had on its surface. An early 19th century Irish monochrome painted pine dresser, fetched £1,500 on the merit of its attractive colour combination, and retained paint surface on the backboards and shelves. This is not an uncommon feature on dressers, corner cupboards and delft racks and one which may add considerably to their value.

Polychrome decoration is most prized on painted furniture as it demands more artistic ability and epitomizes the soul of 'folk art'. A simple child's moneybox, late 18th century, made and painted to imitate a Georgian house, fetched £500. Seventeenth and early 18th century British free-hand painting is extremely rare and highly prized on furniture, but a certain amount of 'leopard spotted', 'striped' or 'chequerboard' decorated early furniture does come on the market, initialed and occasionally dated. The rarity of these pieces always ensures a healthy price, as was the case with the aforementioned bun-footed chest of drawers.

The simulated finish covers items made from ordinary oak or pine, which is then painted to imitate a finer or more exotic timber (often walnut or imaginary burrwood). A mid-17th century English oak joint stool, a rare example of imitation walnut, fetched £2,000. This scumble-type decoration – achieved by drawing a comb, hard brush or feather through a wet dark glaze laid over a lighter coloured ground – became popular in the 18th century and common in the 19th century.

As fashions and tastes changed, much of the early painted furniture was redecorated to cover the cracks, chips and decoration of years gone by, and later added paint serves to protect the original from further damage. To remove these later layers, it is imperative that skilful and careful restoration of the furniture takes place as harm is easily done. Non-original layers of paint added later, should be carefully scraped off with a scalpel or chisel to avoid damage to the original. Known as dry scraping, this slow but worthwhile process leaves a powdery, slightly rough finish, returning the item close to its original condition, complete with blemishes and chips. Only in very exceptional circumstances should chemical paint removers, solvents or hot air guns be used as they seriously damage the original surface.

Dry scraped furniture is the most desirable and easily identifiable. To avoid pitfalls such as claims that later paint has been 'washed off', which usually means that much or all of the 'old' paint has been 'washed on', follow a few guidelines. When examining an 'antique' or 'original' paint surface, look out for any 'original' paint found in worm holes, or worm tracking, on or towards the bottom of feet, on repairs or patches, replaced hinges, and be wary of a paint surface without a ground. Bear in mind that brush strokes shouldn't be visible after 100 years and that a bubbled surface is easily achieved with a blowlamp! A black or coloured wax finish also indicates there may be something to hide.

Evidence of age is proudly displayed in original or dry scraped pieces – faded sun-bleached colours (especially blues, salmon pinks and turquoise greens), paint worn through to wood, built-up patina around handles, and bleached-out areas around polished handles, are all to be cherished. Look too for natural blistering, stains, water damage, and wear around feet.

Many pieces of country furniture were already 50 to 100 years old when painted, so naturally, the question of originality occurs, even though a good piece of such furniture is now worth more than its equivalent in oak. It seems that the painted furniture market has now established its own rules in this respect. If the paint has not been touched up or otherwise enhanced, or if the paint is antique but not necessarily contemporary with the item, it may be considered acceptable. But bear in mind that 17th century furniture with original paint is very rare.

The furniture is simply a vehicle for the paint, which was not applied to deceive or copy, but merely to decorate and brighten up the home. This is British folk art, produced by ordinary unskilled people, but to be considered valuable and desirable, it must have character, colour, originality of design – basically the 'look'. This 'look' can lift a piece of painted furniture from the ordinary and everyday, to a much prized and valuable level.

Robert Young

A carved and painted pine schrank, with deep carved double moulded cornice above a panelled case with shelved interior and 2 drawers in base, Pennsylvania, c1770, 69in (175cm) wide.
**£21,000–23,000**  *S(NY)*

A Hungarian painted pine coffer, c1850, 43in (109cm) wide.
**£675–725**  *UC*

A Hungarian painted pine dower chest, with original finish, c1850, 46in (116.5cm) wide.
**£675–725**  *UC*

A painted pine base, with 3 drawers and one door, c1880, 38in (96.5cm) wide.
**£635–665**  *AL*

An Irish painted pine open rack farmhouse dresser, with original finish, c1850, 55in (139.5cm) wide.
**£2,000–2,200**  *UC*

A Bohemian painted pine armoire, with canted corners, original finish, c1820, 48in (122cm) wide.
**£2,250–2,500**  *UC*

An Irish painted pine two-part hutch dresser, with original finish, c1860, 50in (127cm) wide.
**£1,925–1,975**  *UC*

An Irish painted pine fiddle front farmhouse dresser, original paint worn, c1850, 51in (129.5cm) wide.
**£2,000–2,300**  *UC*

A painted pine chest of drawers, original finish, fitted with glass knobs, c1870, 41in (104cm) wide.
**£535–565**  *AL*

A Romanian painted pine bed, with original finish,
c1880, 39in (99cm) wide.
**£450–500** *UC*

A painted pine coffer, with original
painted finish, on bracket feet, 18thC,
42in (106.5cm) wide.
**£300–400** *SWN*

A Danish painted iron bound
pine seaman's chest, c1850, lined
with newspaper dated '1893',
53in (134.5cm) wide.
**£750–900** *UC*

A painted pine chest of drawers, with
upstand, 2 short and 2 long drawers,
c1840, 42in (106.5cm) wide.
**£540–560** *AL*

A painted chest of drawers, with
2 small and 2 long drawers,
c1880, 36in (91.5cm) wide.
**£400–425** *AL*

A European painted pine cupboard,
with elaborate floral design, 1806,
50in (127cm) wide.
**£800–1,200** *AnD*

A painted pine dresser, with
3 drawers, from southern England,
c1750, 42in (106.5cm) wide.
**£3,500–4,000** *SWN*

A painted pine stool, c1920,
13in (33cm) high.
**£35–45** *Ber*

A painted pine chest, from southern
Germany, c1860, 48in (122cm) wide.
**£275–375** *AnD*

A Russian pine dresser,
with original paint, c1840,
30in (76cm) wide.
**£300–350** *AnD*

A painted pine marriage chest, decorated with
a tulip design, 18thC, 49in (124.5cm).
**£600–700** *SWN*

A painted pine toy cupboard, with
turned baluster columns, late 18thC,
31in (78.5cm) wide.
**£400–450** *SPa*

A Victorian painted pine
washstand, 30in (76cm) wide.
**£140–180** *FOX*

A child's painted latrine,
c1880, 25in (63.5cm) high.
**£65–75** *Ber*

A painted pine corner cupboard,
the door with 4 panels, and a
dentil cornice, mid-18thC, 29in
(74cm) wide.
**£400–500** *SWN*

*r.* A painted pine corner
cupboard, with original finish,
19thC, 25in (63.5cm) wide.
**£340–385** *FOX*

A painted pine food cupboard,
mid-18thC, 33in (83.5cm) wide.
**£500–600** *SWN*

A painted pine stool, with lifting
lid, 19thC, 16in (41cm) wide.
**£80–100** *SWN*

A pine candle stand, with a stool
base, the top painted, c1760, 16in
(41cm) wide.
**£850–1,000** *RYA*

A hanging meat safe, with original paint and iron hooks, c1840, 52in (137cm) high.
**£300–400** *COT*

A five drawer hanging spice cabinet, with original paint, c1880, 18in (46cm) high.
**£125–150** *COT*

A West Country pine box settle, painted to simulate oak, 36in (91.5cm) wide.
**£1,000–1,500** *SWN*

A late Georgian spoon rack, with a salt box and spice drawers, with original grained finish, c1810, 18in (46cm) wide.
**£250–300** *COT*

An early Victorian astragal glazed corner cabinet, with original grained paint, c1840, 30in (76.5cm) wide.
**£350–400** *COT*

A set of 3 North Country spindle backed chairs, with original paint, c1800, 18in (45.5cm) wide.
**£650–750** *RYA*

A vinegar grained box, inscribed 'George Winchester - 12 years old - His Box', c1880, 11in (28cm) wide.
**£30–40** *WaH*

A painted pine country shelf, c1920, 49½in (125cm) wide.
**£135–155** *Ber*

A pine 'Tri-ang Stores' toy shop, with original paint, 24in (61cm) wide.
**£100–125** *COT*

A Victorian set of spice drawers, with porcelain knobs, c1880, 24in (61cm) high.
**£50–75** *COT*

A painted chest of drawers, with 2 short and 2 long drawers, damaged, c1830, 35½in (91cm) wide.
**£400–500** *WaH*

A painted pine chest of drawers, c1925, 35½in (90cm) wide.
**£150–175** *BEL*

An Edwardian pine sewing box, with swag decoration, on cabriole legs, with original paint finish, c1900, 24in (61cm) wide.
**£150–200** *COT*

A Victorian dressing chest, painted to simulate burr walnut, c1860, 38in (96.5cm) wide.
**£300–400** *COT*

A Victorian pine painted dressing chest, c1880, 40in (101.5cm) wide.
**£350–450** *COT*

A Regency pine washstand, with gallery back, original paint finish, c1830, 38in (96.5cm) wide.
**£500–650** *COT*

A Georgian pine butler's cupboard, grain painted, blue painted interior, 2 brushing slides, mother-of-pearl roundels on ebony handles, c1800.
**£1,250–1,500** *COT*

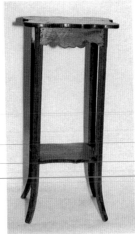

A pine plant stand, with painted legs, c1840, 32in (81cm) high.
**£80–95** *Cou*

A grained pine cooking box, complete with tins, c1860.
**£100–150** *COT*

A Georgian three-drawer dresser base, with original powder-blue paint, c1800, 69in (175cm) wide.
**£650–800** *COT*

A mid-Victorian grain-painted child's play crib, 20in (50.5cm) long.
**£100–150** *COT*

A painted pine wardrobe, c1770,
71in (180cm) wide.
**£1,500–1,700** *BEL*

An Austrian painted cupboard,
c1830, base moulding replaced,
36in (91.5cm) wide.
**£2,450–2,850** *RYA*

A Georgian corner
cupboard, with arched
doors, with original
grained paint, c1780,
39in (99cm) wide.
**£1,250–1,500** *COT*

One half of an Austrian corner bench, 18thC,
repainted in 1905, 74in (188cm) wide.
**£700–900** *COT*

An early Victorian grain-painted
chest of 3 drawers, with a gallery
back, c1830, 28in (71cm) wide.
**£400–500** *COT*

A dresser base, with 3 drawers above 2 panelled doors,
60in (152cm) wide, and an architectural delft rack,
with 3 shelves and fluted column ends, some original
blue paint, c1780.
**£3,800–4,800** *RYA*

An early Georgian pine lace or campaign
chest, the hinged lid enclosing a small well,
above 2 drawers with original handles, with
original finish, c1740, 24in (61cm) wide.
**£500–650** *COT*

An Orkney shepherd's chair,
made from recycled timber,
traces of old paint, c1840, 21½in
(54cm) wide, with a cushion.
**£800–900** *RYA*

A West Country painted pine
dresser, with glazed cupboard
doors above, c1770.
**£10,500–12,500** *RYA*

An Austrian painted
cupboard, c1830, base
moulding replaced, 36in
(91.5cm) wide.
**£2,000–2,250** *RYA*

A painted floor standing
corner cupboard, with a
carved mask, c1730.
**£3,500–4,000** *RYA*

An Austrian painted bed, initialled
and dated '1796'.
**£2,500–3,500** *RYA*

An armoire, painted to simulate
marble, with floral decoration,
the central cartouche with
initials 'IK' and dated '1793',
56in (142cm) wide.
**£1,000–1,200** *RYA*

A Victorian pine chest of
2 short and 3 long drawers, with
later paint, 35in (89cm) wide.
**£200–250** *FOX*

A hand painted pine armoire,
decorated with folk art depicting
horsemen, dated '1836', 48in
(122cm) wide.
**£3,500–4,500** *RYA*

An American rocking chair,
the back panel painted with
fruit decoration, c1830.
**£400–500** *JBL*

A Georgian glazed wall cabinet, with original grained paint, c1780. **£300–400** *COT*

A Victorian pine grain-painted chest of 5 drawers, c1880, 40in (101.5cm) wide. **£350–450** *COT*

A painted pine chest of 4 long drawers, c1870, 37in (95cm) wide. **£250–275** *BEL*

An Irish carved bed settle, with original paint finish, c1820, 78in (198cm) wide. **£1,450–1,650** *UC*

A painted pine trunk, inscribed inside 'James Ferguson - Sea Cook - Cutty Sark - Presented by E. R. Ferguson for the benefit of the Prince of Wales' Boys', 23½in (60cm) wide. **£300–400** *WaH*

A Georgian pine clerk's table, with original varnish, c1780, 38in (96.5cm) wide.
**£200–300** *COT*

A painted pine wall cupboard, 19thC, 18in (45.5cm) high.
**£75–85** *Cou*

A late Georgian elm child's chair, c1820, 16in (40.5cm) wide.
**£100–125** *COT*

A painted pine wardrobe, with one door, c1900, 41½in (105cm) wide.
**£240–260** *BEL*

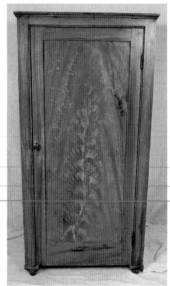

A grained pine cupboard, c1860, 30in (76cm) wide.
**£300–350** *COT*

A painted pine wardrobe, with 2 doors, c1840, 59in (150cm) wide.
**£450–485** *BEL*

A painted pine coffer, c1890, 38½in (97cm) wide.
**£250–300** *MCA*

A Victorian pine grain-painted blanket box, with 2 drawers inside, and a candle box, c1850, 48in (122cm) wide.
**£200–250** *COT*

A Queen Anne painted pine dresser, in original condition, 60in (150cm) wide.
**£8,000–9,000** *AP*

A Continental painted pine cupboard, mid-18thC, 29in (73cm) wide.
**£1,500–1,700** *AP*

A French painted pine food cupboard, mid-18thC, 30½in (76cm) wide.
**£1,500–1,700** *AP*

An East Anglian painted pine chest, in original condition, 18thC, 25in (63cm) wide.
**£900–1,000** *AP*

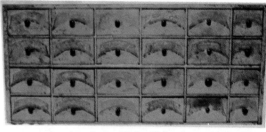

A painted pine flight of drawers, c1830, 44½in (112cm) wide.
**£900–1,000** *AP*

*r.* A pine rack, for storing wooden spoons, c1850, 12in (30cm) wide.
**£250–300** *AP*

*l.* A French painted pine hanging cupboard, containing a collection of children's plates, 18thC, 31in (78cm) wide.
**£2,250–2,750** *AP*

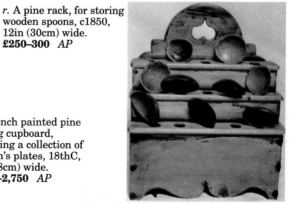

*r.* A pine box, decorated with paper, c1740, 16in (40cm) wide.
**£400–500** *AP*

A miniature fruitwood spoon rack, with shaped cresting, containing bone spoons, c1760, 15in (38cm) high.
**£600–750** *RYA*

A Scandinavian food box, 19thC.
**£150–175** *SWN*

A Welsh stepped spoon rack, with a collection of old cawl spoons, paintwork original, early 19thC, 11in (28cm) high.
**£700–750** *RYA*

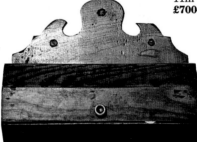

A hexagonal elm salt box, with shaped cresting, c1800, 11½in (29.5cm) wide.
**£250–300** *RYA*

A wooden bucket, with a metal handle, c1900, 12in (30.5cm) high.
**£40–50** *FOX*

A Northumbrian beehive riddle board, c1760, 16½in (42cm) wide.
**£200–250** *RYA*

A Scandinavian food box, 19thC.
**£125–150** *SWN*

A pine cutlery tray, 12in (30.5cm) long.
**£20–30** *FOX*

A pine cheeseboard, 19thC, 25in (63.5cm) long.
**£25–30** *AnD*

An eastern European wooden trough, 19thC, 31in (78.5cm) long.
**£65–70** *AnD*

Two wooden pine mashers, 1870s,
10in (25cm) high.
**£30–40 each** *CEMB*

A peck measure, 12in (31cm) diam.
**£65–70** *MIL*

A housemaid's pine box,
c1890, 14in (35.5cm) wide.
**£60–70** *MIL*

A pair of elm bellows,
c1880, 21in
(53cm) long.
**£50–55** *MIL*

A potato basket, 25in (54cm) wide.
**£60–80** *MIL*

A French grape basket, 19in (48cm) long.
**£35–40** *MIL*

A Victorian wooden rolling pin,
16in (41cm) long.
**£4–8** *TaB*

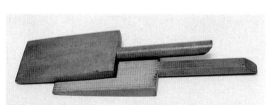

Two small wooden butter pats, 8in (20cm) long.
**£8–10** *TaB*

A French wooden coffee grinder, c1920–30,
6½in (16cm) high.
**£20–25** *CEMB*

A Romanian butter maker,
c1870, 28in (71cm) high.
**£70–80**  *OPH*

A terracotta dairy pail, the inside
glazed, with a wicker handle,
15in (38.5cm) high.
**£30–40**  *TaB*

An eastern European pine stand, with
a pine tray, stand 28in (71cm) high.
**£100–125**  *NWE*

A small Victorian range,
26in (66cm) wide.
**£250–300**  *WaH*

An enamel cereal bin, c1920,
14in (35.5cm) high.
**£15–20**  *OPH*

A French cheese press, c1920,
17in (43.5cm) high.
**£55–65**  *OPH*

An enamel washing boiler, c1920,
11in (28cm) high.
**£50–60**  *OPH*

Two wicker baskets, largest 27in (69cm) long.
**£15–18 each**  *NWE*

Two copper saucepans, with lids, c1860, largest 9in (22.5cm) diam.
**£100–120 each** *MIL*

A set of 3 tin and brass measures, largest 10in (25cm) high.
**£50–60** *MIL*

A milk can, with brass handle, stamped with the name of the dairy, early 1900s, 7½in (19cm) high.
**£60–70** *TaB*

A blue enamel Universal Ham Cooker, 15in (38cm) high.
**£25–30** *TaB*

A tin and brass pint bottling measure, 9in (22.5cm) high.
**£30–35** *MIL*

A tin cream bowl, with handles on each side, c1880, 20in (50.5cm) diam.
**£30–35** *MIL*

A metal cream skimmer, 8in (20cm) diam.
**£12–15** *TaB*

Four tin and brass cream cans, one gill to 2 pints, largest 4½in (11.5cm) high.
**£300–320** *MIL*

An iron skillet, with spout, c1850, 14in (35.5cm) diam.
**£40–45** *MIL*

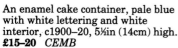

Two German galvanized wash boards, c1920, largest 22in (56cm) wide.
**£6–10 each** *NWE*

An enamel cake container, pale blue with white lettering and white interior, c1900–20, 5⅓in (14cm) high.
**£15–20** *CEMB*

A metal cream can, with a brass screw stopper, 5in (13cm) high.
**£75–85** *MIL*

A pewter pillar ice-cream mould, c1868, 6⅓in (16cm) high.
**£150–200** *CEMB*

A metal egg whisk, with original pottery basin, c1930s, 10⅓in (26.5cm) high.
**£20–22** *TaB*

*l.* A copper fish kettle, c1860, 20in (51cm) wide.
**£220–240** *MIL*

A set of Salter household scales, with a cast-iron body with tin pan, c1930, 10⅓in (27cm) high.
**£20–25** *CEMB*

A metal cream can, 9in (23cm) high.
**£75–85** *MIL*

A tin and brass 2 gallon milk can, 13in (33cm) high.
**£75–85** *MIL*

An Eastern European pine blanket box, with candle box, lock and key missing, 22in (56cm) wide.
**£200–300**  *HGN*

A small pine estate desk, with internal drawers, c1800, 23in (59cm) wide.
**£425–475**  *PEN*

A pine stool, c1870, 38in (96.5cm) long.
**£100–125**  *PEN*

A painted pine occasional table, 17½in (44.5cm) wide.
**£300–375**  *PEN*

A pine cricket table, with painted base, original paint, c1840, 28½in (71cm) diam.
**£250–325**  *PEN*

A French pine folding table, c1850, 35in (89cm) diam.
**£200–300**  *PEN*

*l.* A Regency glazed pine hanging cupboard, c1810, 31in (79cm) wide.
**£450–500**  *PEN*

A Regency painted pine simulated rosewood occasional table, 18in (45.5cm) wide.
**£350–400**  *PEN*

A Georgian pine sideboard,
38in (96.5cm) wide.
**£450–500** *PEN*

A Welsh sycamore painted
stool, original paint, 13½in
(34cm) high.
**£30–40** *PEN*

A green painted stool, c1850,
15in (38cm) wide.
**£30–40** *PEN*

A set of painted pine
library steps, c1840,
27in (69cm) high.
**£200–220** *PEN*

A painted simulated bamboo chest of
drawers, original paint, c1880, 42½in
(107cm) wide.
**£500–570** *PEN*

A northern French
chestnut armoire, with
terracotta wash, c1785,
51in (129.5cm) wide.
**£1,300–1,600** *PEN*

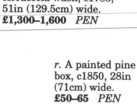

*r.* A painted pine
box, c1850, 28in
(71cm) wide.
**£50–65** *PEN*

*r.* A painted pine
cupboard, with
shelves, 36in
(91.5cm) wide.
**£500–595** *PEN*

*l.* A Scandinavian painted
pine cupboard, with
single door, dated '1804',
47in (119cm) wide.
**£800–900** *GD*

A Scandinavian painted beech
spinning wheel, c1860, 37in
(94cm) high.
**£170–190** *RK*

A German painted and decorated
pine marriage bedstead, the
shaped headboard painted with a
lady and a gentleman standing in
a landscape, with floral and leaf
motifs in polychrome, and an
inscription 'Johann and Maria
Katharina' and the date '1824',
with turned footposts, the tester
panel overhead painted with
bucolic landscapes within
medallions in polychrome, 50½in
(128cm) wide.
**£3,000–3,500** *S(NY)*

A child's black painted
Windsor armchair, with
shaped fan-back above
7 spindles and flat-shaped
set back arms over a
saddle seat, on splayed
baluster turned legs
jointed by a bulbous turned
H-stretcher, 19thC.
**£600–800** *CNY*

A pine chest of drawers, with
simulated bamboo decoration,
40in (101cm) wide.
**£800–1,000** *PH*

A Victorian painted pine
box/chest, with original
decoration, 37in (94cm) wide.
**£150–200** *AL*

A German painted pine box,
c1850s, 24½in (62cm) wide.
**£150–200** *WHA*

A painted pine marble topped
washstand, with original
paintwork and handles,
c1860, 36in (92cm) wide.
**£350–400** *AL*

An original painted pine washstand,
c1870, 36½in (93cm) high.
**£200–250** *AL*

A painted pine box, with original lock and key,
dated '1868', 44in (111.5cm) wide.
**£425–475** *CHA*

A painted pine wedding chest, possibly
Scandinavian, 30in (76cm) wide.
**£400–500** *PH*

A Scandinavian painted pine coffer, original paint, dated '1808', 46in (116.5cm) wide.
**£420–480** *GD*

A Scandinavian original painted pine coffer, 18thC, 50in (127cm) wide.
**£420–480** *GD*

*l.* A paint decorated poplar blanket box, New Jersey, painted black with red amber mottling and amber faux marble veining, minor imperfections, early 19thC, 32in (81cm) wide.
**£450–550** *SK(B)*

A French buffet, with block fronted doors, re-painted, 1870s, 51in (129.5cm) wide.
**£580–650** *GD*

A red painted high post bedstead, Texas, with shaped headboard with scalloped crest above a row of spindles, the footposts similarly chamfered, on square tapering legs, mid-19thC, 52½in (133cm) wide.
**£2,700–3,000** *CNY*

A joined panelled and painted chest, Boston or Coastal Massachusetts, the pine top above an oak six-board chest with fielded side pine panels, and a single drawer, the painted panels and drawer outlined with black applied mouldings, c1800, 42in (106.5cm) wide.
**£1,500–2,000** *SK(B)*

A painted blanket box, New England, with applied mouldings, original red paint, 18thC, 43in (109cm) wide.
**£550–650** *SK(B)*

*l.* A pine chest, New England, with applied half-round moulding, lidded till and early stained brown surface, early 19thC, 44½in (112cm) wide.
**£1,500–2,000** *SK(B)*

A Bavarian pine coffer, with panelled top and boarded sides, with iron carrying handles, the plinth base with name and date '1793', 18thC, 58in (147cm) wide.
**£1,000–1,500** *S(S)*

A Victorian original painted
pine bookcase, Cumbrian,
c1850, 83in (210.5cm) high.
**£1,200–1,500** *BH*

A bowfront chest of drawers,
painted in blue, c1820, 41½in
(105cm) high.
**£800–1,000** *RP*

A blue painted kitchen chest of
drawers, with brass knobs, late
19thC, 61in (155cm) wide.
**£500–600** *PCh*

r. A painted pine chest of drawers,
c1830, 36½in (92cm) high.
**£500–600** *RP*

A painted pine linen chest,
c1830, 43in (109cm) wide.
**£1,400–2,000** *RP*

A painted pine chest of drawers,
c1840, 42in (106.5cm) wide.
**£500–600** *RP*

An original painted pine chest of drawers,
c1850, 41in (104cm) wide.
**£600–700** *AP*

A painted pine chest of drawers, 40in (101.5cm) wide.
**£600–700** *AL*

An oak and pine jointed chest with drawer, Massachusetts, old finish, c1700, 43in (109cm) wide.
**£2,800–3,500** *SK(B)*

An American carved and painted pine blanket chest, Berks Country, Pennsylvania, dated '1788', the moulded hinged top opening to a deep well with till, two drawers below, 18thC.
**£21,000–24,000** *B*

A jointed oak and pine carved chest over drawers, Connecticut Valley, probably Hadley area, the centre panel with initials 'S.K.' above two drawers, old refinish, c1700, 41in (104cm) wide.
**£13,500–14,000** *SK(B)*

*r.* A Continental painted oak chest, with 2 panelled doors painted with flowering plants flanking florally painted central panel above scalloped apron and block feet painted with trees, possibly Austrian, 54in (137cm) wide.
**£2,600–3,000** *LHA*

A child's paint decorated pine blanket chest, signed 'Jonathan Maitz', Pennsylvania, dated '1871', 27in (69cm) wide.
**£9,000–12,000** *S(NY)*

A fan-back Windsor side chair, New England, old black paint, c1780.
**£1,500–1,800** *SK(B)*

A George III oak and painted comb-back armchair, with solid seat and splayed legs, late 18thC.
**£1,300–1,500** *S(S)*

*r.* A fan-back Windsor armchair, New England, old black paint imperfections, c1780.
**£950–1,200** *SK(B)*

*l.* A sack-back Windsor armchair, New England, painted black, c1780.
**£1,200–1,500** *SK(B)*

A Windsor armchair, probably Rhode Island, old black paint, c1780.
**£1,200–1,500** *SK(B)*

A pine corner cupboard, with painted dome, c1760, 50in (127cm) wide.
**£4,000–5,000** *PH*

A Federal pine corner cupboard, with blue painted interior, plate grooves, scallop surround, reeded lower section with hinged door opening to a shelf, American, early 19thC, edges of shelves scalloped at later date, 52in (132cm) wide.
**£4,000–5,000** *S(NY)*

An Austrian painted armoire, c1807, 73in (185cm) high.
**£6,000–7,000** *CHA*

A painted pine bowfronted corner cupboard, with panelled doors, original paint, 19thC, 46in (118cm) wide.
**£1,000–1,250** *BEL*

*l.* A Swedish painted pine marriage chest, 18thC, 43in (109cm) wide.
**£500–600** *DN*

A painted pine armoire, with domed top, 48in (122cm) wide.
**£400–500** *LAM*

A Napoleon III pine and simulated bamboo tall chest, with 6 drawers, c1860, 28in (71cm) wide.
**£800–900** *S(S)*

A German original painted pine box, c1854, 45in (114cm) wide.
**£750–800** *CHA*

A chest of drawers, recently painted floral theme, no handles or knobs, 1860–80.
**£240–270** *PIN*

A Scandinavian painted pine secrétaire, with fitted interior, c1845, 36in (93cm) wide.
**£950–1,200** *BEL*

A pair of French cream painted pine console tables, with cloven hoof feet tied by a curved stretcher surmounted by a figure of a putto playing a harp, originally gilt, 18thC, 36in (92cm) wide.
**£2,500–3,000** *HSS*

A Belgian painted armoire, c1820, 72in (182.5cm) high.
**£1,000–1,500** *UP*

A Scandinavian pine bench, painted with flowers on a brown and green ground, 19thC, 51in (130cm) wide.
**£900–1,000** *DN*

A glazed painted pine hanging cupboard, c1840, 42in (106.5cm) wide.
**£250–300** *KEY*

A French pine and faux bamboo (beechwood turned to look like bamboo) escritoire, 39in (99cm) wide.
**£350–450** *MCA*

A German painted pine cobbler's cupboard, 27in (68.5cm) wide.
**£150–200** *CHA*

A German painted pine armoire, c1840, 55in (139.5cm) wide.
**£550–600** *BEL*

A painted and decorated chest of drawers, the top with a ship within a painted oval reserve above 2 short drawers over 3 long drawers, on compressed ball feet, the entire surface painted brown and embellished with yellow highlights, the drawer fronts inscribed '1871/The Liberty/800 Tons/Falmouth', 39in (99cm) wide.
**£850–1,000** *CNY*

A Galway painted housekeeper's 18/19thC.
**£2,500–3,000** *B*

A Victorian chiffonier, with original stain, 36in (91.5cm) wide.
**£270–300** *CCP*

A Romanian pine presser, original finish, c1850s, 37½in (95cm) wide,
**£500–600** *OPH*

A Victorian table, with original finish, c1860, 27in (69cm) wide.
**£350–400** *COT*

A red painted pine cupboard, Texas, the rectangular projecting cornice above a pair of recessed panelled cupboard doors opening to an interior fitted with 3 shelves over a scalloped apron, on square tapering legs, mid-19thC, 50in (127cm) wide.
**£1,600–1,800** *CNY*

An American empire painted slant front desk, the fall front opening to reveal a fitted interior, the base with single drawer, on turned legs, lid inscribed 'The Flower and the Fern', c1840.
**£380–420** *MMG*

*r.* A Queen Anne brown painted yellow pine architectural cupboard, Virginia, one side unfinished, late 18thC, 31in (79cm) wide.
**£2,800–3,200** *S(NY)*

*l.* An American painted pine architectural corner cupboard, with moulded fluted cornice above a pair of arched glazed mullioned hinged doors opening to a painted shelved interior, two hinged panelled doors below opening to a shelf, c1780, 55in (139.5cm) wide.
**£1,800–2,200** *S(NY)*

A painted pine low dresser, c1700, 60in (152cm) wide.
**£2,000–2,500** *OSc*

A painted ship's box, c1880, paint restored, 17in (43cm) wide.
**£100–150** *MCA*

A pair of painted chairs, 17in (43cm) wide.
**£500–600** *PH*

A painted sycamore cupboard, East German or Polish border, c1818, 24in (61cm) wide.
**£500–700** *CHA*

A painted pine corner cupboard, with original glazing, 46in (116.5cm) wide.
**£2,000–2,500** *PH*

A painted pine dressing table, 18thC, 42in (106.5cm) wide.
**£800–1,000** *AP*

A late Victorian painted chest, with graduated drawers and compartment, and a painting of birds on top, 15in (38cm) wide.
**£200–250** *W*

A Scandinavian painted pine chest of drawers, 37in (94cm) wide.
**£350–375** *BEL*

A painted arched top dresser, 19thC, 98in (249cm) wide.
**£2,000–2,500** *RK*

A Scandinavian painted pine chest of drawers, recently painted, c1890, 38in (96.5cm) wide.
**£375–400** *BEL*

*l.* A German painted pine chest, 19½in (49cm) wide.
**£275–325** *CHA*

A Victorian grey painted pine bookcase, in the Gothic taste, the upper section with a moulded cornice, the base with panelled cupboard doors, on a plinth, slightly reduced in length, late 19thC.
**£30,000–35,000** *Bon*

A Queen Anne painted table, New England, with original blue-green paint, early turned pull handle, minor repairs, 18thC, 43in (109cm) wide.
**£10,000–11,000** *SK(B)*

*r.* A Victorian table, with single drawer, original colour wash, c1860, 40in (101.5cm) wide.
**£300–400** *COT*

An early Victorian lyre-ended side table, with 2 frieze drawers, gallery back, original painted decoration, c1840, 44in (111.5cm) wide .
**£400–500** *COT*

A painted pine 8-day clock, c1848.
**£850–950** *BEL*

A late Federal painted washstand, New England, with splashback, painted yellow and embellished with black highlights and trailing fruit vines, c1810, 28in (71cm) wide.
**£850–950** *CNY*

A pair of green and tan-painted headboards, each with ring turned baluster toprail flanked by turned finials, the waved board painted with foliate arabesques, on ring turned tapering legs, lacking side rails 47in (119cm) wide.
**£550–650** *C*

A painted pine pot cabinet, with gallery back, c1870, 32in (81cm) high.
**£140–160** *ASP*

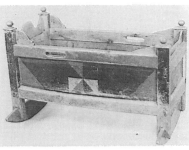

A wood cradle, painted in red, yellow and black with geometric patterns, 19thC, 33in (84cm) wide.
**£220–280** *EL*

*l.* A doll's house front, early 19thC, 28in (71cm) high.
**£300–400** *SWN*

A painted Windsor cradle, New England, retains old brown paint over blue-green, some damage, c1810, 38in (96.5cm) long.
**£1,600–2,000** *SK(B)*

*r.* A pine cot, hand painted using buttermilk paints, c1920, 30in (76cm) wide.
**£100–125** *POT*

*l.* A Georgian mule chest, with original paint, on bracket feet, moulding on top replaced, c1820, 39½in (100cm) wide.
**£200–300** *POT*

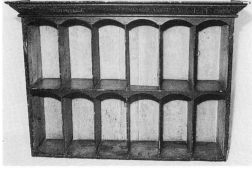

A hanging shelf unit, with numerous arches and original paint, c1830, 51½in (130cm) wide.
**£275–325** *POT*

A pine box, with original paint, with unusual hinge, c1820, 31in (79cm) wide.
**£150–185** *POT*

A painted pine hanging corner cupboard, with fielded panels, c1750, 31½in (80cm) wide.
**£450–550** *POT*

A French painted ash farmhouse ladderback chair, with rush seat.
**£100–150** *AF*

A George III pine dresser, the associated raised back with moulded cornice above a painted frieze and open shelves, the base with 3 central drawers flanked by a pair of fielded panel cupboard doors, on stile feet, cornice partially lacking, 63in (160cm) wide.
**£2,000–2,500** *S(S)*

An Austrian painted pine cupboard, with one bottom drawer, original lock and key, c1770, 78in (198cm) high.
**£2,000–3,000** *AF*

*r.* A Bohemian pine box, with original paint, dated '1771', 45½in (115cm) wide.
**£500–600** *AF*

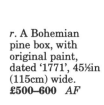

*r*. A European pine box, original paint, 38in (96.5cm) wide.
**£250–300** *AF*

A Georgian Dutch style box, painted in Pennsylvania, with original hinges and candle slide inside, on bracket feet, 48in (122cm) wide.
**£600–700** *AF*

An eastern European painted pine box, dated '1889', 58in (147cm) wide.
**£200–300** *OCP*

An Austrian painted pine mule chest, with carved owl corbels, 2 false drawers and one bottom drawer, 47in (119cm) wide.
**£700–800** *AF*

*r*. A European pine mule chest, with single drawer, original paint, 44in (111.5cm) wide.
**£450–500** *AF*

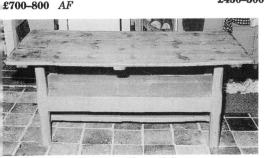

An Irish painted settle table, 18thC, 65½in (166cm) long.
**£600–700** *AF*

A Georgian painted pine corner cupboard, with carved cornice, astragel glazed door, with bracket feet, original paint, c1800, 78in (198cm) high.
**£800–900** *AF*

A Georgian Irish pine alcove cupboard, repainted, c1780, 84in (213cm) high.
**£750–850** *AF*

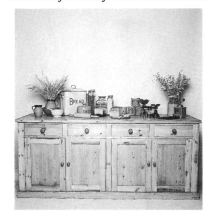

An Irish pine country chair, original paint, 34in (86cm) high.
**£55–75** *AF*

A painted pine captain's chair, c1890.
**£110–140** *DFA*

A captain's chair, c1890.
**£110–140** *DFA*

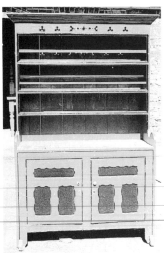

An Irish painted pine dresser, Co. Galway, c1860, 50½in (128cm) wide.
**£600–750** *DFA*

A painted pine davenport, c1860, 22in (56cm) wide.
**£650–700** *DFA*

An Irish painted pine dresser, c1860, 49in (124.5cm) wide.
**£600–700** *DFA*

*l.* A painted pine desk, on tapered legs, c1880, 48in (122cm) wide.
**£300–350** *DFA*

A painted pine drop-leaf table, c1880, 48in (122cm) long.
**£120–140** *DFA*

A late Georgian Irish painted pine food cupboard, c1820, 48in (122cm) wide.
**£600–700** *DFA*

An original painted dressing table, with drawer and cupboard, mirror and towel rail, turned legs, c1860, 37in (94cm) wide.
**£300–360** *DMc*

A painted pine dresser, c1880, 51in (129.5cm) wide.
**£450–550** *DFA*

A painted pine food cupboard, with panelled sides, on bracket feet, c1800, 55in (139.5cm) wide.
**£550–600** *DFA*

A pine dressing chest and chest of drawers, each with 3 deep drawers, glass handles, original paint, c1860, 41in (104cm) wide.
**£1,000–1,400** *AL*

A painted pine box, with original blue paint, c1880, 18½in (47cm) wide.
**£75–85** *AL*

A painted pine trunk, original paint, c1880, 29in (74cm) wide.
**£150–200** *AL*

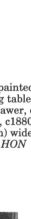

*l.* An Irish painted pine writing table, with one drawer, on turned legs, c1880, 47in (119cm) wide.
**£100–150** *HON*

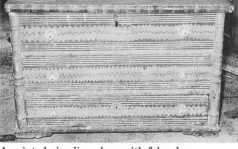

A painted pine linen box, with false drawers, c1875, 45in (114cm) wide.
**£100–120** *DFA*

An Irish painted pine cottage dresser, with fretwork top and panelled doors, c1870, 47in (119cm) wide.
**£600–800** *HON*

An Irish painted pine chiffonier, the carved back with original mirror, 2 drawers and 2 cupboard doors to base, c1880, 46in (116.5cm) wide.
**£200–250** *HON*

An Irish painted pine dresser, with 2 drawers and open base, c1860, 58in (147cm) wide.
**£250–300** *SA*

An Austrian painted pine box, 29in (74cm) wide.
**£200–300** *Byl*

An Austrian painted pine box, with candle box inside, c1870, 42in (106.5cm) wide.
**£300–500** *Byl*

An Austrian painted pine blanket box, original paint, with candle box, c1870, 48in (122cm) wide.
**£300–500** *Byl*

An Austrian painted pine box, c1850, 43in (109cm) wide.
**£300–500** *Byl*

A Georgian carved and stained pine cradle, c1750, 22in (56cm) wide.
**£400–500** *SA*

*r*. An Irish painted pine dresser, with 2 drawers and 2 cupboard doors to base, c1880, 56in (142cm) wide.
**£250–300** *SA*

# Old Court Pine

### *(Alain & Alicia Chawner)*

Old Court • Collon • Co. Louth • S. Ireland

Tel: 041-26270

Fax: 041-26455

International Code: 00-353-41

Irish Dower Chest C1860    Glazed Book case C1880    Cottage Sideboard C1890

Original Cut Open Top Dresser C1880    Armoire C1890    Bed Press C1880    North Antrim Cupboard C1840

Coffee Table C1885    Gallery Back Washstand    Pot board Farmhouse Table C1860

## Up to 1000 pieces of Irish Country Pine at wholesale prices

50 minutes from Dublin Airport -
we can meet you.
Packing and containerisation on the premises.
Fax or ring us in advance.

# KITCHENWARE

The kitchen has been the centre of domestic life for generations of women. While traditional kitchen furniture, such as dressers and tables, have long been desirable pieces, until recently the wide range of kitchen utensils and equipment used has largely been overlooked as a collecting area. The enormous success of the auction of Elizabeth David's Kitchen in London in 1993 played a major part in raising the status of kitchenware, reflecting its established popularity with many collectors and introducing it to a wider audience. In the full glare of the media, cooks and kitchenware enthusiasts from around the world gathered at Phillips auction house for the chance to buy an item from the kitchenware collection of Elizabeth David, one of the century's most important cookery writers.

Elizabeth David's interest in kitchenware is easy to understand as it is a fascinating and diverse field, appealing to a wide range of interests and pockets. Remarkably, it is still possible to find some early pieces of kitchenware from the 18th to the mid-19th century. These pieces offer a fascinating glimpse into pre-industrial society and range from high-quality tea caddies made by craftsmen to simple homemade griddles and herb and spice choppers. Beautiful copper moulds in a wealth of different shapes and sizes were produced from the 1830s onwards and were originally used in the kitchens of wealthy homes. Particularly popular with collectors today, they generally command the highest prices of all kitchenware.

Fortunately, collecting this field can also be easily affordable. The past decade has seen an explosion in popularity of items produced from the 1880s to the 1950s, arguably the most interesting period in the development of kitchenware. The 19th century saw the introduction of many designs that were to remain unchanged until today, such as the balloon whisk and the pastry crimper. In the 20th century, mass production led to the development of kitchenware as a huge international industry, with British makers such as Tala and Nutbrown leading the field.

Although many designs have not altered since the 19th century, different materials have come in and out of fashion. For instance, cast iron was commonly used for pots and pans, along with steel and vitreous enamel. By the early 20th century, aluminium, a lighter and more versatile material, was favoured, especially in North America. From the 1920s onwards, stainless steel became the most popular metal for making cutlery.

Collectors today have an enormous range from which to choose. Favourite subjects include storage jars, wooden spoons and pie funnels, while other popular items are whisks, pudding basins, waffle makers and rolling pins. Some collectors prefer to concentrate on a specific type of material, such as wirework or enamel. Wirework has recently come back into fashion and items must always be examined carefully to make sure they are not modern reproductions. Early pieces will be of far higher quality and the wire will be twisted rather than soldered.

Whatever you choose to collect, most of these implements and utensils are still easy to find today, often for only a few pounds, and much enjoyment can be had from tracking them down in car boot sales, auctions, specialist kitchenware shops, markets or even junk shops. Prices reflect the diversity of these sources and vary according to geographical location, the availability of particular items and the overheads of the dealer. However, one of the joys of kitchenware is that owning a collection of pie funnels which would cost tens of pounds can be as enjoyable as having a set of enamelled storage jars which would set you back over £100.

Perhaps the best and most inexpensive source of kitchenware is direct from your mother or grandmother, who can explain first-hand how a particular item was used in her kitchen. However, as kitchenware has grown in popularity, items that at one time were readily available are now not appearing on the market, with families keeping what would once have been discarded. At the same time, collectors are becoming more discerning and appreciate the craftsmanship and quality of older kitchenware items.

Finally, make the most of your kitchenware by, where possible, using an item for its original purpose. Remember though that older items will need more looking after than new ones, so take extra care with washing and drying up, and always store kitchenware safely in a dry place to prevent rust damage.

Christina Bishop

A rub-a-tub, 16½in
(42cm) diam.
**£30–35** *AL*

A wooden trough, 18in (46cm) wide.
**£15–20**
A meat cleaver.
**£10–15**
A wooden butterpat.
**£5–10** *LAM*

A meat tenderiser.
**£10–15** *AL*

*l.* A pair of scales, for
weighing babies, 15in
(38cm) high.
**£40–50** *AL*

An enamel candlestick.
**£10–12** *AL*

A thatcher's wrought iron needle, 19thC.
**£30–35** *PCA*

A chemist's ball, 21in (53cm) high.
**£600–630** *JeB*

A metal bound oak tub,
19thC, 14in (36cm) high.
**£80–100** *PCA*

An oak costrel, with glass ends,
19thC, 10½in (26cm) high.
**£80–100** *PCA*

*r.* A lacemaker's lamp, with
hollow baluster stem and
plain moulded foot, c1880,
10½in (27cm) high.
**£100–150** *P*

An oak silk thrower, 18thC,
25½in (64cm) long.
**£80–100** *PCA*

A Victorian butcher's scales table, with brass plaque marked 'Chayney & Co, Ramsgate', 36in (91.5cm) wide.
**£350–400** *WaH*

A selection of cutlery trays, c1900, largest 14in (36cm) long
**£15–20 each** *ASP*

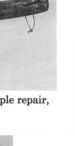

*r.* A pine butter churn, c1870, 17in (43cm) high.
**£55–75** *ASP*

An early Georgian corn ladle, old staple repair, c1740, 15in (38cm) long.
**£60–80** *COT*

A pine trug, c1870, 31in (79cm) long
**£35–45** *ASP*

An oak butcher's block, 30in (76cm) wide.
**£200–225** *PEN*

A pine hanging rack, c1880, 21in (53cm) wide
**£65–75** *ASP*

A pine plate rack, c1870, 29in (74cm) wide.
**£110–130** *DFA*

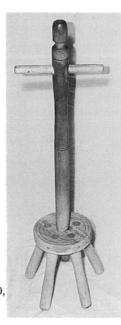

*r.* A wash dolly, c1880, 36in (91.5cm) high.
**£30–40** *DFA*

A beech and maple butcher's block on 19thC pitch pine stand, 24in (62cm) wide.
**£100–250** *HNG*

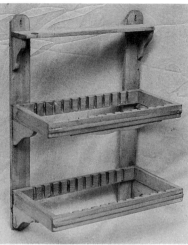

A pine dish rack, c1880, 24in (61cm) high.
£35–45 *ASP*

A pine knife box, c1830, 40in (101.5cm) high.
£40–50 *DMe*

An elm chopping block, c1820, 30in (76cm) wide.
£190–220 *GD*

An Irish pine separator, for extracting the buttermilk from butter, c1870, 39in (99cm) long.
£150–200 *HON*

A willow banded bucket, c1900, 13in (33cm) diam.
£100–110 *WAC*

A pine trug, 36in (91.5cm) wide, on a modern wrought iron stand, 32½in (82cm) high.
£125–150 *ASP*

An Irish pine open wall rack, with drawer, c1870, 39in (99cm) high.
£125–150 *ASP*

A Continental pine apple barrel, c1880.
£90–110 *ASP*

## Locate the source

*The source of each illustration in* Miller's Pine & Country Buyer's Guide *can easily be found by checking the code letters at the end of each caption with the Key to Illustrations located at the front of the book.*

A pine plate rack, c1840, 36in (91.5cm) wide.
£250–300 *DFA*

A wooden wall egg rack,
15in (38cm) high.
**£30–35**
Two china eggs.
**£3–5 each** *AL*

A wooden bread slicer.
**£60–80** *LAM*

An Edwardian
marmalade slicer.
**£25–45** *LAM*

An egg rack.
**£20–25** *LAM*

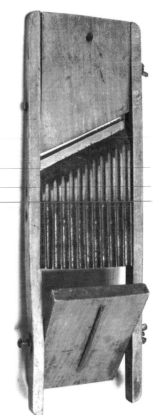

*l.* A wooden
draining spoon.
**£7–10** *LAM*

A Spong miniature knife
sharpener and cleaner.
**£30–50** *LAM*

A grater/slicer.
**£25–30** *LAM*

*l.* A pine
sleeve board.
**£12–15** *LAM*

*l.* A pine plate rack.
**£70–80** *LAM*

*r.* A wooden rolling pin.
**£15–20** *LAM*

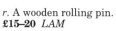

A pine spice rack,
28in (71cm) wide.
**£150–250** *LAM*

A miniature chest of spice
drawers, c1890, 18in
(46cm) high.
**£250–300** *AL*

A pine lead-lined double trough,
46in (116.5cm) wide.
**£400–500** *PH*

An oak spice cupboard, with
rosewood inlay, c1690, 12in
(31cm) square.
**£450–500** *OSc*

A pine dough bin, 19thC,
34in (86cm) wide.
**£450–600** *FF*

A pine spice cabinet, with oak
drawers, 18thC, 16in
(41cm) wide.
**£200–250** *AL*

A pine box, 14½in (36.5cm) wide.
**£100–140** *AL*

A fitted pine wine cellaret,
c1850, 20in (51cm) wide.
**£200–250** *AL*

A dough bin, 19thC,
32in (81cm) wide.
**£75–100** *WHA*

A pine specimen chest,
15in (38cm) wide.
**£100–150** *AL*

A pine salt box, carved 'Home
Sweet Home' on box, and
'W. J. Bothwell', 18in (46cm)
high. **£80–100** *AL*

A pine cutlery box, c1850,
7½in (19cm) wide.
**£45–50** *W*

A pine butcher's block, c1880,
72in (182.5cm) wide.
**£500–600** *UP*

A pine plate rack,
22in (56cm) wide.
**£175–200** *LAM*

A pair of glass candlesticks, early 20thC, 7½in (19cm) high. **£15–20** *AL*

A green glass bottle, late 19thC, 18in (47cm) high. **£20–25** *AL*

A Victorian picnic set, 19thC, 8in (20cm) wide. **£150–200** *AL*

A glazed multi-brown jug, chipped, late 19thC, 12in (31cm) high. **£7–8** *AL*

An Alexandra Inhaler, glass tube missing, 19thC, 5in (13cm) high. **£35–45** *AL*

Three pottery Virol jars, late 19thC, largest 5in (13cm) high. **£10–15 each** *AL*

A Brown and Polson's Blanc-Mange mould, late 19thC, 5in (13cm) diam. **£35–45** *AL*

*l.* A brown pottery drainer, 19thC. **£30–40** *AL*

Two pottery jugs, early 20thC, 8in (20cm) high. **£15–20 each** *AL*

Various jugs, 20thC. **£15–20 each** *AL*

Two pestles and mortars, late 19thC. **£30–40 each** *AL*

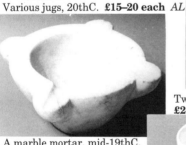

A marble mortar, mid-19thC, 5½in (14cm) wide. **£60–80** *AL*

Two pieces of Cornishware, early 20thC. **£20–30 each** *AL*

A brown transfer-printed pottery jug, mid-19thC, 8in (20cm) high. **£30–40** *AL*

A white pottery shaving mug, late 19thC, 4in (10cm) wide. **£15–20** *AL*

*l.* A white pottery jug, late 19thC. **£16–20** *AL*

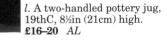

*l.* A two-handled pottery jug, 19thC, 8½in (21cm) high. **£16–20** *AL*

An Irish plate rail dresser, c1800, 61in (155cm) wide.
**£900–1,100** *UP*

A large dough bin, with a scrubbed top used for a work surface, c1820, 34in (86cm) wide.
**£450–600** *AL*

An Irish cheese press, with 4 doors and 2 drawers, c1850, 78in (198cm) high.
**£650–700** *LC*

A pine meat safe, c1890, 24in (61cm) wide.
**£80–100** *SPA*

An elm dough bin, with 2 compartments, slight woodworm, c1800, 43in (109cm) wide.
**£600–800** *OB*

A pine plate rack, with drain hole in bottom, c1840, 36in (90cm) wide.
**£200–250** *AL*

An elm dough bin, on a stand, late 18thC.
**£700–900** *Max*

A primitive oak chopping block, 19thC.
**£150–200** *ARK*

r. A pine bread rack, 28in (71cm) wide.
**£200–300** *W*

A butcher's block with shelf, c1850, 48in (122cm) long.
**£450–550** *AL*

A Victorian egg basket, 6½in (16cm) high. **£30–40** *AL*

A stone hot water bottle, now filled with sand for use as a door stop, 12in (30.5cm) long. **£20–30** *AL*

A spot pattern jug, by T. G. Green & Co., 4in (10cm) high. **£12–15** *AL*

Two enamel scoops, largest 4½in (11.5cm) long. **£6–10 each** *AL*

A spot pattern plate, by T. G. Green & Co., 7in (18cm) diam. **£8–11** *AL*

A clothes dryer, 32in (81cm) high. **£40–50** *AL*

Two Cornish Kitchenware oval cups and saucers, by T. G. Green & Co. **£12–14 each** *AL*

An Easimix bowl, with platform for easy mixing. **£14–17** *AL*

A selection of Cornish Kitchenware, by T. G. Green & Co., marked 'Sultanas' and 'Flour', 5in (12.5cm) high, 'Sugar' 4in (10cm) high. **£20–30 each** *AL*

A bee collection box, and comb, 18in (46cm) wide. **£50–70** *AL*

*r.* Two wooden flour barrels, largest 10in (25.5cm) high. **£60–80 each** *AL*

Three milk cans, tin with brass rim, 8 to 3in (20.5 to 7.5cm) high. **£25–40 each** *AL*

A garden fork, trowel and hoe.
**£10–12 each** *AL*

An onion hoe, 14in (35cm) long.
**£12–15** *AL*

A bag hook, 12in (30cm) long.
**£6–10** *AL*

A metal chocolate mould, 5½ by
3in (14 by 7cm).
**£25–35** *AL*

A metal chocolate mould, 8
by 2½in (20 by 6cm).
**£20–30** *AL*

A metal folding milk bottle crate.
**£30–40** *AL*

A wooden coffee mill,
7in (17.5cm) high.
**£14–16** *AL*

A wooden leaf dish, 15in (37.5 cm) wide.
**£20–30** *AL*

A metal cutter, 3in (7.5cm)
diam. **£10–15** *AL*

A wooden cutter,
14½in (36cm) long.
**£15–20** *AL*

A wooden spoon,
12in (30cm) long. **£1–2** *AL*

A metal hook, 10in (25cm) long.
**£15–20** *AL*

An orange/lemon squeezer,
4½in(11cm) diam.
**£10–15** *AL*

A wooden plane,
7½in (19cm) long. **£6–7** *AL*

A brass letter box, 8½in (21cm) long.
**£20–30** *AL*

*l.* A wooden roller, 8in (20cm) long.
**£8–12** *AL*

A selection of chopping blades.
**£12–20 each** *AL*

A wrought iron revolving grill, early 19thC.
**£150–200** *PCA*

An oak candle box, 18thC, 17½in (44cm) high.
**£80–90** *PCA*

A rhubarb forcer, 28in (71cm) high.
**£70–100** *WRe*

A set of ceramic feet, for standing a dresser on stone floors.
**£40–60** *AL*

A selection of Mauchline ware napkin rings, with transfer picture of the Isle of Wight and Beachy Head.
**£10–25 each** *DEL*

A bell-shaped tin chocolate mould, 5½in (14cm) high.
**£25–30** *AL*

*r.* A Macintosh's 'Golden Pats' tin, 16in (40.5cm) high.
**£30–40** *AL*

A copper saucepan, stamped 'H. E. Cars'.
**£30–40** *ONS*

Three toffee hammers:
*top:* Sharps, 4in (10cm) long.
**£8–10**
*centre:* Blue Bird, 4in (10cm) long.
**£8–10**
*bottom:* with bone handle, 5in (12.5cm) long.
**£15–20** *AL*

A selection of tin scoops, 5½ to 12in (14 to 30.5cm) long.
**£12–15 each** *AL*

A pair of brass and iron fire dogs, 19thC, 7in (18cm) wide.
**£45–50** *AL*

A selection of tin scoops, 19thC.
**£12–15** *AL*

Two plated brass ice cream scoops, early 20thC.
**£16–25 each** *AL*

A pair of brass candlesticks, mid-19thC, 10in (25cm) high.
**£60–80** *AL*

An iron foot last, 19thC.
**£10–12** *AL*

A pine and glass egg timer, 7in (18cm) high, 19thC.
**£20–30** *AL*

A selection of knives, late 19thC.
*from top to bottom:*
A butter knife, 8in (20cm) long. **£12–15**
A bread knife, 16in (40.5cm) long. **£16–20**
A bread knife, 15in (38cm) long. **£16–20**
A bread knife, with ivory handle, 15in (38cm) long. **£20–25** *AL*

A wire waste paper basket, 23in (59cm) high.
**£12–15** *AL*

*r.* An oak and iron bound pump action butter churn, c1880.
**£200–250** *CGC*

A wicker basket, early 20thC, 18in (46cm) wide
**£10–12** *AL*

A Cadbury's tin display stand, early 20thC, 13in (33cm) wide.
**£30–40** *AL*

A pine tub, early 20thC, 16in (41cm) high.
**£15–20** *AL*

A wire egg basket, 19thC, 14in (36cm) high.
**£20–25** *AL*

A housemaid's tin black and red painted box, 19thC, 12in (31cm) high. **£40–45** *AL*

A wire cake stand, 14in (36cm) wide.
**£10–15** *AL*

A brass and iron fire-guard, early 20thC, 19in (48cm) wide.
**£45–65** *AL*

A Sussex trug, early 20thC, 21in (53cm). **£25–35** *AL*

A wicker basket, early 20thC, 14in (36cm) wide. **£12–16** *AL*

A wicker basket, early 20thC, 16in (41cm). **£12–16** *AL*

A wood and hair sieve, 19thC, 8in (20cm) diam. **£15–20** *AL*

A pine flour barrel, 19thC, 7in (18cm) high. **£40–50** *AL*

Three wood and wire garden sieves, late 19thC, largest 22in (56cm) diam. **£12–15 each** *AL*

A basket shopping trolley, c1920. **£25–35** *AL*

Three elm grain measures, early 20thC. **£25–35 each** *AL*

*l.* A pine York County Hospital money box, 19thC, 9in (22.5cm) wide. **£25–30** *AL*

*r.* An elm and pine flax crusher, c1850, 34in (86cm). **£65–70** *AL*

A mahogany knife box, mid-19thC, 18½in (59cm) wide. **£30–50** *AL*

A pine shoe cleaning box, 19thC, 12in (31cm) wide. **£11–13** *AL*

A pine knife box, 19thC, 14in (36cm) wide. **£25–35** *AL*

A pine letter rack, 19thC, 14in (36cm). **£30–40** *AL*

A pine knife box, 19thC, 13in (33cm) wide. **£20–35** *AL*

A sycamore bowl, early 19thC, 13in (33cm) diam. **£70–80** *AL*

Two small wooden rakes. **£15–20 each** *AL*

A sycamore bowl, 14½in (37cm) diam. **£70–80** *AL*

A pine duck board, with copper nails, 19thC, 26in (66cm) long. **£20–25** *AL*

*r.* A wooden bath rack, early 20thC, 27in (69cm). **£20–30** *AL*

A sycamore bowl, early 19thC, 18½in (47cm) diam. **£90–120** *AL*

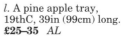

*l.* A pine apple tray, 19thC, 39in (99cm) long. **£25–35** *AL*

A brown and pale green crock, mid 19thC, 11in (28cm) wide. **£20–30** *AL*

A brown crock, glazed inside and outside, mid-19thC, 12in (31cm) diam. **£35–60** *AL*

A crock, mid-19thC, 10in (25cm) high. **£20–30** *AL*

A bread crock, 10in (25cm) high. **£50–60** *AL*

A Zero Cool butter cooler, early 20thC, 11in (28cm) long. **£10–15** *AL*

Two brown pottery jelly moulds, 19thC, 4in (10cm) diam. **£20–25 each** *AL*

A glazed jug and basin, early 20thC, 17in (43cm) diam. **£35–38** *AL*

A brown and cream pottery casserole, 8in (20cm) diam. **£10–15** *AL*

A crock, mid-19thC, 14in (36cm) high. **£40–50** *AL*

A set of iron balance scales and weights, late 19thC, 16 and 22in (41 and 56cm). **£75–100** *AL*

A candle lamp, mid-19thC, 10in (25cm) high. **£10–11** *AL*

A hurricane lamp, early 20thC, 16in (41cm) high. **£10–15** *AL*

A set of platform scales, by W. & T. Avery, for butter and cheese, with brass weights. **£180–220** *BHW*

A set of miller's beam scales, fully restored and painted, complete with weights. **£550–750** *CGC/FRM*

A Kenrick brass and iron coffee mill, 19thC, 6in (15cm) diam. **£60–80** *AL*

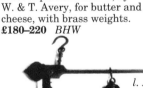

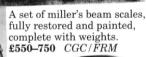

*l.* An iron steelyard, mid-19thC, 20in (51cm) wide. **£25–30** *AL*

An iron kettle, 19thC, 13in (33cm) wide. **£40–50** *AL*

A brass kettle on stand, 19thC, 13in (33cm) wide. **£60–65** *AL*

*l.* Brass spring scales, early 20thC, 17in (43cm) long. **£20–30** *AL*

*l.* A brass blow lamp, early 20thC, 12in (31cm) long. **£11–13** *AL*

*l.* A tin coffee pot, 19thC, 8in (20cm) high. **£20–30** *AL*

Two Victorian copper jelly moulds.
**£12–15 each** *AL*

*l.* A pair of sugar nips, late 19thC.
**£15–20**
*c.* A saltglaze jelly mould, early 19thC.
**£25–35**
*r.* A white jelly mould. **£30–40** *LAC*

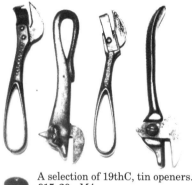

A selection of 19thC, tin openers.
**£15–20** *MA*

A pair of butter stamps,
2in (5cm) and 3in (8cm) long.
**£40–70 each** *AL*

A Victorian nutmeg grater, with
compartment for spare nutmeg
in the handle, 7½in (19cm) long.
**£35–45** *AL*

A selection of brass pastry
jiggers, 19thC.
**£25–35** *MA*

A Peugeot wooden coffee grinder,
19thC. **£30–40** *MA*

Three treen pastry/butter rolling
moulds, 18thC.
**£40–70 each** *Bon*

An Edwardian cheese press,
12in (31cm) high.
**£70–100** *AL*

A Victorian egg basket,
10in (25cm) diam.
**£9–11** *AL*

A Regency cane basket,
11in (28cm) long.
**£25–40** *AL*

A Victorian wicker egg
basket, 8in (20cm) diam.
**£15–20** *AL*

*from left to right.*
A leather pricker, late 19thC. **£8–10**
A pastry marker, late 19thC. **£12–15**
Two butter prints. **£10–12 each** *LAC*

A set of Victorian black glazed pottery food weights, largest 10in (25cm) diam.
**£15–20** *AL*

A pine spoon rack, 19thC.
**£150–200** *MAT*

A Victorian miniature pine chest of 2 drawers, 12½in (32cm) wide.
**£30–40** *AL*

A Victorian small pine chest of drawers, 17in (43cm) wide.
**£150–250** *AL*

*l.* A Victorian pine cat box, 11in (28cm) wide.
**£40–50** *AL*

A Guernsey cream can and cover, made of tin, the bottom impressed 'De La Rue, maker Guernsey', c1880, 8in (20cm) high.
**£20–35** *AL*

An Edwardian tin string container, with cutter at side, 7in (18cm) high.
**£25–35** *AL*

An Edwardian string holder, Sandows patent, 6½in (16cm) wide.
**£5–7** *AL*

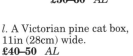

A Victorian pine fire screen, 18in (46cm) wide.
**£50–60** *AL*

A George V wooden gallon measure, with duty mark, woodworm in base, 5in (13cm) high.
**£40–65** *AL*

An Edwardian tea tin, 13in (33cm) high.
**£40–60** *AL*

An Edwardian green painted tea tin, 15½in (39cm) high.
**£75–100** *AL*

An Edwardian string holder, 12½in (32cm) wide.
**£15–20** *AL*

A Victorian miniature pine cupboard.
**£45–50** *AL*

# Irons

It was not until the 16thC that Europeans used a heated tool to smooth clothes. Earlier they used a mangle, or rubbing devices, to flatten cloth while it was damp.

It is not clear whether the idea of using a hot iron arose spontaneously in the west, or whether it was introduced from the Orient. The Dutch probably introduced ironing to add to the white woman's burden. And what a burden! So that the iron should retain its heat as long as possible it was made as heavy as a woman could handle – often weighing 6lbs or more.

At first there were two kinds of iron: the sad iron, heated on the stove, and the box iron, hollow and kept hot by a pair of solid iron slugs heated in the fire and inserted alternately into its body. The box iron was the aristocrat – often made of brass and elaborately embossed. The sad one, made of iron, was a functional, blacksmith-made affair, heavy, practical and ponderous – in fact, the true middle-English meaning of the word 'sad'.

As use of the iron spread during the 17th and 18thC, the need for a self-heating iron became obvious. In the 19thC designs appeared which allowed for a charcoal fire to burn inside the iron. These mainly originated in America and were immediately popular. The Bless and Drake foundry produced 100,000 of them in the year 1856 alone! Then came all sorts of variations, including improvements in draught control so that charcoal or coke would burn more evenly. Then there were methods of burning gas, paraffin, vegetable oil, petrol and methylated spirits.

In 1870, a Mrs Potts of Iowa, USA, fed up with her old sad iron, decided to improve it. First, she designed one that was pointed at both ends for ironing into odd corners. Then she patented one with a detachable handle and two soles. The soles were heated on the stove and the handle attached alternately to each so that it never got too hot.

Electricity came in the 1880s. The old-timers fought on well into the 20thC, but now a flex trails where once wafted smoke and fumes.

A lace iron, late 19thC,
4in (10cm) long.
**£25–35** *FA*

A cap iron, early 19thC,
5in (12.5cm) long.
**£15–20** *FA*

A tailor's iron, by Levine & Sons,
35 Greenfield Street, London W1,
19thC, 8in (20cm) long.
**£30–35** *FA*

A French flat iron No. 5,
late 19thC, 6in (15cm) long.
**£15–20** *FA*

A Belgian flat iron No. 4, late
19thC, 6½in (16.5cm) long.
**£15–20** *FA*

A Kenrick No. 3 smoothing iron,
5in (12.5cm) long.
**£15–25** *FA*

*r.* A straight chimney charcoal iron,
made in Hong Kong at the end of
WWI for the eastern market,
8in (20cm) high.
**£40–50** *FA*

A Vulcan chimney iron, with
vulcan head damper, mid-
19thC, 7in (17.5cm) long.
**£45–50** *FA*

A Victorian plaited rush basket, woodworm in handle, 13in (33cm) wide. **£15–20** *AL*

A Victorian wicker and rush egg basket, 13in (33cm) wide. **£15–20** *AL*

A Victorian wicker and plaited rush basket, 10in (25cm) diam. **£15–20** *AL*

A Victorian heavy wicker egg basket, 13in (33cm) diam. **£20–30** *AL*

A Victorian wicker bread basket, 13in (33cm) diam. **£25–35** *AL*

A Victorian wicker shopping basket, 15in (38cm) wide. **£15–25** *AL*

A Victoria willow and wicker basket, 9in (24cm) diam. **£15–20** *AL*

A Victorian wicker basket, 14in (35.5cm) wide. **£15–20** *AL*

A Victorian willow basket, 10½in (25cm) diam. **£15–20** *AL*

A wicker eel trap, 19thC, 31in (78.5cm) high. **£25–30** *AL*

A Victorian wicker basket, 13in (33cm) wide. **£15–20** *AL*

A wicker basket, early 20thC, 18in (45.5cm) long. **£12–16** *AL*

A wicker basket, early 20thC, 14in (35.5cm) wide. **£12–16** *AL*

A pine bread board, carved with ears of wheat, early 10thC, 11½in (29cm) diam. **£12–20** *AL*

A pair of Victorian Irish bellows, 32in (81cm) wide. **£55–75** *OA*

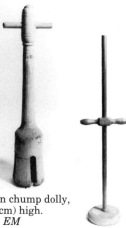

A wooden chump dolly, 34in (86cm) high. **£45–60** *EM*

A wooden poss stick, 46in (116.5cm) high. **£45–60** *EM*

A pine bread board, carved with ears of wheat, 12in (30.5cm) diam. **£15–25** *AL*

*l.* A Victorian pine washboard, 24in (61cm) high. **£30–40** *EM*

Two poss sticks, with copper bases, largest 21in (53cm) long. **£15–25 each** *EM*

A pair of wooden sock driers, 23in (59cm) long. **£40–50** *EM*

A Victorian pine bread board, carved with 'Our Daily Bread', 12in (30.5cm) diam. **£40–50** *AL*

A wooden napkin press, 15½in (40cm) long. **£75–100** *EM*

A copper posser, with valve, by Paul Birkett, 23in (58.5cm) high. **£15–18** *EM*

A fruitwood linen press, 24in (61cm) wide. **£60–80** *EM*

A metal washboard, in a wooden frame, 22in (56cm) high. **£12–15** *EM*

A wooden hanging soap container, 12½in (32cm) high. **£25–35** *EM*

A Victorian metal and brass cheese press, on a wooden base, 10in (25cm) long. **£16–20** *AL*

A Victorian metal bound cheese press, constructed of oak, pine and poplar, 10in (25cm) diam. **£25–35** *OA*

A mahogany coal box, fitted with brass handles, with a scoop in the drawer, c1900, 15in (38cm) high. **£200–250** *BB*

A cheese vat, 20in (50.5cm) diam. **£150–250** *MPA*

A wooden 'Hudson's Extract of Soap' box, 16in (41cm) wide. **£20–30** *EM*

A wooden ladle, 18thC, 11in (28cm) long. **£12–15** *OA*

A pine egg rack, c1860, 21in (53cm) wide. **£40–50** *AL*

A stone pestle, with a wooden handle, 19thC, 13in (33cm) long. **£10–12** *OA*

An Edwardian inlaid oak coal box, with metal liner and fitted scoop, 18in (45.5cm) wide. **£100–150** *Ph*

A pair of Victorian boxwood butter pats, 11in (28cm) long. **£8–12** *OA*

A wire sieve and mortar, 19thC, 8in (20cm) wide. **£9–11** *AL*

An iron raisin pipper, dated '7th October 1897', 12in (30.5cm) wide. **£8–9** *AL*

Two Victorian pastry cutters, 5½in (14cm) long. **£15–20** *OA*

A Victorian earthenware colander, 9in (22.5cm) diam. **£30–40** *AL*

A mahogany knife box, c1840, 16½in (42cm) wide. **£60–75** *AL*

An iron trivet, 19thC, 7in (17.5cm) wide. **£8–10** *AL*

A cottage biscuit barrel, by Price Bros., c1930, 7½in (19cm) high. **£30–40** *GWe*

An earthenware butter tub, with glass liner, 1920s, 6in (15cm) diam. **£10–12** *AL*

A Victorian stoneware double walled butter tub, 6in (15cm) diam. **£8–12** *OA*

*l.* A stoneware jar, with moulded decoration, 6in (15cm) high. **£10–15** *OA*

A Scottish earthenware bread crock, 19in (48cm) wide. **£150–175** *MPA*

A stoneware storage jar, 10in (25cm) high. **£8–12** *OA*

A Spong knife polisher, c1910, 17in (43cm) high. **£100–140** *Ph*

A Victorian Beranger wooden box counter weighing machine, 16in (40.5cm) wide. **£45–55** *EEW*

A Royal mangle, with rubber rollers, pressure adjustment and fixing clamps, 17in (43cm) wide. **£20–25** *EM*

A cork press, by Townson & Mercer Ltd., late 19thC. **£60–70** *Be*

A galvanised metal automatic washer, the central tub with brass tap at the base, c1910, marked 'The Dream', 19in (48cm) high. **£20–25** *EM*

*r*. A set of tinplate scales, c1890, 10½in (27cm) high. **£25–30** *AL*

A Victorian child's wooden mangle, metal frame, on rubber tyred wheels, 20in (50.5cm) high. **£30–35** *EM*

An orange slicer, early 20thC, 16in (40.5cm) long. **£15–20** *BHW*

An American tin 'No. 4 Three Minute Bread Mixer', awarded Gold Medal at St. Louis Exposition 1904, 12in (30.5cm) high. **£40–50** *AL*

A set of cast iron household scales, marked 'British Made', c1890, 12⅝in (32cm) high. **£25–35** *AL*

A single beam iron sweet scale, with brass pans, c1850, 16in (40.5cm) wide. **£80–100** *EEW*

A hand-operated child's washing machine and mangle, with a wooden lid, 27in (68.5cm) high. **£40–50** *EM*

A set of cast iron and brass vegetable scales, by Morgan & Sons, c1900, 23in (59cm) wide. **£100–150** *AL*

A brass and cast iron set of scales, c1900, 9in (22.5cm) long. **£80–100** *BB*

A cast iron steelyard, 18thC, 18in (46cm) long. **£25–30** *AL*

A tin watering can, early 20thC, 16in (40.5cm) high. **£12–15** *AL*

A tin urn, with brass tap, 19thC, 12in (30.5cm) high. **£12–15** *AL*

A tin watering can, early 20thC, 15in (38cm) high. **£10–12** *AL*

A tin milk can, 19thC, 18½in (47cm) high. **£12–15** *AL*

Two tin cheese graters, early 20thC, largest 8in (20cm) high. **£4–8 each** *AL*

A blue enamel mug, early 20thC, 3in (7.5cm) high. **£8–10** *AL*

A selection of wooden and iron chopping utensils, 19thC, largest 6in (15cm) wide. **£8–10 each** *AL*

A brass bowl, early 19thC, 12in (30.5cm) diam. **£40–45** *AL*

A blue enamel mug, late 19thC, 3½in (9cm) high. **£12–15** *AL*

A two-handled chopping knife, with boxwood handles, steel blade, 19thC, 13in (33cm) long. **£15–18** *AL*

An iron and wood marmalade chopper, late 19thC, 16in (40.5cm) wide. **£15–20** *AL*

Two iron string holders, 19thC, 8in (20cm) wide. **£10–12 each** *AL*

An iron and blue enamel tongue press, 19thC, 10in (25cm) high. **£30–35** *AL*

*r.* a copper ladle, 18thC, 15in (38cm) long. **£20–25** *AL*

A red and white enamelled iron mincer, late 19thC, 12in (30.5cm) high. **£8–10** *AL*

Two wrought iron game hooks, 19thC, 7in (17.5cm) long. **£12–15 each** *AL*

An iron keel, 19thC, 21in (53cm) long. **£15–20** *AL*

A wood and iron wallpaper roller, 19thC, 8in (20cm) long. **£5–10** *AL*

# GLOSSARY

**Acanthus** A leaf motif used in carved and inlaid decoration.

**Apron** The shaped skirt of wood that runs beneath the legs of a table or feet of a chest.

**Armoire** The Continental term for a large tall cupboard originally used for storing armour.

**Astragal** A small semi-circular moulding in architecture, and in furniture a term often applied to the glazing bars of cabinets and bookcases. Astragals are sometimes in brass.

**Backboard** The unpolished back of wall furniture.

**Bacon settle** Long, backed seat with boxed base, or on legs, with a storage press in the back.

**Baluster** The shaped turning, or slender pillar with a bulbous base, used on the legs and pedestals of tables.

**Banding** Decorative veneer used around the edges of tables and drawers.

**Barley twist** The spiral shape much favoured for turned legs of the second half of the 17thC.

**Bevel** The decorative angled edge of a mirror.

**Bow front** The outward curved front found on chests of drawers from the late 18thC.

**Bracket foot** A squared foot, the most commonly found foot on 18thC cabinet furniture.

**Breakfront** The term for a piece of furniture with a protruding central section.

**Brushing slide** The pull-out slide found above the to drawer of some small 18thC chests.

**Bun foot** A flattened version of the ball foot.

**Bureau** A writing desk with a fall front, enclosing a fitted interior, with drawers below.

**Bureau bookcase** A bureau with a bookcase above.

**Cabriole leg** A gently curving S-shaped leg found on tables and chairs of the late 17th and 18thC.

**Cellaret** 18thC term for wine coolers and containers, and the drawer in some sideboards designed for storing wine.

**Chamfer** An angled corner.

**Chest on stand** A two-part tall chest of drawers, also known as a tallboy or highboy.

**Cheval mirror** A tall dressing mirror, supported by two uprights.

**Chiffonier** A side cabinet with or without a drawer and with one or more shelves above.

**Children's furniture** Usually small scale furniture for children's usage.

**Coffer** A joined and panelled low chest with handles but without feet, made for travelling, usually of oak, with a lid.

**Commode** A highly decorated chest of drawers or cabinet, often of bombé shape, with applied mounts.

**Corbel** Projecting bracket found on the frieze of cabinet furniture.

**Cornice** The projecting moulding at the top of tall furniture.

**Country/Provincial furniture** The functional furniture made away from the major cities and main centres of production.

**Cross banding** A veneered edge to table tops and drawer fronts, at right angles to the main veneer.

**Dentils** Small rectangular blocks applied at regular intervals to the cornices of much 18thC furniture.

**Dished table top** A hollowed out solid top, associated with tripod tables with pie-crust edges.

**Drop-leaf** Any table with a fixed central section and hinged flaps.

**Dummy drawer** A decorative false drawer, complete with handle.

**Escritoire** A cabinet with a hinged front, which provides a writing surface, and a fitted interior.

**Escutcheon** Brass plate surrounding and protecting the edges of a keyhole – sometimes with a cap or cover on a pivot.

**Etagère** A small work table consisting of shelves or trays one above the other.

**Fall front** The flap of a bureau or secrétaire that pulls forward to provide a writing surface.

**Fielded panel** A raised panel with a bevelled or chamfered edge that fits into a framework.

**Finial** A decorative turned knob applied to the top of fine bureau bookcases etc.

**Fluting** Decorative concave, parallel grooves running down the legs of tables and chairs.

**Foliate carving** Carved flower and leaf motifs.

**Fretwork** Fine pierced decoration.

**Frieze** The framework immediately below a table top.

**Gadroon** A decorative border, carved or moulded, comprising a series of short flutes or reeds.

**Gallery** A wood or metal border around the top edge of a table or washstand.

**Harlequin** A set of chairs that are similar but do not match.

**Intaglio** An incised design, as opposed to a design in relief.

**Joined** Method of furniture construction from 15thC until the end of the 17thC using mortice and tenon joints secured by pegs or dowels, without glue.

**Joined stool** A stool, usually in oak, of joined construction.

**Lowboy** A small side table on cabriole legs, from the early 18thC.

**Married** The term used for an item that has been made up from two or more pieces of furniture, usually of the same period.

**Mule chest** A coffer with a single row of drawers in the base.

**Ogee** A double curve of slender S-shape.

**Ormolu** A mount or article that is gilded or gold coloured.

**Patina** The build-up of wax and dirt that gives old furniture a soft mellow look.

**Pedestal desk** A flat desk, usually with a leathered top, that stands on two banks of drawers.

**Pediment** The gabled structure that surmounts a cornice.

**Platform base** Three or four-cornered flat bases of tables supporting a central pedestal above and standing on scrolled or paw feet.

**Plinth base** A solid base, not raised on feet.

**Potboard** The bottom shelf of a dresser or court cupboard, often just above the floor.

**Reeding** Parallel strips of convex flutes found on the legs of chairs and tables.

**Secrétaire** A writing cabinet with a mock drawer front that lets down to provide a writing surface, revealing recessed pigeon holes.

**Secrétaire bookcase** A secrétaire with a bookcase fitted above.

**Serpentine** Undulating front for a case piece – convex in the centre and concave at the ends. Used for cabinets, chests, sideboard and so on, late 18thC.

**Settle** The earliest form of chair to seat two or more people.

**Spandrel** A decorative corner bracket, usually pierced and found at the tops of legs.

**Splat** The central upright in a chair back; loosely applied to all members in a chair back.

**Stiles** The vertical parts of a framework, usually associated with early furniture.

**Stretchers** The horizontal bars that unite and strengthen the legs of chairs and other furniture.

**Tester** The canopy or ceiling over a bed.

**Tripod table** A small table with a round top supported by a three-legged pillar.

**Whatnot** A mobile stand with open shelves.

**Windsor chair** A type of wooden chair with a spindle back.

# INDEX TO ADVERTISERS

An unusual Austrian pine
kneehole desk, with leather top,
centre section pulls out,
on turned feet, late 19thC,
49in (124.5cm) wide.
**£1,200–1,300** *HeR*

A Scandinavian pine settle, with
corner cupboard, c1820, 124in
(315cm) wide.
**£525–575** *BEL*

# DIRECTORY OF SPECIALISTS

*If you would like to contact any of the following dealers, we would advise readers to make contact by telephone before a visit, therefore avoiding a wasted journey.*

# Country Furniture

## Cumbria

Anvil Antiques,
Cartmel,
Grange over Sands,
LA11 6PZ.
Tel: 01539 536362

## Hampshire

Cedar Antiques Ltd,
High Street,
Hartley Wintney,
RG27 8NY.
Tel: 01252 843252

Millers of Chelsea,
Netherbrook House,
Christchurch Road,
Ringwood,
BH24 1DR.
Tel: 01425 472062

## Kent

Berry Antiques,
Kay Parkin,
The Old Butchers Shop,
Goudhurst,
TN17 1AE.
Tel: 01580 212115

Flower House Antiques,
90 High Street,
Tenterden,
TN30 6JB.
Tel: 01580 763764

Foxhole Antiques,
James Rourke,
High Street,
Goudhurst,
TN17 1AL.
Tel: 01580 212025

Old Bakery Antiques,
St David's Bridge,
Cranbrook,
TN17 3HN.
Tel: 01580 713103

Sparks Antiques,
4 Manor Row,
High Street,
Tenterden,
TN30 6HP.
Tel: 01580 766696

Swan Antiques,
Cranbrook,
Tel: 01580 291864

## Shropshire

Clegg, John & Anne,
12 Old Street,
Ludlow,
SY8 1NP.
Tel: 01584 873176

No 7 Antiques,
7 Nantwich Road,
Woore,
CW3 9SA.
Tel: 01630 647118

# Wales

Country Antiques
(Wales),
31 Bridge Street &
Castle Mill,
Kidwelly,
Dyfed, SA17 4UU.
Tel: 01554 890534

## West Midlands

Pierre of LP Furniture,
Short Acre Street,
Walsall, WS2 8HW.
Tel: 01922 746764

## Wiltshire

Combe Cottage Antiques,
Castle Combe,
BA13 4SY.
Tel: 01249 782250

# Kitchenware

## Berkshire

Below Stairs,
103 High Street,
Hungerford,
RG17 0NB.
Tel: 01488 682317

## Lancashire

Old Bakery, The,
36 Inglewhite Road,
Longridge,
Nr Preston,
PR5 6AS.
Tel: 01772 785411

## London

Bishop, Christina,
Westway,
Portobello Road Market,
W11.
Tel: 0171 221 4688

## Shropshire

No 7 Antiques,
7 Nantwich Road,
Woore,
CW3 9SA.
Tel: 01630 647118

## Suffolk

Tartan Bow, The,
3a Castle Street,
Eye, IP23 2RG.
Tel: 01379 783057/
870369

## Sussex

Lingard, Ann ,
Ropewalk Antiques,
Ropewalk,
Rye, TN31 7NA.
Tel: 01797 223486

## West Midlands

Dog House, The,
309 Bloxwich Road,
Walsall,
Tel: 01922 30829

# Yorkshire

Halifax Antiques Centre,
Queens Road/Gibbet
Street,
Halifax, HX1 4LR.
Tel: 01422 366657

# Painted Pine

## Kent

Fox Hole Antiques,
High Street,
Goudhurst,
TN17 1AL.
Tel: 01580 212025

Page, Angela,
15 Cumberland Walk,
Tunbridge Wells,
TN1 1UJ.
Tel: 01892 522217

## London

Young Antiques, Robert,
68 Battersea Bridge Road,
SW11 3AG.
Tel: 0171 228 7847/
Fax 0171 585 0489

## Somerset

Gilbert & Dale Antiques
The Old Chapel,
Church Street,
Ilchester,
Nr Yeovil,
BA22 8LA.
Tel: 01935 840444

# Pine

## Avon

Pennard House Antiques,
3-4 Piccadilly,
London Road,
Bath,
BA1 6PL.
Tel: 01225 313791/01749
860260

## Bedfordshire

Adams Pine & Design,
9-11 High Street,
Langford,
SG18 9RP.
Tel: 01462 700064
Fax: 01462 700059

## Berkshire

Hungerford Pine Company,
14/15 Charnham Street,
Hungerford,
RG17 0EF.
Tel: 01488 686935

## Cambridgeshire

Adams Furniture Centre,
The Old Post Office,
George Street,
Huntingdon,
PE18 6AW.
Tel: 01480 435100
Fax: 01480 454387

Adams Pine & Design,
The Old Post Office,
George Street,
Huntingdon,
PE18 6AW.
Tel: 01480 414814
Fax: 01480 454387

Antique Centre, The,
Stephen Copsey,
George Street,
Huntingdon,
PE18 6AW.
Tel: 01480 435100

Midloe Grange Antiques
(TRADE ONLY),
Rectory Lane,
Southoe,
St Neots,
PE18 9YD.
Tel: 01480 404029
Fax: 01480 471658

## Cheshire

Hopwood Antiques, Maria,
Hulgrave Hall,
Tiverton,
Tarporley,
CW6 9UQ.
Tel: 01829 733313

Richmond Galleries,
Watergate Building,
New Crane Street,
Chester,
CH1 4JE.
Tel: 01244 317602

## Cleveland

European Pine Imports,
Riverside Park Industrial
Estate,
Middlesborough,
TS21 1QW.
Tel: 01642 584351

## Cumbria

Ben Eggleston Antiques,
The Dovecote,
Long Morton,
Appleby, CA16 6BJ.
Tel: 01768 361849

Utopia Antiques,
Lake Road,
Bowness-on-Windermere,
LA23 2JG.
Tel: 01539 488464

## Devon

Cullompton Old Tannery
Antiques,
The Old Tannery,
Exeter Road,
Cullompton,
EX15 1DT.
Tel: 01884 38476/266429

Fagin's Antiques,
The Old Whiteways
Cider Factory,
Hele, Exeter,
EX5 4PW.
Tel: 01392 882062

Fine Pine,
Woodland Road,
Habertonford,
Nr Totnes,
TQ9 7SX.
Tel: 01803 732465

**Dorset**

Overhill Antiques,
Wareham Road,
Holton Heath,
Poole,
BH16 6JW.
Tel: 01202 621818/
665043

**Essex**

English Rose Antiques,
7 Church Street,
Coggeshall,
CO6 1TU.
Tel: 01376 562683

**Gloucestershire**

Campden Country Pine
Antiques,
High Street,
Chipping Campden,
GL55 6HN.
Tel: 01386 840315

Country Homes,
61 Long Street,
Tetbury, GL8 8AA.
Tel: 01666 502342

Waterloo Antiques,
20 The Waterloo,
Cirencester, GL7 2PZ.
Tel: 01285 644887

**Hampshire**

Pine Cellars, The,
39 Jewry Street,
Winchester, SO23 8RY.
Tel: 01962 867014

Pine Company, The,
104 Christchurch Road,
Ringwood, BH24 1DR.
Tel: 01425 476705

**Humberside**

Bell Antiques,
68A Harold Street,
Grimsby,
DN35 0HH.
Tel: 01472 695110

Wilson, Paul,
Perth Street West,
Hull, HU5 3UB.
Tel: 01482 447923

**Ireland**

Bygones of Ireland,
Westport Antiques
Centre,
Lodge Road,
Westport,
County Mayo.
Tel: 00 353 98 26132

Delvin Farm Antiques,
Gormonston,
Co Meath,
Tel: 00 353 18412285

Forsythe, Albert,
Mill House,
66 Carsonstown Road,
Saintfield,
Co Down,
BT24 7EX.
Tel: 01238 510398

Honans Antiques,
Crowe Street, Gort,
County Galway.
Tel: 00 353 91 31407

Ireland's Own Antiques,
Alpine House,
Carlow Road,
Abbeyleix,
Co. Laois.
Tel: 00 353 502 31348

Old Court Pine,
(Alain Chawner),
Old Court, Collon,
Co. Louth.
Tel: 00 3531 412 6270

Somerville Antiques &
Country Furniture Ltd,
Moysdale,
Killanley,
Ballina,
Co Mayo.
Tel: 00 353 963 6275

**Kent**

Antique & Design,
The Old Oast,
Hollow Lane,
Canterbury,
CT1 3TG.
Tel: 01227 762871

Country Pine Antique
Company,
The Barn,
Upper Bush Farm,
Upper Bush Road,
Nr Rochester, ME2 1HQ.
Tel: 01634 296929

Old English Pine,
100 Sandgate High
Street, Sandgate,
Folkestone,
CT20 3BY.
Tel: 01303 248560

Up Country,
The Old Corn Stores,
68 St John's Road,
Tunbridge Wells,
TN4 9PE.
Tel: 01892 523341

Warehouse, The,
29-30 Queens Gardens,
Worthington Street,
Dover, CT17 9AH.
Tel: 01304 242006

**Lancashire**

Enloc Antiques,
Birchenlee Mill,
Lenches Road,
Colne, BB8 8ET.
Tel: 01282 867101

**Leicestershire**

Hartwell Antiques,
152 Station Lane,
Scraptoft, LE7 9UF.
Tel: 0533 416695

Richard Kimbell Antiques,
Riverside,
Market Harborough,
LE16 7PT.
Tel: 01858 433444

**London**

Antique Warehouse,
9-14 Deptford Broadway,
SE8 4PA.
Tel: 0181 691 3062

**Nottinghamshire**

Jack Spratt Antiques,
Unit 5,
George Street,
Newark, NG24 1LU.
Tel: 01636 707714

**Scotland**

Times Past Antiques,
Broadfold Farm,
Auchterarder,
Perthshire,
PH3 1DR.
Tel: 01764 663166

**Somerset**

Milverton Antiques,
Fore Street,
Milverton,
Taunton,
TA4 1JU.
Tel: 01823 400597

Westville House Antiques,
Littleton,
Somerton,
TA11 6NP.
Tel: 01458 273376

**Staffordshire**

Aspleys Antiques, John,
Compton Mill,
Compton,
Leek, ST13 5NJ.
Tel: 01538 373396

Johnsons,
Park Works, Park Road,
Leek, ST13 8SA.
Tel: 01538 386745

**Surrey**

Cherub Antiques of
Carshalton,
Spring House,
Benhill Road,
Sutton, SM1 3RN.
Tel: 0181 661 7427
24 Hours - 0181 643 0028

**Sussex**

Bob Hoare Pine Antiques
Unit Q, Phoenix Place,
North Street,
Lewes, BN17 2QJ.
Tel: 01273 480557

Drummer Pine,
Hailsham Road,
Herstmonceux,
BN27 4LH.
Tel: 01232 833542

Graham Price Antiques
Ltd.
Unit 4, Chaucer
Industrial Estate,
Dittons Road,
Polegate, BN26 6JD.
Tel: 01323 487167

Libra Antiques,
81 London Road,
Hurst Green,
Etchingham,
TN19 7PN.
Tel: 01580 860569

Lingard, Ann,
Ropewalk Antiques,
Ropewalk,
Rye,
TN31 7NA.
Tel: 01797 223486

Mary Sautter Pine
Furniture,
6 Station Road,
Lewes, BN7 2UP.
Tel: 01273 474842

**The Netherlands**

Van der Tol, Jacques,
Antennestraat 34,
1322 A E Almere-Stad.
Tel: 00 31 3653 62050

**Wales**

Heritage Restorations,
Maes Y Glydfa,
Llanfair Caereinion,
Welshpool,
Powys, SY21 0HD.
Tel: 01938 810384

Pot Board, The,
30 King Street,
Carmarthen,
Dyfed, SA31 1BS.
Tel: 01267 236623/01834
871276

Cottage Pine Antiques,
19 Broad Street,
Brinklow, Nr Rugby,
CV23 0LS.
Tel: 01788 832673

Old Pine House, The,
16 Warwick Street,
Royal Leamington Spa,
CV32 5LL.
Tel: 01926 470477

**Wiltshire**

Crudwell Furniture, The
Paint and Varnish
Strippers,
The Workshop,
Oddpenny Farm,
Crudwell, SN16 9SJ.
Tel: 01285 770970

North Wiltshire
Exporters,
Farm Hill House,
Brinkworth,
Nr Chippenham,
SN15 5AJ.
Tel: 01666 510876

Sambourne House
Antiques, Minety,
Malmesbury, SN16 9RQ.
Tel: 01666 860288

**Yorkshire**

Byrne Antiques, Simon,
Unit 16, Eastburn Mills,
Eastburn,
Keighley, BD20 7SJ.
Tel: 01535 656297

Smith & Smith Designs,
58A Middle Street,
North Driffield,
YO25 7SU.
Tel: 01377 256321

# Publications

**West Midlands**

Antiques Bulletin
HP Publishing,
2 Hampton Court Road,
Harborne,
Birmingham,
B17 GAE.
Tel: 0121 428 2555